Date Due

The Rockingham Connection and
the Second Founding of the Whig Party

The Rockingham Connection and the Second Founding of the Whig Party is a study of the ideological development of the Rockingham Whigs in Britain between 1768 and 1773 and a re-examination of the party system in the later part of the eighteenth century. W.M. Elofson traces the transition of the Rockingham Whigs from court-centred supporters of the status quo to proponents of parliamentary reform, illustrating the central role the party played in the evolution of "liberal" philosophy that preceded the massive reform movement in the next century.

Elofson reveals that the Rockinghams, far more than previously recognized, were governed by a coherent set of constitutional ideals and argues that they saw "party" not primarily as a means to office but as a vehicle for public-spirited men to "secure the predominance of right and uniform principles" in the operation of the state. He examines the ideological writings of Edmund Burke, the party's noted and prolific publicist, placing them in their political context and providing a new analysis of Burke's renowned pamphlet *Thoughts on the Cause of the Present Discontents* (1770).

Throughout, Elofson illustrates the ways in which the Rockinghams altered and redefined the Whig Party and its principles as they took the first halting steps towards a program of constitutional amendment, establishing their place not only in Whig but also in British constitutional thought.

W.M. ELOFSON is assistant professor of history, University of Calgary.

The Rockingham Connection and the Second Founding of the Whig Party, 1768–1773

W.M. ELOFSON

McGill-Queen's University Press
Montreal & Kingston • London • Buffalo

© McGill-Queen's University Press 1996
ISBN 0-7735-1388-4

Legal deposit second quarter 1996
Bibliothèque nationale du Québec

Printed in Canada on acid-free paper

Canadian Cataloguing in Publication Data

Elofson, W.M.
  The Rockingham connection and the second
  founding of the Whig Party, 1768–1773
  Includes bibliographical references and index.
  ISBN 0-7735-1388-4
  1. Whig Party (Great Britain) – History – 18th
  century. 2. Great Britain – Politics and government –
  1760–1789. I. Title.
  DA510.E46   1996   324.241'02   C95-900972-8

This book was typeset by Typo Litho Composition Inc.
in 10/12 Palatino

For Betty Lou, Shane, Brett, and Wade.
We are and for ever will be together.

Contents

Preface

The Marquis of Rockingham and his friends, whom Lord Macaulay labelled "the second founders of the Whig party," have for some years been the subject of considerable controversy amongst historians. On the one side they have been viewed as a highly principled and virtuous group, concerned more about constitutionalism and the public good than about their own political ambitions; and on the other, as ruthless opportunists preoccupied for the most part with self-aggrandizement. Posterity's views of these men have been so divided and so definite partly because when contemplating them it is difficult not to become excessively moralistic. To a considerable extent, this is a reflection of the fact that the Rockinghams were inclined to be noticeably moralistic about themselves. Through the works of their celebrated and prolific publicist, Edmund Burke, and in their private correspondence, they constantly glorified their own motives and aspirations in relation to ethical standards that were very important to them. As a result, it has been convenient or perhaps natural for historians to assess the party according to the same standards. This has not only created distortions, it has been somewhat wasteful. The purpose here is to study the Rockinghams in detail during a short but immeasurably significant phase of their career, when they were forced to come to grips with the idea that the Whig party's position had, of necessity, changed from one of almost unlimited governmental power to one of more or less futile opposition.

I should like to express my thanks for the assistance which, in the course of research, I received from the staff of the following institutions: the British Library; the Public Record Office; the House of Lords Record Office; Northamptonshire, Staffordshire, and Warwickshire record offices; the Bodleian Library; Nottingham University Library; Sheffield City Library; New York City Library; Huntingdon

Library; and the History of Parliament Trust. I should also like to acknowledge my debt to Earl Fitzwilliam for permission to consult the great collections of manuscripts now at Sheffield and Northampton, and to the Social Sciences and Humanities Research Council of Canada for crucial funding.

*The Rockingham Connection and
the Second Founding of the Whig Party*

Introduction

The Marquis of Rockingham[1] and his friends took over the leadership of the largest Whig following in the British Parliament during their first brief administration of 1765–66. When they went into the political wilderness, just a year after that administration was formed, they lost most of the ambitious politicians of the "old Whig" following, who chose to stay with the court rather than risk political obscurity. What was left was a collection of country aristocrats and gentlemen, who were to remain in opposition for some sixteen of the next seventeen years, in part because they were suited to and satisfied with that role.

Among the important figures who were with the party from the earliest days, only Edmund Burke[2] demonstrated the consistent interest in national politics that might be considered a genuine thirst for governmental power. Some five years before his death, Burke wrote a sort of apologia for his long devotion to the Rockingham cause. His words describe his colleagues as landlords, whose greatest virtue was the independence they had been able to achieve as a result of private wealth and property:

The party with which I acted had ... been ... by the wise and good always esteemd and confided in – as an aristocratick Party. Such I always understood it to be in the true Sense of the word. I understood it to be a Party, in its composition and in its principles, connected with the solid, permanent long possessed property of the Country; a party, which, by a Temper derived from that Species of Property, and affording a security to it, was attached to the antient tried usages of the Kingdom, a party therefore essentially constructed upon a Ground plot of stability and independence; a party ... equally removed from servile court compliances, and from popular levity, proscription and precipitation.[3]

The Marquis of Rockingham and the men Rockingham most respected, including his second-in-command, the Duke of Portland,[4] his leader in the House of Commons, William Dowdeswell,[5] and his close personal friends, Lord John Cavendish[6] and Sir George Savile,[7] bore a close resemblance in some important respects to the stereotypical country-party country gentleman identified by Sir Lewis Namier.[8] Indeed, it is ironic (considering Namier's opinion of the Rockinghams)[9] that only their loyalty to their party and to certain court Whig preconceptions prevent the historian from using the above phrase without qualification to describe them. They were all large landholders whose lives revolved more around social and business matters in their localities than in the world of political intrigue and power mongering at Westminster. In comparison to other connections, they were unmoved by the attractions of place and pension in the national government;[10] and as will be demonstrated, in the course of years in opposition they became deeply concerned about the two matters that aroused fear in all country parties of the eighteenth century – government financial mismanagement and the potential inability of the House of Commons and the electorate to act with independence, because of ministerial exploitation of the patronage of the crown.[11]

Considering the Rockinghams' relative indifference to political power, one might think that they would have been able to make a smooth transition to opposition after leaving office in 1766. In fact, they did not. The major obstacle they had to overcome was their self-image. These men considered themselves the authentic successors of the court Whig oligarchy that had governed the nation for nearly half a century under the first two Hanoverian kings. The Rockinghams constantly identified with such figures as Robert Walpole[12] and Henry Pelham,[13] and they found it difficult, particularly early in their career, not to view the political world in general through the eyes of the court Whigs. Therefore, it took some time for them to feel comfortable in an opposition role. The central purpose of this study is to document the transition – that is, to demonstrate how, during several crucial years, the Rockinghams led their connection away from a strictly court Whig approach and moulded it into something closely resembling a country party. This process was in all practical respects completed in the late 1760s and early 1770s. Before then, the Rockinghams were largely controlled by a political and constitutional philosophy that was essentially still court Whig. By the end of this period, however, country-party values had become just as powerful in governing their actions. The Rockinghams were never to abandon the past completely. Their attitude towards the constitution and society in general would always be significantly affected by principles they shared with power-hungry Whigs of the previous reign. But by the time they were forced to face the East India Company controversy in 1773, the party leaders had in most practical respects begun to act like a more or less permanent fixture of opposition and had learned to channel all their major political stands towards the objectives of reducing the cost of government and the undue influence of the crown.

This development is important, firstly for the light it sheds on eighteenth-century British politics. Recently, revisionists have questioned the prevalence, if not the very existence, of Namier's country-party country gentlemen. To many scholars they have become "an ideal type rather than a widespread species."[14] The Rockinghams were able to command the loyalty of some one hundred Parliamentary supporters for more than a decade and a half in the political wilderness.[15] It seems logical to assume that most of these supporters shared their leaders' values. If, notwithstanding their partisan Whiggishness, the Rockinghams became something very close to a country party, that element may well have been considerably more important in British politics than some historians currently believe. Further, the Rockinghams' example helps show that modern historiography still has some distance to go before it can claim to have offered a thorough description of the party system in the late eighteenth century. Peter D.G. Thomas has explained most effectively of late some of the problems with the Whig-versus-Tory interpretation. Among other things, he has pointed out that during Lord North's ascendancy, not only the Rockinghams but a number of their allies in opposition and a large majority of the men who comprised the ministry all identified themselves with the same Whig label.[16]

To argue successfully that the Rockinghams became a country party creates another problem for the Whig-Tory interpretation. It enables one to demonstrate that at critical times British politics had a tendency to break down into a distinctly court-country struggle and thereby to nullify the rather limited rivalry that did survive between advocates of the traditional parties. In George III's Parliament, one other identifiable country interest, besides that which the Rockinghams represented, was a Tory interest. In the seventies, it included country gentlemen such as Sir Roger Newdigate,[17] Sir William Bagot,[18] Sir Charles Mordaunt,[19] and a number of others, whose roots were Tory but who were independent in that they were uninterested in places or pensions in the national government and were not members of any clearly discernible parliamentary political following. In normal circumstances, these men tended to support North's predominantly Whig administration, but they were able to keep alive some of the traditional party animosities by regularly dividing against the Rockinghams and other Whigs in opposition. Once the American Revolutionary War began to go badly, however, these men, along with many other independents, generally began to turn against the North regime. Increasingly, they sided with Rockingham and his friends in support of a country-party program of "economical reform."[20] When the war was lost, country Whigs and country Tories not only stood together against the court, but they shared a common country platform. One supposes that these two groups did not suddenly feel a strong sense of kinship for one another; but for a significant period, their country values did more to draw them together than their party allegiances could do to push them apart.

If the Rockinghams pose difficulties for the Whig-Tory interpretation, they also do not fit comfortably into the "Namierite three-part analysis,"[21] which divides MPs into a court party of office holders, independents, and political factions. They were too disinterested to be called either a court party or a faction competing for power, and though they were free from real concern about office, most of them displayed far too much party loyalty to be labelled independents. It is likely, moreover, that if the Rockinghams do not suit extant theories, other political groups of their time also do not. Before a really satisfactory understanding of political alignments can be established, the aspirations and ideals of a number of connections and alliances need to be examined in detail. It is hoped that this study will offer some important insights with respect to the Rockinghams in particular, which may eventually help make the overall picture somewhat clearer.

The transition which the Rockinghams underwent in the early 1770s was also extremely significant in the evolution of Whig liberalism. Despite the fact that in a number of respects the marquis and his friends were unlike the men who had led the party before them, they unquestionably had a right to call themselves the Whigs. Considering that they emerged in conjunction with such politicians as the Duke of Newcastle,[22] the Earl of Albemarle,[23] and the Duke of Devonshire[24] and that in their midst were such names as Cavendish, Wentworth, and Bentinck, their connection with the Whig leaders of the previous reign is undeniable. Moreover, while many important politicians outside their fold considered themselves Whigs, the Rockinghams were the largest of several groups in Parliament that did so. The most convincing reason for conceding their right to the title, however, is that they aspired to be called Whigs and sought to identify with Whig ideals more than any other political group of their time, and that most of their contemporaries accepted their claims.[25] If they and the society in which they lived believed they were the Whigs, then surely they were. Yet Rockingham and his friends seriously altered the party and its principles before passing the mantle to their successors. In the process, they forged an essential link in the chain connecting the Whigs who defended the constitution from alteration in the first half of the eighteenth century to those who championed the cause of change in the early nineteenth century.

Before the reign of George III, the court Whigs had emerged as the staunchest supporters in British politics of the status quo.[26] To a considerable degree, this was because, over the years, they had come to represent the status quo. Their party had played a very large role in the revolution settlement, and it had virtually monopolized governmental power between 1714 and 1760. Therefore, they had learned constantly to defend the system that seemed to be their own and to provide for their power and authority. In the late eighteenth century, however, the party was to follow Charles James Fox[27] in propagating parliamentary reform, and in 1832 it was to rally behind Lord John Russell[28] and Earl Grey[29] to champion no less significant a measure than the first Reform Bill. In the historical development of Whiggism, the Rockinghams' importance is that they presided over the party when it made its first cautious moves in this direction. The marquis and his friends were never as anxious for change as the men who carried the Whig banner after the marquis's death in 1782. By late-eighteen century standards, their program was considered very mild. It sought significant reductions in the crown's influence and in government spending, but it did not advocate substantive amendments to the structure or conventions of Parliament or to the system of representation, and it did not call for an extension of the franchise.[30] Yet, arguably, it was a necessary first step that foreshadowed the more far-reaching schemes that Whigs espoused in later years.

The Rockinghams' drift in the direction of reform can be detected in the evolution of their attitude towards the constitution. Their earlier view is found in Edmund Burke's celebrated pamphlet, *Thoughts on the Cause of the Present Discontents*, written in 1770. This work was regarded by the Rockingham leaders as the "creed" of their party. It reflected their combined mind-set at the end of the first decade of George III's rule.[31] One of its least complicated arguments was that in recent British history, greatness had been achieved when monarchs had been wise enough to place their faith in the hands of men who possessed the "name of Whig, dear to the majority of the people."[32] This thesis prompted Burke to wax positively ebullient about the Walpole-Pelham era – during which, he asserted, reliance on the right men had enabled George II to maintain "the dignity of his Crown connected with the liberty of his people, not only unimpaired, but improved, for the space of thirty three years." The "most ardent lover of his country," Burke insisted, "cannot wish for Great Britain an happier fate than to continue as she was then left."[33] Since the beginning of the new reign, the Rockinghams had witnessed the downfall of the "old Whigs," and except for a very brief period,[34] their own version of the party had been relegated to the political wilderness. Consequently, even though they were not personally very ambitious, they were inclined to look back nostalgically to a time when their party's pre-eminence and the existing constitution had gone hand in hand. At this stage, their particular biases encouraged them to believe that everything that was wrong in Britain could be remedied, not by change but simply by placing trustworthy Whigs at the helm to direct all the institutions of government which they had controlled a short time ago.[35]

Less than a decade after the publication of the *Thoughts*, the Rockinghams were to champion their economical reform legislation. Although this was moderate in comparison with other proposals of the time, it was (as its initial failure on the floor of the House of Commons demonstrates) too extensive for many of the politically influential in Britain to stomach.[36] Eventually, when the Rockinghams returned for their last short term of office in 1782, they encompassed this program in three new acts. Crewe's Act disfranchised revenue officials in national elections;[37] Clerke's Act removed from the Commons some 15 to 20 government contractors;[38] and Burke's Establishment Act, a watered-down edition of a bill he had unsuccessfully submitted to the Commons more than two years earlier, removed 134 offices in the royal household and the ministry (22 of them tenable with a seat in the Commons), abolished the Board of Trade and the third secretaryship of state, and brought changes to the civil list which placed it for the first time under parliamentary control. If nothing else, this program was a milestone in Rockingham constitutional thought. The party had moved away from its earlier court Whig background just far enough to accept that the system could in fact be changed for the better.

More than anything else, what enabled the Rockinghams to take this step was their relative indifference to power and the sense of fulfilment they derived from carrying on the battle against the undue influence of the crown. It was precisely this combination of country-party values that enabled them to accept life out of office without the feeling of dejection which more ambitious politicians might have experienced when exiled to the political wilderness for so long.[39] It encouraged them as well to identify on a regular basis with the "outs" rather than the "ins" and to develop a sense of outrage at apparent abuses of patronage by courtiers and professional politicians in the North regime. Eventually, therefore, it also prompted them to believe that certain measures should be instigated to restrain government. The Rockinghams could become reformers only at the point where their country suspicion of ministerial power became as strong in controlling their thinking as their court Whig empathy for the system. One argument here is that this occurred as a result of experience gained by the party leaders during their early years in active opposition, and that for all practical purposes it was complete by 1773.

This study focuses on the five-year period following the election of 1768. It must be admitted that pragmatic incentives helped establish the autumn of 1768 as the starting point. John Brooke, in his seminal work *The Chatham Administration*, concluded a thorough and illuminating analysis of parties with the resignation of Lord Chatham[40] in October 1768, and my intention is to add to rather than overlap and in a sense compete with his valuable work. This is not to suggest that my assessment meshes exactly with that in *The Chatham Administration*. Professor Brooke looked closely at all the major groups competing for power in the late 1760s. He clearly did not disagree with the opinion expressed here, that there were far too many connections operating with their own complexions and personnel to think of imposing a Whig-Tory or any other two-party analysis on them.[41] On the other hand, I do not mean to endorse Brooke's view (which both he and Sir Lewis Namier promulgated in *Their History of Parliament*),[42] that the Rockinghams were a rather unscrupulous faction prepared at any moment to trample on ideals in order to force their way into office. Historians have an understandable tendency to look at the politicians of the past through modern eyes. In the twentieth century, we almost automatically assess their strategies and organizations as if they were involved in a never-ending struggle for office. One of the lessons that is reinforced from a closer scrutiny than has previously been made of the Rockinghams' activities in opposition is that this can be misleading. The principal members of the party, I shall argue, went into politics to demonstrate and augment their standing in their home counties and to display their virtue to the nation – indeed, to the entire world. Essentially, they were a group of aristocrats and gentlemen who wanted to be known as Whigs but who, at critical times, forsook the attractions of place and pension to stand up for what they believed in.

It should be understood from the beginning that the objective is not to supply sustenance for an outdated and far too elementary Whig interpretation of the party.[43] Rockingham and his friends do not merit the type of accolades that were heaped on them by nineteenth-century historians, including G.O. Trevelyan[44] and T.B. Macaulay.[45] They were men not saints, and as will be seen, their policies lacked the insight – and their dedication to parliamentary politics, the resolution – to warrant praising them to the skies. Moreover, one must be careful not to applaud them too loudly for sacrificing power for their principles; for in doing so, they did not have to give up anything they cared about very much. Nevertheless, what follows is a less cynical picture than the Rockinghams' harshest critics have painted.[46] I have tried to delve below the surface in all the major issues which the marquis and his friends faced between 1768 and 1773, in order to illustrate their real motives and priorities and to compare them with all the other groups in opposition. What becomes evident is that the Rockinghams were governed by coherent constitutional philosophies much more than their allies were – and far more than we have previously recognized. The marquis and his friends saw "connection" or "party" not primarily as a means to office but as a vehicle through which public-spirited men could "secure the predominance of right and uniform principles" in the operation of the state.[47] Thus, as they moved from a predominantly court-Whig to a mainly country-party perspective, they were careful to maintain, and when necessary to adjust, their ideological framework. This framework was apparent in numerous political stands and in various publications, including Burke's *Thoughts on the Cause of the Present Discontents*. For this reason, it was critical in securing the Rockinghams a prominent place not just in Whig but in British constitutional history.

In establishing late 1768 as the starting point of my study, factors over and above the earlier work of Professor Brooke have also been important. The Marquis of Rockingham and his closest friends left government in 1766, but it was more than a year before they decided to play a vigorous part against the administration and to ask those of their followers who had remained in office under the Earl of Chatham to resign. Consequently, they were just beginning to take an antiministerial stance when the 1761–68 Parliament came to an end. The focusing on one Parliament also provides the luxury of a more or less constant membership in the House of Commons, which in turn enables one to follow the activities of all the important political personalities. This facilitates a more thorough understanding of party affiliations and the basic aspirations not just of the Rockingham Whigs but, to a useful extent, of the other important political groups as well.

CHAPTER ONE

The Rockingham Whigs in Opposition, 1766–1768

Recently, thorough studies by Professors Frank O'Gorman and James Bradley have focused on local politics in England in the late eighteenth century and have discovered the continuance, in many cases, of a partisan duality of a Whig-Tory nature.[1] This duality was not overlooked by the Rockinghams. During the petitioning movement of 1769, Burke wrote repeatedly to his political colleagues about the Whig and Tory responses in the counties,[2] and some eight years later, when examining the state of affairs at Bristol and other boroughs, he said that he could see "manifest marks of the resurrection of the Tory party." He explained: " They no longer criticize, as all disengaged people in the world will, on the acts of Government; but they are silent under every evil, and hide and cover up every ministerial blunder and misfortune with the officious zeal of men, who think they have a party of their own to support in power ... embodied, united with their natural head the Crown, and animated by their Clergy ... As to the Whigs I think them far from extinct. They are what they always were."[3]

Rockingham himself, in at least one of the constituencies his supporters represented in Yorkshire, could not afford to forget that a Tory alternative was available to those who might wish to challenge his authority.[4] To accept that a dichotomy often existed at the local level, however, and that most politicians do seem to have considered themselves either Whigs or Tories, does not force one to embrace Professor B.W. Hill's thesis that the two-party system was a conspicuous feature of national politics in the early decades of George III's reign.[5] In fact, as is well known, this system faded considerably for two major reasons. The first was the elimination of the Jacobite threat after the defeat of Bonnie Prince Charlie at Culloden in 1746. This freed Tories from the taint of Jacobitism and allowed them a greater degree of political acceptability than they had had for years. Over the course of time, many of them were successfully courted in Parliament by various Whigs, and their cohesion suffered.[6] The second reason was the ascendancy of George III in 1760.[7] The young king was determined to escape the Whig oligarchy which he believed had imprisoned his grandfather. As he struggled to find someone he could work with, he saw to the establishment, in one way or another, of six different ministries in ten years. Small personal followings coalesced around the principal politicians while in office; and when they left office, these groups stayed together to compete for support in Parliament. In combination with Tory diffusion, this provided for the development of a complex admixture of small alliances and connections that obscured two-party politics until at least the early 1780s and arguably until the polarization of British society that accompanied the French Revolution.[8]

In the 1760s and 1770s, the traditional party labels continued to be used, but they reflected a whole range of possibilities. A politician who successfully ran as a Whig in the 1768 election could continue to refer to himself as such while joining any of a number of mutually exclusive groups in the House of Commons.[9] These groups included the Chathams, the Grenvilles,[10] the Bedfords,[11] the Rockinghams, the Graftons,[12] and, after early 1770, the Norths.[13] They also included the radicals who encircled politicians from the City of London such as William Beckford[14] and James Townsend.[15] All of these groups were predominantly Whig, and for considerable periods of time they managed to retain their own identities.[16] Then again, a person might prefer to be an independent Whig and thus either free in all practical respects from any affiliation or loosely associated with one of the personal followings.[17] Anyone who considered himself a Tory could also be independent (in which case, he would have found himself siding with country gentlemen such as Sir William Bagot and Sir Roger Newdigate). Alternatively, he could have joined the court in the 1760s or the North regime after early 1770, and he could even have made cause with the Rockingham, Grenville, or Chatham connections, all of which had small segments which, at least at one time, would have been considered Tory.[18] At Westminster, a Whig or a Tory was likely to spend a considerable amount of his time in conflict with men who claimed the same title and in alliance with men who did not.

It could also be said that just as the Whig-Tory conflict was disrupted in the early part of the reign, so, in normal circumstances, was the court-country conflict. Since the late seventeenth century, the burgeoning fiscal military state and the proliferation of public offices it facilitated[19] had produced a large country interest in the House of

Commons consisting of both Whigs and Tories whose main concern was their fear of an increase in the influence of the crown. Place and pension bills, oaths against bribery in elections, and shorter Parliaments had thus been promulgated time and time again.[20] However, in the 1760s, the political followings fragmented the country element in the House of Commons. As will be seen, a number from this element became associated with the Rockinghams; some seem to have been careful to avoid all connections;[21] some, including Newdigate and Bagot, simply maintained the Tory label;[22] others kept the Whig label;[23] some supported Grenville until his death in 1770;[24] and still others moved closer to Grafton and then North.[25] Partly because of this, country measures that had been marshalled so often against the court before the Seven Years' War did not reappear with any regularity until the Rockinghams began to promote them near the end of the American Revolution.[26] Those that did reappear were inspired by radical voices in the City of London rather than by politicians linked closely to country gentlemen in the House of Commons. Such was the case, for instance, with Beckford's bill in 1768 to make MPs swear that they had not corrupted their electors,[27] a spate of proposals in Parliament in 1770,[28] and John Sawbridge's[29] motions, beginning in 1771, for annual parliaments.[30]

In every respect, then, two-party politics declined at the national level in the early years of George III's reign. The point here is not to criticize the regional studies; what these have done is make us aware of the importance of the constituencies in preserving traditional distinctions at a time when they might otherwise have tended to disappear. However, one needs to keep firmly in mind that circumstances at Westminster did not always mirror those in the regions. In attesting that Rockingham headed the Whig party in Yorkshire, one is acknowledging that he and his friends were pre-eminent. But in speaking of his stature as the leader of the Whigs in Parliament between 1766 and 1782, one must add the caveat that his party was merely the largest and most persistent of several small opposition groups that claimed the title. Recognition of this is fundamental to an understanding of the parliamentary environment in the 1760s and 1770s. It also helps us see the marquis and his friends not as the aggressive competitors in national affairs that have been described by some historians,[31] but as the rather nonprofessional and phlegmatic group they more often were. To amass and direct their following, they did not need to be skilled organizers capable of coordinating an enormous party machine that somehow stretched across the country.[32] What they really did was bring together, in a largely informal manner, a number of personal friends, relatives, and other associates, most of whose interests were one way or another linked with their own in the counties.[33]

If the Rockinghams lacked the depth of personnel and the infrastructure that would characterize the Whig party in later years, they also (as Paul Langford alone among their present-day chroniclers has discerned) were not endowed with the drive and determination of the "old Whigs," the members of the Pelham-Newcastle oligarchy, whom they considered to be their predecessors.[34] It is remarkable how little time Rockingham, Portland, Cavendish, and Dowdeswell spent planning political strategies or drawing up division lists, or estimating voting or party affiliations in the House of Commons. The kinds of concern which some of their predecessors had been addicted to, they regarded as onerous duties and often neglected altogether.[35]

In the late 1760s, a few of the old corps were still in the party, but their influence had declined dramatically. Since the Duke of Newcastle had fallen from power in 1762, he had been pushed steadily into the background both of his own connection and of politics generally, and his complaints to Rockingham about the failure of his younger friends to consult him regularly or to heed his advice had grown louder and become more frequent over the years.[36] In the spring election of 1768, Newcastle brought only three personal followers into the Commons who had been with him before 1762. They were James West,[37] who in the fifties had served Henry Pelham and Newcastle as a secretary of the Treasury and had remained Newcastle's faithful man of business in opposition; and John Hewett[38] and John Offley,[39] who were landowners from Nottinghamshire and Staffordshire, respectively. None of these men was ever of much consequence in the House. West attended regularly but in thirty years spoke only once. Hewett was a disinterested country gentleman who seldom attended, and Offley, though he had held minor offices under Newcastle in the fifties, later showed little ambition and appears never to have spoken in the debates.

Besides Newcastle, there were only three old-corps leaders who still acted with the Rockinghams in the late 1760s, and their influence was also on the decline. The Earl of Albemarle,[40] the head of the Keppel family, was suffering from age and the infirmities that go with it; until his death in 1772, his interest in politics and his attendance in Parliament were at best spasmodic. His friends the Earl of Winchilsea[41] and the old Earl of Bessborough[42] no longer concerned themselves much with public affairs or attempted to make their voices heard in the upper echelons of the party.

Among the younger men who took over the Whig traditions in the 1760s, the most noticeable characteristic was a tendency towards inertia in national political affairs, which made quick or decisive action almost impossible. Rockingham displayed this characteristic excessively and for this reason was severely handicapped politically. Even so, by the time he left office in 1766, he had developed some of the attributes that were necessary to justify his high stature among his friends. He seems to have had a natural air of authority and a gift for dealing with people. This enabled him to get his followers to support party policies in difficult situations. William Dowdeswell, who was quite competent in this regard, was well aware of his leader's talent. In early 1771, for instance, when Rockingham was kept from London for personal reasons, Dowdeswell wrote to him, at one point almost in a panic, pleading for his appearance to help enforce obedience among their friends on a course about which many felt uneasy: "The public ... at this critical moment stands much in need of Your Lordships presence here for a few days ... If Your Lordship could pass 40 hours in London, it might be of much service ... It is material as well for the preservation of my weight among ... [our friends] as for confirming them & bringing Them to an attendance."[43] In similar circumstances, the Duke of Portland wrote in January 1773:

Your presence here is of the utmost consequence to conciliate differences & moderate opinions which the strictest honesty in some, & vanity may have suggested in others, but which, be the motives what they may, ought to be modelled if possible to such a shape as may enable us to exert all our powers in resisting a plan which my ideas are gloomy enough to represent to me as consequentially involving in it the total ruin of this Country ... There is no other person capable of undertaking it but Yourself; & Therefore would most earnestly exhort you to it.[44]

Rockingham was highly respected by all his colleagues and was eminently capable in working with them. As his death in 1782 was to demonstrate, he was "the Centre of our Union, without [whom] ... we should become a rope of Sand."[45] It is perhaps unfortunate that he was seldom able to combine his abilities with aggressiveness. In dealing with parliamentary affairs, he always moved slowly and hesitantly. This appears to have been partly the result of a lack of self-confidence. As one of his friends once pointed out, "Lord Rockingham's disposition is always to deferr, & by too fine spun schemes to bring about what he wishes. He loses many opportunities by being always too late & while he is talking and scheming perhaps to prevent a thing, it is done."[46] Rockingham's dilatoriness was also the result of a lack of consistent interest. While he could, on occasion, become quite enthusiastic about an issue, he was also inclined, especially during the parliamentary recess, to neglect politics completely for long periods in order to pursue other matters.

His health was not the best. He often complained of stomach troubles and boils. However, it is evident that he seldom allowed illness to interfere with interests about which he genuinely cared. His love of the turf and the amount of time, money, and energy he put into breeding and training horses is well known. Furthermore, he was a most industrious farmer. When his father died in 1750, the marquis inherited a great fortune in land, situated in Ireland, Northumberland, and his home county, Yorkshire.[47] The celebrated agriculturalist Arthur Young, after making one of his famous tours in 1768, commented, "The husbandry of the Marquis of Rockingham is much more worthy of attention than that of any palace; the effects which have and must continue to result from it are one of the noblest and most truly national kind." Young added that Rockingham's operations demonstrated "how much an extensive tract of country is obliged to this patriotic nobleman for introducing a cultivation unknown before."[48]

Rockingham was also active in the local politics of Yorkshire. His influence came as a result of noble bloodlines and landed wealth, and it was secured by a demonstrated respect for the attitudes of the largest landholding classes in the county. Ten of the twenty MPs who supported the party in the Commons were elected with direct support from the Marquis or, as in York, from the politically motivated Rockingham Club. However, few of these men could have felt assured of success without the approval of the important landed gentry in their districts. Six were themselves independent country gentlemen, whose inclinations towards the party reflected their respect for the marquis and his close friend Sir George Savile. To maintain his standing, what Rockingham needed more than anything else was a thorough understanding of the values, aspirations, and biases of the landed gentry. He seems to have recognized this from the beginning,[49] and as is evinced in particular by his performance during the petitioning movement of 1769, it forced him at times to move with extreme caution in undertaking political objectives.[50]

Rockingham seldom showed as much affinity for politics on the national level as he did on the county level, and he rarely allowed national affairs to interfere with his farming, horse breeding, or racing. If Newcastle was the archetype courtier, concerned chiefly for power and office, Rockingham was above all a country aristocrat. This does not imply that he was totally unconcerned about parliament. Indeed, he must have realized that success there would do much to augment his standing in Yorkshire. However, it does help to account for the fact that his attention to parliamentary affairs was less consistent than that of many of his contemporaries. In Yorkshire he felt at home and enjoyed unparalleled prestige. In the House of Lords he was somewhat out of his element – and early in his career was often a source of amusement to his critics. Ostensibly because of innate shyness, he spoke in the Lords only four times before 1770, and two of these occasions were during his ministry when a few words from the first lord of the Treasury were essential. His inadequacy in this regard was well known. In 1768 lady Mary Coke[51] wrote: "Lord Rockingham ... will [not], I dare say, leave any thing untry'd to raise as much disturbance as he can, with no other view then [sic] placing himself again at the head of Affairs, Which he wou'd be incapable of, was there no other reason, then [sic] he's [sic] not being able to speak in the House of Lords."[52]

Rockingham's somewhat cavalier approach is to a greater or lesser extent evinced in the actions and attitudes of all his most noteworthy parliamentary supporters. Foremost among these in the early years was William Dowdeswell. Dowdeswell exemplifies just how weak the lines separating the traditional parties could be, for before he joined the Rockinghams in 1765, he had been a Tory. He converted to the Whigs partly because of "coinciding territorial and personal interests in the West Country,"[53] but it is also clear that one of the main reasons why he and two Tory friends[54] were able to stay with the Rockinghams over the years was that they were comfortable with the party's casual attitude towards politics in general. Dowdeswell was the leader of the party in the House of Commons and spoke more often for the Whigs than anyone else in the connection, including Burke.[55] He was also central in framing party policies in both the long and the short term. The Duke of Portland once justly described him as "our great Bulwark in the House of Commons & our great luminary in all private consultations ... whose clearness in explaining & judgement in determining are equaled by his disinterestedness & integrity."[56] But for all Dowdeswell's importance in the party and his abilities in the House of Commons, he cannot be compared with the political opportunists of the Pelham-Newcastle era. Although he worked energetically in Parliament, he resembled the independent country gentleman to a significant degree. Between sessions he retired to his farm in Worcestershire and lost all contact with public and political life. For instance, in October 1772, when the crisis in the East India Company was causing a great deal of controversy and public alarm and when the administration announced that Parliament would meet earlier than usual to deal with the crisis, Dowdeswell wrote to Burke, "We are to meet in November. If You do not think this place too distant from Yours, mount your horse & come & tell Me why. There must be something in agitation worth attending to: and I am so Uninformed, so little versed in politics, *during the summer*, that I have not a guess about it."[57] One of the best overall descriptions of this man came from Burke. After the party fell from power in 1766, he lamented that it had no other leader in the House of Commons "but Dowdeswell, who though by far the best man of business in the King-dom, and ready and efficient in debate is not perhaps quite strenuous and pugnacious enough for that purpose."[58]

It is not surprising that the one man in the Rockingham fold who demonstrated some dissatisfaction with Dowdeswell on these partic-ular grounds was Burke. He was the most energetic and consistently active member of the party. Over the years, he not only kept himself and his friends informed of all the important political matters on the national scene, but he regularly acted as the chief publicist for the party. His two major works in this period were his *Observations on a Late State of the Nation* (1769) and *Thoughts on the Cause of the Present Discontents* (1770). It is impossible to avoid the conclusion that in some ways Burke was unsuited by nature to be a Rockingham and that he might have felt more comfortable with politicians such as Robert Walpole, Newcastle, or William Pitt the Younger[59] – who de-voted their entire lives to politics and political intrigue and who wanted constantly to be at the forefront of affairs. Dissatisfaction with his leaders' ways was often recorded in Burke's letters. When the Rockingham ministry fell in August 1766 and the marquis retreated quietly to the country, Burke sent his first gentle admonition for ne-glect of duty: "I begin almost to fear, that your Lordship Left Town a little too early. I think your friends must since then have wanted your advice on more than one occasion."[60] Such complaints were to be-come increasingly frequent and at times betrayed a distinct feeling of frustration and dejection.

However, Burke's loyalty was limitless. In 1765 the marquis had befriended him and given him paid employment, and from then on Burke was emphatically prepared to face many years in the wilder-ness with him. Thus, for instance, in January 1767 he told a friend that the Rockinghams were "by a good deal the strongest, of any, sepa-rated from Government, and their connection the closest":

They certainly stand fairest in point of character; but that fairness which they have kept, and are determined still to keep, goes against their practicability; which is a quality you know and feel to be indispensible ... [in the pursuit of power] ... Their turn never can be next, whilst any party, of not more strength, and practicability, may be found; and it may very easily. I look therefore upon our Cause, viewed on the side of power, to be, for some years at least, quite desperate.[61]

Ironically, Burke's devotion to the Whigs helped to prevent him from giving the party the full benefit of his prodigious intellect. Before the death of Dowdeswell in 1775,[62] he was seldom able to be the decisive force that some historians would like us to see.[63] This does not mean that the picture those historians have painted is entirely wrong. I would agree with Conor Cruise O'Brien, for instance, that Burke deserves something much better than the harsh assessments of the Namierite school.[64] Throughout his life, he tried repeatedly to do what was right. He fought to help those he considered oppressed, including the Irish, African slaves, and religious minorities. As I have recently indicated elsewhere, he also displayed considerable courage and devotion to principle in seeking fair treatment for unpopular elements that he personally found distasteful. During one particular short stretch in 1780, these included the Gordon rioters, naval mutineers, and, perhaps most remarkably, two sodomites.[65] However, in attempting to explode the Namierite myth, we should not write another. If we are ever going to understand Burke fully, we have to recognize that he was a human being with human qualities. Distinct amongst these was his bias for the men with whom he operated in national politics. Burke worshipped his party and all its ideals and values. His aristocratic friends were men of "temperate, permanent, hereditary virtue" who had "redeemed the present age, and would have adorned the most splendid period in ... history,"[66] whereas he himself and others of the same common stamp were as "annual plants that perish with our Season and leave no sort of Traces behind."[67] Consequently, in the early years, it was particularly difficult for Burke to step forth as any sort of leader.

In the House of Commons, he nearly always worked under the direction (or, as Paul Langford has put it, "in harness with") Dowdeswell. His responsibility was to endorse and bolster, after his partner had taken the initiative by "putting motions or amendments, opposing ministerial proposals, developing the basic arguments against the government's measures, and generally setting up the framework on which the typical debate developed."[68] With respect to policy, Burke normally acquiesced in the line prescribed either by Dowdeswell or Rockingham. Consequently, through the entire period of this study, he was not instrumental in determining a single major strategy. As will be seen, the conditions on which the Rockinghams were prepared to accept office in 1767 and the decision to become involved in the petitioning campaign of 1769 were largely Dowdeswell's business. The Jury Bill of 1771 and the subsequent challenge to the undue influence of the crown were Rockingham's preoccupations. And the "broad and comprehensive" ministry was a vision of both men. Burke at times actually found himself going against his better judgment to work with his colleagues. Thus, he not only supported the fruitless movement to establish a union among the opposition between 1767 and 1770,[69] but as O'Brien acknowledges, for the party's sake Burke helped temper its stand with respect to the American colonies.[70] He also materially reworked the *Thoughts* to fit the cause of union.[71] In 1773, moreover, he helped defend the East India Company from government regulation, though he foresaw that regulation might well be necessary to prevent abuses by the company's servants.[72]

After Dowdeswell's death in 1775, Burke's stature in the party necessarily rose.[73] In the later seventies, he spoke more often than any of his friends in either of the Houses of Parliament, he demonstrated considerable independence on important matters such as constitutional reform, and he regularly participated in policy formulation. This, however, was a different Burke, one forced by circumstances to exert a more controlling hand. For the period of this study, the facts are unavoidable. Burke stood a solid step below the most commanding figures in the Rockingham fold. To say this is not to suggest that he did not have his own opinions on consequential issues; historians have recently uncovered convincing evidence that during the Rockinghams' first administration, Burke recognized the need to repeal the Stamp Act before any of his friends did.[74] What it does mean, however, is that Burke's role in the early years, both in and out of government, was normally not that of a decision maker; it was one of publicist, informant, and worker. To be sure, in this particular connection, the fact that he could fulfil his duties in these areas made him indispensable. Because Rockingham and Dowdeswell lacked Burke's energy, eloquence, and knowledge of events, they relied on him a great deal and rarely made a move without consulting him. In reality, there was no one else they could turn to, because the vast majority of their supporters were afflicted with the same country-gentleman mentality as themselves.

First and foremost among the men who normally backed the party's central core was Sir George Savile, Rockingham's friend and a pillar of his influence in Yorkshire. Savile's major attribute was respectability. In Yorkshire, where he owned large estates, he was the leading member of the gentry class, without whom Rockingham would most likely never have achieved his predominance. The county's twenty-thousand-strong electorate was the largest in Britain. Yet from 1761 to 1783, Savile was unopposed in filling one of its two seats in the House of Commons and he essentially chose who should have the other.[75] He was looked on by his neigbours and the members of the House of Commons as a man of strict moral rectitude, and he was once referred to by a leading political figure as "the most Virtuous character in this country" because of "his constitutional, as well as his private integrity."[76] For the purposes of the Rockingham connection, Savile's major shortcoming was his independence. People considered him a virtuous person largely because, by eighteenth-century standards, he was just that. He had no desire for political power. He refused office under Rockingham in both 1765 and 1782, and although he was a firm friend of the marquis and often attended meetings of the party leaders, he was liable to refuse to support his friends when to do so might violate his strict moral code or constitutional ideals.[77]

The two other really important members of the connection, the Duke of Portland and his cousin Lord John Cavendish, also did not exude the qualities of the professional politician. Both were Rockingham's close friends and were influential enough in the north of England to contribute significantly to his strength. Neither, however, was consistently active in parliamentary politics. Portland's priorities seem to have been much like those of the marquis. He was reasonably active at the local level and in 1768 was instrumental in returning six MPs.[78] For the most part, Portland was also unable effectively to extend his interest to the national theatre. He was perpetually involved in business or social activities in the country, and he attended irregularly and seldom spoke in the House of Lords. Cavendish was the brother of the fourth Duke of Devonshire,[79] for whom Newcastle and his friends had resigned in 1762. He too brought considerable numerical strength to the party. Since Devonshire's death, he had become the leader of a circle that included his brothers Lord Frederick[80] and Lord George Cavendish,[81] his cousin Henry Cavendish,[82] and three friends in the House of Commons.[83] Lord John was respected for his good sense and moderation and was quite a competent public speaker. In the heat of debate he was able to keep his head. Under "the appearance of virgin modesty, he had a confidence in himself that nothing could equal."[84] However, he tended to lack resolve in undertaking political objectives. In 1767 Burke considered contesting the borough of Lancaster for a seat in Parliament, but he hesitated to commit himself without the approval of Lord John and his family, who had some interest there. A mutual friend gave a fairly accurate description of the Cavendishes' general attitude to politics when he told Burke, "I think you right not to look for it, but with the entire desire of the Cavendishes, for they are right Men, and good Men; and I am persuaded too, they are your friends, but dont let their Idleness and Your Delicacy cooperate to hurt you all."[85]

In the House of Lords the Rockinghams had only one competent speaker after Newcastle's death. He was Albemarle's cousin, the third Duke of Richmond.[86] Richmond had first become closely connected with the party towards the end of the 1765–66 administration, when Rockingham had appointed him northern secretary. He left office with the party and eventually determined to stay with it, though torn between his loyalty to Rockingham and to his brother-in-law Henry Seymour Conway,[87] who remained in power in the Chatham ministry.[88] Because of his willingness to engage in public debate, Richmond was a valuable asset. This was particularly marked on occasions when he was "the only Ld in the opposition that was a speaker."[89] He had "an anxious, busy mind,"[90] but he too was rather spasmodic in attending to political business. Burke put his finger squarely on the problem when he told Rockingham that "Work must be cut out for him … If this be done, I am sure he will be faithful and resolute; and I am persuaded he is an essential part of the Strength of your body."[91] When Richmond felt that a course of action was clear and he had an important role to play in pursuit of a cause, he threw all his efforts into party activities. Thus, for instance, he was very active in the negotiations between the Chatham administration and the Rockinghams and other parties in 1767[92] and in championing the cause of the East India Company against government interference in 1772–74.[93] But at other times he was likely to go into a state of stagnation from which it was very difficult to extricate him. Rockingham recognized Richmond's abilities, and he attempted to keep in touch with him as much as possible. However, this was not easy. Richmond lived far to the south in Sussex and therefore missed many of the important meetings at which the marquis and his friends in the northern counties made some crucial decisions. He therefore felt "how little weight my opinion is of with our Friends in the Lump"[94] and was less effective than he might otherwise have been.

Two people who merit mention because of the frequency with which they were consulted were Albemarle's brother, Admiral Augustus Keppel,[95] and the latter's close friend, Sir Charles Saunders.[96] Both men had mapped out careers for themselves in the navy and had served under Pitt during the Seven Years' War. Both had also been lords of the Admiralty in the first Rockingham administration. Keppel and Saunders attended regularly but spoke infrequently in the House of Commons and mostly on matters concerning the navy, where their real ambitions lay.

The rank-and-file Rockinghams were men who were connected territorially or through family or friendship with the leaders and who, for various reasons, were content to stay with a group of men who were not very tenacious in pursuing political objectives. In the House of Lords, where Rockingham had some twenty supporters,[97] they were people such as the Duke of Devonshire,[98] "a very bashful young man," in 1768, who "speaks very little and is *bien sauvage et bien gauche*";[99] the Earl of Fitzwilliam,[100] Rockingham's nephew and heir; Lord Archer,[101] who married the daughter of James West; the Earl of Stamford,[102] Portland's brother-in-law; Lord Abergavenny,[103] an old Whig who in the fifties had been connected through marriage with the Pelhams; and Sir George Savile's close friend from Yorkshire, the Earl of Scarborough.[104] None of these men had anything much to contribute except the occasional vote. In general their attendance record was poor, their interest short-lived, and their parliamentary talents negligible.

In the House of Commons, I estimate the Rockinghams' numbers to have been about eighty-five.[105] This calculation is considerably larger than that of some other historians.[106] Our main difference seems to be over where to draw the line between MPs who could be classified either as independents or as Rockinghams. It is in some measure a reflection of the rather casual approach to politics by members of the party, at all levels, that a substantial percentage of the men who normally followed the lead of Dowdeswell, Burke, and Lord John Cavendish were quite independent. They not only displayed no desire for national office, but (despite a bias in the Rockinghams' favour) they generally disliked party and prided themselves on their ability to decide every issue on its merits. Like Savile, they might refuse to support the party when careful attention was not paid to their moral or constitutional principles. Such men were John Hanbury,[107] MP for Monmouthshire, whose father had been a prominent old Whig in the previous reign; Charles Turner,[108] who came into Parliament with Rockingham's support in York but refused to join the Rockingham Club there and made the marquis's life uncomfortable on occasions when he spoke out against peers meddling in elections;[109] William and Thomas Frankland,[110] who represented Thirsk; and George René Aufrere,[111] MP for Stamford. Based largely on their voting patterns between 1766 and 1782, or on their friendship with one or more of the leaders of the party, I have classified most of these men as independent Rockinghams (and therefore in the following).[112]

Whether my assessment or a narrower one is used, the general picture that emerges of the politicians who supported the Rockinghams in the Commons is the same as in the Lords. Few appear to have had much interest in making their mark in national politics. Of course, there were one or two noteworthy exceptions. Robert Walsingham,[113] for instance – who was connected through marriage to the Cavendish family and had won his seat with Rockingham's backing at Knaresborough – attended regularly and spoke often, despite the fact that politics were secondary to his career as a naval officer. Similarly, George Dempster[114] and Robert Gregory[115] attained influence in the Commons, though they were primarily concerned with their interests in the East India Company, of which they were substantial stockholders and at various times directors. More typical of the Rockingham following in the Lower House were country gentlemen such as William Weddell,[116] Beilby Thompson,[117] Nathaniel Cholmley,[118] and Fontaine Wentworth Osbaldeston,[119] who appear to have entered Parliament largely to demonstrate their standing among the leading gentry families in the regions.

The majority of the Rockinghams in the House of Commons were men who had inherited a family tradition of identification with Whig ideals. Paradoxically, however, there was a noticeable Tory element in the party.[120] Most of the Rockingham Tories were in general representative of many who had become associated with that title under the first two Hanoverians. They were country gentlemen who had a natural aversion to courts and no desire to attain power, and who looked on Parliament primarily as a means of promoting regional objectives. Some of them, such as Sir Anthony Abdy[121] who came from a Tory family well known in Surrey and Essex, and his friend John Luther,[122] were rather independent. Others, such as William Dowdeswell's friends, Sir William Codrington[123] and Charles Barrow,[124] were more strongly committed to the party. All of them found that their disinterested approach was acceptable to the Rockingham Whigs, and they therefore had little difficulty remaining on good terms with them.

One of the most interesting things about the Rockingham party is that it stands as evidence that before George III's reign, the line separating many of the Whigs from many of the Tories had been extremely blurred. Under George I and George II, the Whig party had been thought to consist primarily of those who, in conjunction with Walpole, Pelham, and Newcastle, aspired to keep a firm grasp on the reins of power. They were thought to be professional, ambitious politicians. Yet there was always a substantial number of them who could not be described that way. People such as John Hewett, John Offley, and Sir George Savile were Whigs because they had inherited the tradition or because they had come into Parliament with the support of known Whigs. In the 1760s, the Rockinghams took over the lead of many such men – country Whigs, who had as much in commmon with the country Tories in the House of Commons as with any of the other groups, Whig or Tory. This points to the danger of assuming that an eighteenth-century political figure can, without careful attention to the circle he moved in, automatically be categorized with others who were identified with the same party label. Clearly, the Rockingham Tories were not normally aligned with Sir Roger Newdigate or William Bagot in the sixties and seventies. And one wonders if scholars have too readily assumed that such men should be lumped together earlier in the century.[125] If, in George III's reign, Abdy and Luther were connected not with numerous other Tories but with country Whigs such as Savile and Turner and were loosely associated with Rockingham, almost anything is possible.

Linda Colley has argued that under the first two Hanoverian kings, Tories developed an uncommon taste for some radical expedients, whose objective it was to keep MPs attuned to their constituents rather than to the influence of the crown.[126] Her thesis is beyond dispute. However, it seems appropriate to point out that in the long eighteenth century, all country-party politicians – Whig and independent as well as Tory – supported that objective.[127] The degree to which non-Tory country politicians responded in the first half of the century to the idea of employing extraparliamentary instructions, associations, and other radical measures to achieve it needs to be examined more closely. One would assume that there was considerable sympathy among the group that H.T. Dickinson has described as "radical Country Whigs" at least.[128] There is little doubt, however, that country advocates of all leanings supported such measures late in the century. Thus, for instance, near the end of the American Revolution, men such as Savile and Turner promoted Christopher Wyvill's association movement, annual Parliaments, and changes to the system of representation.[129] Of the association itself, which was to be a new institution to give the landed interest in particular a stronger voice in the government process, Savile claimed that he "had long ardently wished ... he had even hungered and thirsted for some such measure."[130]

Much of this study will focus on the Rockinghams' considerable efforts to draw under their leadership not only country gentlemen but all sorts of politicians and personal followings, and thus build the Whig party into the great connection they believed it had been in the past. One of the conclusions this will lead to is that the Rockinghams' efforts to create unity actually helped drive wedges between themselves and other groups, and thus reinforced division to the point where only the death and attrition of principal players could possibly overcome it. This is just one of a number of ironies that a close examination of the Rockingham Whigs helps to illuminate. These men were Whigs who attracted significant Tory support; they were also country aristocrats and gentlemen who genuinely believed that they were the direct descendants and the only true representatives of the courtiers and professional politicians who had been known as the court Whig oligarchy before their time. These contradictions were, as will be seen, reflected in many of their approaches to parliamentary politics in Britain during their career. In the earliest years of opposition, however, the contradictions are most apparent in the perception that Rockingham and his friends had of self.

The historian going over the Rockinghams' correspondence of the late 1760s, becomes aware of an ambivalence about the party's proper role in British society and government. In the first place, unmistakable from the time they went into opposition in late 1766 is an acceptance by them all that they might not follow the example of their court Whig predecessors in rising to ministerial office. The Rockinghams unquestionably realized (and were not significantly disquieted by) the distinct possibility that they might spend a considerable portion of their career in the political wilderness. This has already been demonstrated in the case of Burke, who very early on wrote that his leaders were too principled and lacked the drive and pragmatism to be successful in competition with rival parties. The other leading members of the connection were not endowed by nature with Burke's facility with words, but in their own way most of them at one time or another made similar acknowledgments. Like Burke, they saw their willingness to forgo the pleasures of ministerial appointment as something about which they could be most proud. In July 1767 Dowdeswell, who did more than anyone else to determine Rockingham policy, counselled the marquis never to accept a mandate from the king to form an administration unless he had complete control over the designation of offices and certain assurances regarding principles. This, he realized, might keep his party out of power for a considerable period of time. "I confess that I see no fair prospect before us" of an early return, he observed. However, he insisted that the party must not yield, and he was prepared without hesitation to accept the consequences: "Standing still is the only thing we can do. This may possibly weaken us as a party: it depends upon the virtue of our friends whether it will or will not but I am sure it will do us honour as Individuals. In these unhappy times when we find ourselves well in the opinion of mankind the wisest thing we can do is to stand still & enjoy the reputation which we have, Not risque it for something new the chances of which are so much against us."

The leading members of the party also took pains to publicize the fact that they were prepared to decline office over matters of principle. In 1769 Burke acknowledged in the *Observations on a Late State of the Nation* that his connection would "be charged … with a dangerous spirit of exclusion and proscription, for being unwilling to mix in schemes of administration, which have no bond of union, or principle of confidence."[131] A year or so later, after a good deal of input from all the leading members of the party, he produced the *Thoughts*, in part because of a desire to justify "to our friends and to the world, the refusal, which is inevitable, of what will be thought very advantageous Offers. This can only be done by shewing the ground upon which the Party stands; and how different its constitution, as well as the persons who compose it are from the Bedfords, and Grenvilles, and other knots, who are combined for no publick purpose; but only as a means of furthering with joint strength, their private and individual advantage."[132]

The historian also finds expressed frequently in the Rockinghams' early writings the conviction that, as court Whigs, their rightful place was at the head of government and society.[133] This forced them to see it as their responsibility to return to power at some time in the future. Thus, for instance, when speaking of potential allies in opposition, Rockingham always gave priority to those whom he felt would be suitable if they were ever "called upon to form a Ministry in concert" with his own following.[134] In the *Observations*, he and the rest of the party leadership, while warning of the possibility that they might decline appointments, also espoused the opinion that they could well be called on to accept them. The "proper remedy" to all the nations' problems was for the men "who act steadily" on a certain set of principles "to be very serviceable to their country; in one case, by furnishing … an administration formed upon ideas very different from those which have for some time been unfortunately fashionable."[135] Similarly, while attempting in the *Thoughts* to explain the reasons why they might reject office, they also meant "to form and to unite a party upon real and well founded principles – which would in the end prevail and re'establish order and Government in this country."[136]

In the 1760s this ministerial perspective was still relatively strong among the Rockingham leaders, partly because they had so recently been in office. They had not spent enough time in the political wilderness to learn instinctively to view themselves in the long term as a party of opposition, and therefore it was easier than it would eventually become for them to believe that a resurrection of the court Whigs under their own direction was a realistic possibility. Nothing more plainly demonstrates this than their response to one of the most enduring and polemical issues of the entire decade – the one centring on Lord Bute[137] and the apparent problem of favouritism in the early administrations of George III's reign.[138] This issue provided the central focus for the Rockinghams' early political activities. A thorough understanding of their position is essential in marking the evolution of the party away from its court Whig roots and towards its country Whig future.

When they left office in July 1766, the Rockingham Whigs were very unsure of themselves.[139] They had originally formed their government not on their own volition but under the direction and close control of the king's uncle, the Duke of Cumberland.[140] After Cumberland's premature death just a few months into the administration, the party leaders had proved to be poor courtiers. Instead of rising to the challenge of office, they had looked frantically to others for leadership, had stumbled onto momentary expedients in dealing with American resistance to the Stamp Act, and had failed to convince anyone, most of all the king, that they had the stuff of leadership.[141] Animosity towards Bute and the determination to resist interference by him and his supporters in the governing process gave the central corps of the party a *raison d'être* and held them together in the early years of opposition, when they might very well have come apart at the seams.

The Rockinghams' first major opportunity to take a stand came in July 1767, only a few months after they had decided to play an active parliamentary role against the Chatham ministry. At that time, they were approached by government representatives and asked to consider the possibility of taking part in the formation of a new administration.[142] Subsequently, they entered into negotiations with the other major opposition parties – the Bedfords and the Grenvilles – in an effort to establish a plan for a "broad," "comprehensive," and united ministry. Its purpose was "to rescue his Majesty and this country out of the hands of the Earl of Bute, and to restore strength and energy to the King's government, upon a constitutional footing, free from *favoritism* and the *guidance* of a minister, not in a responsible employment."[143] For this plan, both the other opposition connections expressed full support. The Duke of Bedford said that he was anxious to join the "common cause, for rooting out that maxim of favourites who have got too great an ascendancy over the minds of princes, of *divide and impera*, and of changing administrations almost annually in order to retain their unconstitutional power."[144] And some of the leading members of George Grenville's following apparently claimed that they were "ready, willing and most desirous of supporting an administration with ... Lord Rockingham at the head of the Treasury, upon the great plan of removing the Bute interest from court."[145] For all the men involved, the need to achieve these objectives was firmly grounded in experience gained during the early, rather chaotic, years of George III's reign. However, for the Rockinghams alone, it predominated over all other considerations in national politics.

Perhaps no public figure in British history has ever been as feared, detested, and vilified by politicians as the Earl of Bute was in the 1760s. Initially, animosity towards him had developed because he had seemed to use his friendship with the new king to gain control of the crown and thereby force his way into power at the expense of the politicians who had governed the nation so successfully for most of George II's reign. It was alleged that in 1760, when "he had not had time to learn the course by which he should sail, he drove from the helm the able pilot who had guided the ship in the roughest seas. He expelled from the cabinet the old, the experienced and faithful counsellers ... the firm friends of the House of Hanover, that he might alone, and without controul, dictate in an affair [the peace] where his council should have very little weight, if it was to depend on trial or proof of his abilities." [146]

The "able pilot" was, of course, the popular hero of the Seven Years' War, William Pitt, and "the old, the experienced and faithful counsellers" were the old Whigs who fell from power with Newcastle and Devonshire in 1762. The expulsion of these men by a newcomer to the political world, whose power rested solely on his friendship with the king, provoked a series of direct and often intemperate attacks on the favourite and his alleged accomplice, the king's mother.[147] First amongst the anti-Bute propagandists were Pitt's sympathizers, John Wilkes[148] and Charles Churchill,[149] whose diatribes in the North Briton sparked the general warrants conflict in 1763.[150] For several years thereafter, resentment towards Bute continued to grow because of a combination of events, including apparent confrontations between him and the three parties that in 1767 agreed to unite against him.

After the Duke of Newcastle and his friends fell from power in 1762, Bute took over the Treasury and headed the administration for twelve months. When he resigned, largely as a result of the public outcry against him, George Grenville formed a ministry in conjunction with the Duke of Bedford.[151] During this ministry, a paranoia developed out of the fear that Bute continued to hold onto all effective power because of his ability to reach the king and advise him "behind the curtain."[152] The ministers themselves displayed much of this paranoia, and Grenville's constant suspicion of Bute led to conflicts between him and the king, which eventually brought down the government, despite the fact that it had the support of a large majority in the House of Commons. It was on the fall of the Grenvilles and Bedfords that the Rockinghams formed the administration in 1765, out of which they were to emerge as a party and as the recognized successors of the one-time very powerful Pelham-Newcastle Whigs.[153] Because of the young Whigs' belief in their kinship with the latter party, and because many of them, including Rockingham himself, had earlier resigned or been turned out of office along with the old Whigs, they had reason to feel substantial enmity towards Bute. This and their concern about public opinion prompted them to insist, when they achieved power, on the expulsion of a number of crown appointees whom they believed were Bute's friends and supporters. Partly as a consequence of this, they found that on the crucial issue of the repeal of the Stamp Act, they were unable to command the support of many of the placemen who looked to the king rather than to the politicians for leadership.

This experience gave the Rockinghams an enduring sense of injustice. After the arrangements were made for William Pitt, as the Earl of Chatham, to take over the conduct of government, Rockingham told a friend that as "to Lord Bute and *the Lady*, I give them the Credit of being the secret spring of the late Events and continue on this subject the same Calm Contempt, by which it is said I gave Offence when in office."[154] However, he and his principal colleagues were convinced that their downfall had been a result not only of the secret influence of certain advisers but of a system whereby men who held places under the crown could be turned against an existing government.[155] In his first political pamphlet, Burke, who was fast emerging as the mouthpiece of the party, wrote: "In the Prosecution of their Measures [the late ministers] were traversed by an Opposition of a new and singular Character; an Opposition of Place-men and Pensioners. They were supported by the Confidence of the Nation. And having held their Offices under many Difficulties and Discouragements, they left them at the express Command, as they had accepted them at the earnest Request of their Royal Master."[156] When Chatham took office in 1766, he made no attempt to demonstrate animosity towards the Bute interest or to exclude it from office. This encouraged the opposition groups to believe that some sort of "junction betwixt Lord Bute and Chatham" had taken place.[157] It became accepted theory that resistance to the present ministry and to the favourite amounted to the same thing.

The constitutional platform that developed in the fight against Bute came more from antiministerialist pens in the City than anywhere else. How eagerly the Rockinghams and their allies embraced it, however, is reflected in the amount they exploited it when searching for a common cause[158] and, perhaps above all, how heavily Burke relied on it when looking back on the decade of the sixties in his *Thoughts on the Cause of the Present Discontents*.[159] The parliamentary opposition parties found the anti-Bute stand compelling for two fundamental reasons. The first was that in the unstable conditions of these years, it allowed them all to operate as future ministers. The old Whigs, the Grenvilles and Bedfords, and the Rockinghams had confronted Bute directly (or at least had felt they had done so) while they were in office. In each case, this man had been the central force that had brought to an end (or made impossible to achieve) a long successful administration. The politicians were determined to eradicate his power so that their next term of office would be much less difficult.[160] The second reason was that they could claim ultimately to be fighting for the public good rather than for their own selfish designs. Conveniently, the most basic of the publicists' constitutional ideals was that favouritism had to be resisted because it offered a real threat to the entire government process.

More than anything else, the danger, they argued, resulted from the fact that proximity gave Bute and the small "cabal" of "minions" over which he ruled an opportunity to take complete possession of the king and thereby control and pervert his judgment:

A favourite of a crowned head is one, who, without any merit or recommendation from his country, for any services performed for the public, and glory of the crown, has found means to acquire a great and almost an exclusive influence and power over the mind of his royal master: one, who by an early near admission to his presence, conversation and private recreations, has improved every opportunity to discover his weaknesses, to mark his foibles, and to engratiate himself, till he gains an entire ascendant over his will; and governs him without controul.[161]

This situation, it was claimed, would inevitably do serious damage to every institution in the British constitution. Firstly, it would reduce the authority of the crown, since people would quickly recognize that the king was in effect a prisoner of his own counsellor and that the latter had become the true source of power. "Whenever there is a favourite at court, the King may have the crown upon his head, his hand may be kissed and the sword of his state attend his person but the favourite will be worshipped. The King will be but the picture of Majesty, the Favourite will be the reality and engross the whole tribute of it."[162] Similarly, the ministers chosen by Parliament would become little more than figureheads. They could fulfil their responsibility to advise the king, but only the favourite would be heeded, and in essence their influence over the affairs of state would amount to nothing. Ultimately, this meant that Parliament and therefore the people would lose their voice, since the favourite would be barring the king from the men who had the support of the elected representatives of the nation: "The whole executive power and administration of the state is to be placed in hands superiour to control; too strong for ordinary resistance, and too sacred ... for punishment. In effect, therefore, whenever people can be subdued to the practice of such theory, this principle amounts to perfect and complete despotism."[163]

Throughout the eighteenth century, one of the most consistent opposition themes was that which played on the propertied classes' general and often widespread fear of undue increases in the power and influence of the crown. Writers in the 1760s did not fail to incorporate this theme into their stand against secret influence. They argued that in order to make their controls over the king a source of virtual omnipotence, it had been necessary for Bute and his cohorts to do their utmost to expand the king's authority in Parliament and in the nation as a whole: "Ever since this favourite ... took the ascendant at court, prerogative and the power of the crown, have been founded in a manner of which there is no example, since the illustrious House of Hanover came to the throne."[164] Through bribery and the expansion of royal patronage, Bute had sought to give the crown an unfair advantage in elections and in the House of Commons. "Honours were lavished, obsolete places revived,"[165] and the balance between king, Lords, and Commons upset.

If it was a reflection of the age in which they lived that the Rockinghams and their allies wished to resist those "favorites who have got too great an ascendancy over the minds of princes," it was also to be expected that they would think of doing so by uniting their parliamentary forces. It was widely believed that Bute's success had been a result of the divisions of the politicians and that his "greatest dread was union against him; his constant and repeated practice, to break and divide all parties and connections."[166]

In the beginning, Bute had defeated Pitt and Newcastle by dealing with them separately. He turned them against each other and then was able to push them out of office one at a time. Then he established what Burke later called a "sort of *Rota* in the Court."[167] He influenced the king to have political parties brought into office separately, or with only a few followers, so that they would have to rely on his support. In order to ensure that his ministries were always weak and acquiescent, it had been to his advantage to "humble them by promoting a vigourous opposition to their measures" and then to turn them out and seek "the company of the discontented chiefs."[168] Bute kept repeating this process: after yielding the Treasury in 1763, he put the administration into the hands of the Grenvilles and Bedfords, then turned it over to Rockingham and finally to Chatham. It is interesting that many politicians and theorists of this age had little difficulty explaining what has drawn considerable ink from twentieth-century historians – the reason for the political instability of the first ten years of George III's reign.[169]

By working towards union in 1767, the leaders of the three opposition parties felt that they were pursuing the most effective course of resistance to the king's friends, and they could claim the concomitant noble objective of bringing back stable government to Great Britain. It was believed that when the present ministry fell, the king would be forced to call on the united parties (there would be no viable alternative to them), and that once in office, the parties would have the solidarity and political strength to ensure that government would be returned to the sound footing and just principles of the previous reign. A great new coalition like the court Whig oligarchy of the past would re-establish order in the nation. While both the Bedfords and the Grenvilles supported the idea of union against Bute, neither was to prove as faithful to it as the Rockinghams. The negotiations in July 1767 broke down because the three parties were unable to give up individual pretensions for the sake of unity. A few months later, the Bedfords accepted office under the Duke of Grafton[170] without prior agreement on or consideration of principles.

The Grenvilles were not offered a share of power at this stage, but evidence suggests that if they had been, they would almost certainly have accepted, even if this meant coming to terms with Bute. At the end of July, Alexander Wedderburn,[171] one of George Grenville's friends, who had been on good terms with Bute in Scotland, met the favourite. Wedderburn claimed that he found Bute extremely friendly towards the party and said he had done his utmost to persuade him that in the recent negotiations the party had not intended to use coalition as a means of forcing its way into power.[172] Whether or not Wedderburn's version of this story was genuine, both Grenville's man of business, Thomas Whately,[173] and Grenville himself believed it, and they were noticeably appreciative of his supposed attempts to exonerate them.[174] Whately informed his leader with obvious excitement a few days later that the "open language of Lord Bute's friends now is, that he has the same opinion of you as he had four years ago," when the party had taken over the lead in government. "The similarity of phrase [with that used by Bute] proves that the conversation with Wedderburn was for a purpose," added Whately.[175] On Grenville's death some three years later, the majority of his leading supporters were to make their peace with the government and accept offices. The Rockinghams, on the other hand, were asked to join the administration on their "own bottom" in July 1767, but they declined. Moreover, in a sort of manifesto, William Dowdeswell explicitly declared that in future both coalition with allies and the elimination of secret influence would be absolutely essential for the party to take office. In this extremely significant document, Dowdeswell stated that should the marquis ever again be approached, he must

at his audience ... give the K: to understand as tenderly as He can, but at the same time as truly, the real cause of all the public misfortunes. They must be imputed not to the influence of particular persons but to the prevalence of a political principle which says that the power of the Crown arises out of the Weakness of the administration. The public misfortunes necessarily resulting from that Weakness should be set forth & the distress of the Crown in its income & honour. At the same time that these representations are made with all possible deference & submission there should appear a manly resolution not to maintain the pageantry of administration an hour after it is divested of its necessary weight in the Closet, and its necessary power in other places.[176]

If the king accepted these precepts and still wanted Rockingham to form a government, the marquis was to negotiate again with his allies in an effort to establish a "broad and comprehensive" plan. This plan was to be based on the Rockinghams' predominance so that the ministry could be controlled and held to the proper policies and principles.[177] Rockingham was to have the Treasury for himself and "in all offices of business a manifest superiority for his own Friends." If these negotiations failed, he was to decline the offer to go into power, since any administration formed without union would be "insulted at Home & despised abroad." Moreover, it would still be a weak administration, for it would "consist of Men who will have no opinion of each other, who when they were before in office were always quarrelling with & frequently endeavoring to supplant each other. The Secret Promoter of it & the first Open Actor in it would probably be two Men the least conciliating ... & the most unpopular in the Kingdom."

The Rockinghams could hold out for such conditions largely because they, unlike their allies, felt no real sense of urgency about returning to high office. They were determined to accept places only under the very best of conditions. Their attitude suggests a country-like indifference to ministerial power, but it also demonstrates that at this stage in their career the party leaders still viewed themselves principally as court Whigs. They were not at all desperate to return to office, and they were prepared to bide their time in the political wilderness until the parameters were right; but they clearly saw it as their responsibility to form a strong ministry like those their ancestors had predominated over. It is apparent, moreover, that they considered themselves the only party in existence that was up to the task. A few years later, Burke was to take pains to point out that in the present reign it had only been

during the administration of the Marquis of Rockingham, [that] an attempt was made to carry on Government without ... [the] concurrence [of Bute and his minions]. However, this was only a transient cloud; ... [the King's friends] were hid but for a moment; and their constellation blazed out with greater brightness, and a far more vigourous influence, some time after it was blown over. An attempt was at that time made ... to break their corps, to discountenance their doctrines, to revive connexions of a different kind, to restore the principles and policy of the Whigs, to reanimate the cause of Liberty by Ministerial countenance; and then for the first time were men seen attached in office to every principle they had maintained in opposition.[178]

As they struggled against Bute, the Rockinghams saw themselves as the old Whig oligarchy, temporarily excluded from their rightful place at the head of government. But this perception gradually weakened. As their time in the political wilderness stretched into months and then into years, Rockingham and his friends learned to consider themselves as a more or less permanent vehicle of opposition. In this position, their solutions to the nations' problems and to some extent their basic constitutional philosophy had to be adjusted.

CHAPTER TWO

The Movement for a United Administration, 1768–1769

In the early 1770s, the Rockingham Whigs would find themselves facing, in the regime of Lord North,[1] the first administration of the reign that had the support of the crown, the court, and a substantial majority of the independent members in the House of Commons. By 1773, the greatest symptom of strife in the nation and the constitution would no longer seem to be that government kept collapsing; just the opposite was the case. Government had become so powerful and so secure that it could no longer reflect the will of the people. By then, Rockingham and his friends had stopped viewing themselves as courtiers temporarily removed from the helm and had begun – like the erstwhile opponents of their court Whig predecessors – to attempt to discover what it was that gave ministries apparently unlimited control. It was this preoccupation that diverted their attention away from Bute and his cabal and forced them to concentrate, like many country-party advocates in the past, on the undue influence of the crown. The Rockinghams' transition from the one perspective to the other began in early 1770. From then on, they increasingly saw themselves as victims of strong government rather than its chief proponents. Consequently, the eighteen or so months after the 1768 election was the last substantial period, before the formation of their administration of 1782, when they channelled a major portion of their energies towards the construction of a broadly based court Whig administration.

One of the things the party did from the autumn of 1768 to the spring of 1769 was attempt to define for itself, its allies, and the public at large the conditions on which it was prepared to accept office. In the process, it confirmed everything outlined in Dowdeswell's manifesto. This was important. Once the Rockinghams embraced a policy, their consistency and concern for principles largely prevented them from ever giving it up. To the premises they endorsed now, they remained loyal for the remainder of their career.[2] It was this that obliged them to turn down office in 1770 and again in 1780, and finally, in 1782, to accept it for the last time.[3] Admittedly, in the latter instance, as Professor O'Gorman has demonstrated, the party did compromise.[4] In particular, the marquis failed to stand firm by his insistence that he negotiate directly with the king and get full authority to form the ministry. It might be pointed out, however, that before accepting office, he was able to satisfy himself that all the basic parameters were in place. He had a coalition with the Shelburne[5] following; and he had the Treasury himself and would get key positions for his closest friends. He thus had reason to believe that he would be able to maintain his party's predominance over both measures and men. He also had assurances that important past commitments, including the eradication of secret influence, would be honoured. These requirements had been decided on by the leading Rockinghams in 1767. They had confirmed them and tried to clarify them for their allies and the public in 1768–69, and had then maintained them for nearly a quarter of a century in the political wilderness.

The first of Dowdeswell's prerequisite's which the Rockinghams began to work for in the autumn of 1768 was an amalgamation with any allied connections that had been jarred loose by Bute's divisive schemes. In the weeks just before and during the beginning of the new Parliament, they started once again to seek limited cooperation with just one other set. Early in the new year, however, they seemed, on the surface, to be on the verge of permanently drawing together all the parties in opposition. Had they succeeded, some modern historians would no doubt be even more thoroughly convinced that they should impose a two-party analysis on the politics of these years.[6] A close look at the union movement leads one to the conclusion, however, that what I.R. Christie has told us about the Rockinghams and other Whig groups in the seventies and eighties could well be said of the Rockinghams and all their allies in the late sixties; they were separated by striking differences in "attitudes and concerns" that were not about to go away.[7] The challenge for the principal parties involved during the 1768–69 session was to paper over their differences on important issues, including the American colonies and the volatile Middlesex election question. In future sittings, this was to prove a short-term solution that no longer sufficed when morale could not be buoyed by the happy prospect of victory in the House of Commons.

As the largest opposition party in Parliament, the Rockinghams seemed to be in a comparatively strong position after the 1768 election, for the Chatham administration was in a state of almost total disarray. The bulk of the ministry's problems derived from the fact that the various connections of which it was composed were unable to act even remotely like a single party unit. In dealing with the two major issues that had confronted it over the past two years – the settlement with the East India Company and the American problem – the administration had struggled along unaided by its would-be master, the Earl of Chatham, who had been ill and absent almost continually since January 1767. Consequently, it presented a picture of weakness, disunity, and inefficacy that was "rare, if not unique in British political history."[8] If the Bedfords had given the ministry some added strength in Parliament, they had done nothing whatever to improve its efficacy. From the time they had taken office in 1767, there had been rumours of discord within the cabinet, supposedly arising out of a power struggle between them and the Duke of Grafton. Many people believed that the Bedfords intended to force all Chatham's followers out in order to "draw their friend Mr. Grenville in after them."[9] There had been considerable speculation about this particular source of disharmony by 1768,[10] and another as well, involving Lord Shelburne, the secretary of state for the Southern Department. Shelburne had been on bad terms with his ministerial associates almost from the beginning, apparently because of his personality flaws, and by the spring it was widely believed that both the Bedfords and the Duke of Grafton were seeking his resignation.[11]

As a result of all these circumstances, plus the well-known fact that Grafton felt anything but comfortable as leader of this disreputable and divided government and was likely to resign at any moment, the fall of the ministry was expected throughout 1768.[12] Although Grenville was widely considered to be the logical candidate to replace Grafton, the chances that the Rockinghams with their more impressive following in the House of Commons would be approached with serious offers seemed very good indeed.[13] This unquestionably helped preserve the party's ministerial outlook, but it did little to alter its cavalier approach to politics as a whole. During the period when Parliament was out of session, the leading members of the party characteristically lost contact with the national scene altogether. Perhaps nothing better illustrates the difference between the Pelham-Newcastle Whigs of the forties and fifties and their successors in the sixties than the contrasting attitudes in the autumn of 1768 of the old Duke of Newcastle, on the one hand, and Rockingham and some of his younger friends, on the other. By then, Newcastle was within weeks of his death. He had been suffering from a serious illness since the previous December and had announced his retirement from active politics. Yet through his own efforts he remained in contact with the political world in general and with the Rockinghams in particular, hoping to see his comrades in office again. By September, he could see that this was a crucial time, and in his letters his feeling of utter frustration at the inertia displayed by the central core of the party is unmistakable. Between then and the commencement of the new session in early November, he wrote regularly to Rockingham[14] and others, including Portland[15] and the Duke of Richmond,[16] in an attempt to turn their thoughts to politics and get the party leadership together for strategy sessions. But for all his efforts, he obtained very little recompense. During these months, Rockingham spent most of his time at the Newmarket races, and in early October, Newcastle received a typical report of his activities: "I saw the Marquis this morning, in a great hurry dressing, his room full, no conversation but Pilgrim [his race horse] and the Masquerade, & as I have learnt no news in this house, I can not send your Grace any."[17]

Rockingham spent most of his time at Newmarket until the end of October, despite Lord Chatham's resignation on the twelfth.[18] The other leading members of the party likewise showed little interest. On 26 October, Albemarle informed Newcastle, "The Marquis has desired me to give a dinner to him, & Some of our Friends next Sunday when he returns, but I can find no body in Town."[19] The contrast is clear: on one side, the immutable political tactician, who had spent most of his life pursuing power and office; on the other side, the young aristocrats, who were absorbed in the social life of the country during the parliamentary recess.

It is indicative, however, of their sense of responsibility to take over the reins of power that when they finally did turn their attention to national politics, Rockingham and his friends resumed their efforts to promote the "broad and comprehensive" ministry. In 1767 they had professed to be willing to accept power only in a position of strength in the House of Commons *vis-à-vis* the king and Bute. As Dowdeswell's manifesto had emphasized, this necessitated a union with a significant number of political allies who were prepared to accept the marquis's leadership. In late 1768, the possibility of such a merger with George Grenville and his supporters suddenly presented itself, and once the Rockinghams shook off their summertime lethargy, they proved most interested. The Grenvilles were attractive because they had some thirty-one MPs in the Commons.[20] Thus, although the Grenvilles were a significantly smaller group than the Rockinghams, they were the second largest then in opposition. Currently, there are two main schools of thought about Grenville. First, Sir Lewis Namier and John Brooke[21] have portrayed him as something of a disinterested elder statesman in his later years. They tell us that he came to realize that he was never going to be offered high office again because of the enmity the king had developed for him during the administration of 1763–65.[22] In this situation, he supposedly stopped concerning himself with the pursuit of power (because it was futile) and learned to approach all issues in an objective manner, free from pragmatic political considerations. The second, more recent, view is provided by Philip Lawson.[23] This view sees Grenville as a man of principle who, despite an appetite for ministerial office, was driven more by conviction and the desire to do what was right. On the basis of his performance between 1768 and his death in 1770, it would appear that both interpretations are too generous. The oscillations of Grenville and his closest friends with respect to the other parties in opposition and over major issues, including America and the Middlesex election, strongly suggest that they continued to be opportunists to the very end. Unlike the Rockinghams, they were what Namier designated a faction. Their political activities were consistently aimed at the rise to ministerial office, maintenance of it, or return to it.

Between the negotiations of 1767 and late 1768, Rockingham and his friends stopped viewing the Grenville connection as a prospect for union. This was because its leaders had all but given up the game of opposition, on the expectation that they were about to be asked to join the administration. They had managed to convince themselves that "nothing but Mr. Grenville could restore Government"[24] and that "the idea of the Impossibility that this Administration should continue & of the Necessity of sending for us ... gains ... ground every day."[25] Their expectations were derived not only from the fact that the ministry had continued to look weak and that their old allies the Bedfords were in office, but also from public demand for an authoritarian approach to the handling of the American situation – an approach which they, more than any other connection, symbolized. This demand prompted Grenville to agitate the American issue unrelentingly at a time when the Rockinghams were beginning a period, which was to last until well into the revolutionary war, when they were just as pleased to avoid it.

Since 1765, when the American colonists had begun the resistance to Grenville's Stamp Act,[26] Anglo-American relations had never really been free of tension.[27] In 1766 the Rockinghams had repealed the Stamp Act,[28] but in the next year trouble had flared up again in a brief dispute between New York and the home government over the Mutiny Act.[29] It had then broken out, with new levels of bitterness, with respect to Charles Townshend's[30] celebrated Revenue Act.[31] In 1768 the latter conflict showed no signs of resolution and Britons began to react with a good deal of emotion. Lately, our picture of public opinion has perhaps become somewhat more clouded than it used to be, as a result of some important new studies. On one hand, examinations of local politics, notably by John Sainsbury[32] and James Bradley,[33] have detected strong pro-American sentiments among, respectively, anti-establishment elements in the City of London and the dissenting community in a number of English localities. On the other hand, Peter Thomas, in thorough analyses of British politics and the American conflict in the late 1760s and early 1770s, argues that Britons felt considerable indignation at the colonists' actions and demanded strong measures to substantiate the supremacy of Parliament.[34]

Presumably, both arguments are well founded. If one takes the view of the City of London where, as Nicholas Rogers[35] has recently demonstrated, opposition to government-allied merchants, financiers, and contractors had a long tradition, there certainly seems to have been a good deal of empathy for the American cause. Similarly, the dissenting community, which harboured resentment towards laws that excluded it and favoured the Anglican majority, could be expected to feel admiration for the colonists' apparently libertarian objectives.[36] However, if one looks, as Professor Thomas has done (and as this work does), from the perspective of those entrenched in high politics, where the views of landed Anglicans vastly predominated, exactly the opposite was the case. Opinion generally had become overwhelmingly impatient with colonial defiance and antipathetic to it. Consequently, even many men who had formerly acted as friends of America and had called for conciliatory measures, such as the repeal of the Stamp Act, were in a less than compromising mood. One such individual was Lord Chatham, who had stood virtually alone in 1766 in maintaining that Parliament did not have the right to tax the colonies solely for the purpose of creating revenue. After the partial restoration of his health, Chatham announced, during a speech in the House of Lords, "If [the Americans] ... carry their notions of liberty too far, as I fear they do, if they will not be subject to the laws of this country, especially if they would disengage themselves from the laws of trade and navigation of which I see too many symptoms, as much of an American as I am, they will not have a more determined opposer than they will find in me. They must be subordinate."[37]

There is little need to go to great lengths to add to the substantial evidence that Professor Thomas has supplied. Well-known facts, such as the large parliamentary majorities that supported the government's authoritarian actions during the 1768–69 sitting[38] and then brought forward the coercive measures of 1774, speak for themselves.[39] What is germane here is that in formulating their responses to the American conflict, both of the major opposition parties were heavily swayed by the attitude that prevailed among propertied Anglicans. Initially, this encouraged them to behave in almost totally dissimilar ways. The Grenvilles found themselves in circumstances that enabled them to be very outspoken. Grenville had advocated a firm policy from the time he had found it necessary to defend his Stamp Act. He now recognized that this could only help to demonstrate his suitability for office. Therefore, he became most anxious at every opportunity to raise the matter and to paint himself as the champion of parliamentary supremacy. "In all his Speeches ... [Grenville] never fails to bring in North America," it was noted.[40] It was essentially with a view to furthering his image that he and his friend and publicist, William Knox,[41] collaborated during the summer months in producing a pamphlet entitled *The Present State of the Nation*.[42] In it they asserted "the Sovereignty of the King and Parl[iamen]t ... over all the Dominions belonging to the Crown"[43] and blamed the current chaos in America on those, including the Rockinghams, whose weak measures had encouraged the colonists to fly in the face of British laws.[44]

At this stage the Rockinghams, as former advocates of conciliation and appeasement, were much less comfortable. They were well aware of public opinion. They knew, for instance, of the endless criticism that had been directed at their friend Barlow Trecothick,[45] the London merchant who had been so active in helping them achieve the repeal of the Stamp Act.[46] There can be little doubt, moreover, that the most important members of the party were not totally unsympathetic to the argument that it was time to stand up for the supremacy of Parliament. They were, to be sure, against any more provocative actions by British statesmen. However, as Paul Langford has noted, they felt "a sincere attachment to the right of the mother country to tax America."[47] The evidence is plentiful. In May the marquis wrote personally to the House of Representatives of Massachusetts Bay and, in an effort to discourage further confrontations with British officialdom, announced that while he "would not adopt a system of arbitrary Rule over the Colonies," he would not "do otherwise than strenuously resist where attempts were made to throw off that Dependency to which the Colonies ought to submit."[48] Three months later, William Dowdeswell informed his leader of his sentiments on this subject with an openness that was possible only in a situation of strictest confidence between two friends. It is evident that if the party had not been shackled to its past conciliatory actions, he might even have wished to demand a firm hand. Dowdeswell realized that there was more at stake than the Townshend duties:

Char Townshend's duties are I believe not so heavy as to justify one in saying that they are grievous burdens on the Colonies. [The Americans seem to make their stand] … against the general principle of raising *any* revenue in America & therefore extend their opposition even to a reduced duty on the molasses … A repeated opposition … upon a principle directed against all duties for revenue must be met. It must either be admitted which is timidity weakness irresolution & inconsistency: or it must be resisted & ye aims of this Country must be exerted against her colonies …

If the Americans found their petition upon that principle of right which goes agt raising any revenue at all in America, they ought to pray not only agt Ch Townshend's duties but against all duties *laid for revenue*, against those very duties which a few years ago We were told they were so willing to pay. If They succeed in such petition They obtain a great Charter, depriving this Country in all future circumstances of the power of raising any revenue there for the general support of its own authority … But they do more … The distinction between external & internal taxes has been found frivolous, as indeed I always thought it. And … I have never been able to distinguish between ye right of passing one law & the right of passing another. Their claim of right admitted will give them in my opinion a charter against being bound by any laws passed without their consent. I am afraid therefore, such a petition is not to be supported.[49]

Dowdeswell did, however, feel that if the colonists avoided the question of right, the party could take up their cause, as it had done before. But, he was not at all hopeful that they would, and he therefore could do little but decry the ministry for having aggravated the problem again, and call for moderate measures. He did not advocate an anti-American policy for his party, but he insisted that the colonists could not be supported on the question of right. On this point, Sir George Savile – who warned his friends against "playing too familiarly with a Bear that was given me a pretty little merry good humour'd Cub"[50] – appears to have agreed completely.

Exactly what Burke was thinking is difficult to determine since his correspondence, unlike that of his leaders, was more or less silent on the subject between 1768 and 1773.[51] He does, however, seem to have fallen in line with Rockingham and Dowdeswell.[52] When Burke presented his first major American speech in April 1774,[53] he assailed the government for mishandling colonial relations, and he defended the Rockinghams' past actions, not only in promoting conciliation through the repeal of the Stamp Act but also in bolstering parliamentary authority with the Declaratory Act. It is worthy of note that when the deepening crisis forced Burke to give his views during the election campaign at the end of 1774, he actually stressed his support for the "constitutional superiority of Great Britain" over his desire for lenient measures.[54]

A few members of the connection, including Newcastle[55] and Richmond,[56] seem to have favoured a clearly conciliatory approach in 1768, but none of them carried the weight of Rockingham, Dowdeswell, and Savile. Their opinions merely served to complicate matters. Rockingham was obviously in a difficult position. Because of public sentiments and his own and his supporters' views, he could hardly lead his party on another campaign for repeal of the disputed legislation. Yet he was unable to come forth as the advocate of an authoritarian policy, since to do so would have been tantamount to admitting that the repeal of the Stamp Act had been a mistake and that his party was, to a significant degree, responsible for the current troubles.[57] Consequently, the best approach seemed to be to avoid the issue as much as possible.

Until late 1768, the dissimilarity of their points of view over America, along with Grenville's presumed suitability for power, made any sort of alliance impossible. This was not just because the Grenvilles were uninterested. The union movement of 1767 demonstrates that the Rockinghams were anxious to join forces with any group that could significantly broaden their base in Parliament. However, this was only in a situation that would give them superiority in a future administration. To the marquis and his closest friends, the very fact that Grenville seemed likely to be offered power made him repugnant, because it seemed to allow him too much importance and to give him the standing and status to threaten their assumed right to superiority. Again, the contrast between their attitude and that of Newcastle is striking. In May, Newcastle lamented "the Open Declaration which the Marquis, the Cavendishes & the Keppels are Every Day making ... against George Grenville ... Nothing Material will be done without Him."[58]

Between the time Newcastle wrote these words and the opening of Parliament, the outlook for Grenville changed dramatically. It became clear, not only to Grenville but to politicians in general, that he had no chance of being asked to take office after all, because of the animosity which the king had continued to harbour towards him since the 1763–65 administration.[59] This realization brought a distinct change in the attitudes of both the major opposition parties. It illustrates the extent to which their judgment in some important issues could be skewed by political speculation. For their part, the Grenvilles suddenly began to show more interest in cooperating against the Grafton government. They started to make gestures of goodwill towards the Rockinghams, they began talking opposition politics, and they carefully tempered their language regarding America.[60] On the other side, Rockingham was cautious but not totally unresponsive. Suddenly, he felt less threatened and saw hope that the two groups might be able to establish an understanding. In October he spoke to Alexander Wedderburn with whom he and Burke had formed links, and did some courting of his own. Apparently, his "language was, that it was impossible the several parts of the Opposition could differ now on American measures" and "that in Opposition they should entirely agree."[61] It is not to be implied that the two connections quickly overcame all their misgivings and began channelling their energies into a merger, but it is evident that they had unexpectedly begun to contemplate an accord of sorts against the administration. There can be little doubt, moreover, that they saw America as a potential obstacle to their designs. In November, when the marquis and his friends were planning activities for the coming parliamentary session, the possibility of taking "some notice of America ... was some time debated" but was rejected "least it might draw Grenville up and in case of a division divide us."[62]

It is indicative of their desire to avoid the most important political issue at hand in late 1768 that both parties found it convenient to divert their attention for as long as possible to lesser problems in which they could take decisive action and build on their good will. Two lesser matters existed. One centred on a struggle between the Duke of Portland and Sir James Lowther[63] – a staunch and somewhat powerful supporter of government and a political ally of the Earl of Bute – over property and prestige in the county of Cumberland. The other matter concerned British foreign policy with respect to the Mediterranean island of Corsica.

Corsica had come to the notice of the British public in June 1768 with the news that the Genoese had ceded the island to the French as security for outstanding debts.[64] In face of Corsican resistance, the French invaded the island during the summer, and within a few months a bitter and hard-fought war began, which lasted the best part of a year. Public reaction to the invasion was mixed. There was much admiration for the brave stand the little island was making against Britain's long-standing enemy,[65] and many people criticized the government for not intervening at least in a diplomatic capacity to help the Corsicans.[66] On the other hand, the island was considered economically worthless to England because of its small population and because it lacked natural resources, and few thought it merited a war with France.[67]

The Rockinghams discussed Corsica in early November, and during the meeting at which they agreed not to raise the American question for fear of alienating the Grenvilles, they decided to take action in the House of Commons.[68] They seem to have felt that they could attack the government for not trying to stop the conflict without insisting that it was necessary to go to war. Thus, they would run little risk of seriously alienating any of the independents.[69] On the opening day of the session, Burke brought the matter up in the House by making a plea for information about the ministry's movements since hearing of the dispute.[70] On the seventeenth, Henry Seymour,[71] a Grenville supporter, made a formal motion calling for the laying of relevant papers before the House and an inquiry into the government's actions.[72] His motion was seconded by one of the Cavendishes, and he was supported by all the Grenvilles, the Rockinghams, and two of Chatham's friends who had gone into opposition since their leader's resignation: Colonel Isaac Barré,[73] who had just resigned from his position as joint vice-treasurer of Ireland; and William Beckford,[74] the influential London radical. However, the House agreed with government spokesmen that there was no point in exciting a great military confrontation over a "morsel of rock," and the motion was rejected by a vote of 230 to 84.

The Rockinghams and Grenvilles cooperated closely in Parliament over the Corsican war, and they may even have communicated behind the scenes in order to plan tactics. The affair does not appear to have been something that either party felt very strongly about. They bothered to agitate it primarily, or perhaps only, because none of them was tied to a past stand on the issue. That they were able to draw in some of Chatham's friends augured well for the future. Experience had taught the Rockinghams to distrust Chatham. In 1766 he had refused to give them the support they felt they needed to continue in office; and then, after taking the helm himself, he had seemed to do everything possible to humiliate them.[75] However, as is clear from some of their responses between late 1769 and early 1771, the Rockinghams, along with the British public in general, had a curious respect for Chatham's authority.[76] The position taken by his influential city ally must have seemed a bonus. During the campaign to repeal the Stamp Act, Rockingham and his friends had discovered how public opinion could roll like a tidal wave from London, quickly sweeping across the rest of the kingdom.[77] They unquestionably realized how strong Beckford's support was in the city's burgeoning opposition press.[78] His taking their line over Corsica was to prove timely in the dramatic dispute that broke out before the end of the session, between the House of Commons and the electors of the London county of Middlesex.

Meanwhile, in the other lesser issue – the Portland-Lowther conflict[79] – the various opposition parties were able to strengthen their relationship further – though this was by no means the only important consideration from the Rockinghams' point of view. The quarrel between the two magnates had begun in July 1767 when Sir James Lowther, the Earl of Bute's son-in-law,[80] attempted to extract some of Portlands's electoral influence in Cumberland. He sent a memorial to the lords of the Treasury, alleging that Portland's title to the forest of Inglewood and to the socage of Carlisle Castle was defective and that this property legally belonged to the crown.[81] In the same memorial, Lowther asked that he be allowed to lease the property himself. After the surveyor general had complied,[82] Portland was forced, over a period of several months, to state his own claim to the property in appeals to the lords of the Treasury.[83] However, partly because of what appeared to be prejudicial treatment by them, and by the surveyor general and the surveyor general's deputy,[84] he was unable to do so in a satisfactory manner, and the dispute was taken to the law courts.[85] This began a protracted battle in the Court of Chancery, which was eventually settled in Portland's favour – but not completely until 1777.

Another element in the conflict developed out of the general election of 1768, when two candidates – Henry Fletcher[86] and Henry Curwen[87] – ran, with strong support from Portland, against Lowther and his friend Humphry Senhouse.[88] Previously, Lowther, through his connection with Bute, had been politically supreme in the county and had controlled both seats; but now a large percentage of the independent gentry, who were tired of Lowther's predominance and disgusted at his assault on Portland's property, revolted and voted for the other side. As a result, Curwen was elected outright, and it took some dubious interference by the sheriff to enable Lowther to beat Fletcher.

The leaders of the Rockingham party responded to both sides of the conflict with a diligence which for them was quite extraordinary. In reaction to the dispute over the Cumberland property, a bill to invalidate claims of the crown over land that had been alienated for a period of sixty years or more was drawn up, and on 17 February 1768 it was presented to the House of Commons by Sir George Savile. During the few days before the presentation, Rockingham was indefatigable in summoning his friends in order to ensure that the bill received the best possible support.[89] When it was presented, the members voted 134 to 114 to postpone it, and the Rockinghams determined to submit it again in November. During the recess, Savile and Sir Anthony Abdy revised the bill.[90] In late October and early November, when Rockingham was again able to turn his attention to politics, his major concerns were the Quiet of the Subjects (or Nullum

Tempus) Bill, as it was called, and the Cumberland election. Until both were settled, he, Portland, and the Cavendishes worked vigorously, getting their friends together for discussions and sending out their whips for the relevant days in Parliament.[91] Rockingham at times seemed even more animated than Portland. Although hampered by poor health, he performed his duties to the best of his ability and at one point claimed, with only slight exaggeration, that although his "complaints" continued "exceeding troublesome," he was doing "as well as I can, in not neglecting as far as I am able to see, talk, Converse, send &c to our Friends to forward & convey on all the Business now depending."[92]

On 14 November, Savile presented the Nullum Tempus Bill for the first time in the new Parliament.[93] It passed the Lower House in March 1769.[94] The Cumberland election question was resolved on 15 December 1768, when the Commons, after hearing a petition from Portland's county supporters[95] and having examined evidence from both sides, determined that Lowther should be turned out of the House and Henry Fletcher admitted in his place.[96] Even at this point, the Rockingham leaders were not satisfied that justice had been done, and they continued to seek retribution. They sponsored a motion that Lowther should appear before the House to account for his actions,[97] and on 6 April they saw him declared guilty of altering the election returns, and he was taken into custody by the sergeant-at-arms.[98] Then they sponsored two motions which, respectively, would have had the sheriff who interfered in the election sent to Newgate prison[99] and reprimanded before the bar of the Commons.[100] These motions were defeated, ostensibly because the majority felt that the party was pushing the punishment too far.

The Rockinghams' exuberance resulted from two considerations. Firstly, the issue offered an opportunity to work with their allies to defend private property against enemy forces that included important placemen, court supporters, and friends of Bute, who had apparently used corrupt methods to attain specific aims. Secondly, one of the Rockinghams' leading supporters had much at stake. In the case of Portland and his close relatives the Cavendishes, the latter consideration was undoubtedly the more important, but with Rockingham and several other members of the party, the former appears to have held at least equal weight. When Rockingham first heard the news of the sheriff's actions in the Cumberland election, he told Newcastle, "I grieve that the D[uke] of P[ortland] should have the additional Trouble & Expense of a Petition. I should not else much dislike it, as I think it will be a Scrape not only for Sir J Lowther but also for Ld Bute as I am sure the Publick will naturally see that this Return never could have been, but from the Expectation that the support of that Power would be sufficient to carry the affair thr' the House of Commons."[101] The importance of a common attack against Bute on behalf of general (rather than specific) private property is also evinced by the fact that, largely as a consequence of "a sort of delicacy" among themselves[102] (presumably, about making their bill appear too partisan), the party leaders agreed that the Nullum Tempus Act should be effective as of January 1769. This meant that it did nothing whatever to resolve the specific case of Portland versus Lowther. Some two years later, an unsuccessful bill of amendment was introduced in the Commons to make it effective a year earlier, but the Rockinghams were not the responsible party,[103] though they supported it in debate.

This issue offered the Rockinghams an excellent opportunity not just to promote but to lead the union movement, while displaying their unsullied principles. It may have occurred to them that since the Glorious Revolution, the defence of private property had been a great Whig shibboleth.[104] Regardless, it was unquestionably something for which all men of stature could feel empathy. Standing in defiance of the favourite, of course, was particularly attractive. Ever since their first short administration, resisting Bute had been the obelisk in the Rockinghams' platform. In 1767 Dowdeswell had written it into their constitutional ideology and had insisted that they must always be prepared to stand up for it, whatever the cost. What they were anxious above all to do now was reveal that they were still the most dedicated group in Parliament in pursuing this cause.

Throughout the session they were supported, both in debates and in the divisions, by the Grenvilles, who also found this an attractive issue. In 1767 Grenville had (however pragmatically) announced support for the principle of union in opposition to Bute and favouritism. As success in the divisions in the House of Commons demonstrated, the Rockinghams' stand against Lowther was not on the whole unpopular among independent interests. From their very first overtures to the Rockinghams, Grenville and his men had found it convenient to stress the need for concerted action on this matter when they were being most careful to avoid any mention of America.[105] Now they backed even the most retributive manoeuvres. It seems very likely as well that the few Chatham supporters, including Colonel Isaac Barré, William Beckford, and the radical London politicians who normally followed Beckford's lead, also voted with the Rockinghams, since they had now cut their ties with the Grafton administration and were beginning to support opposition on other fronts.[106]

If it had been necessary to deal only with problems such as Corsica and the Portland-Lowther conflict, the game of opposition could have been almost enjoyable. This, of course, was not the case. As the session progressed, the American question refused to go away, and it caused a good deal of discomfort for the two principal connections on the opposition side. The politicians who consistently fought for the colonists were those who had various personal reasons for so doing. They included William Beckford and Rose Fuller,[107] who had been born in the West Indies and had spent enough time there to develop strong colonial sympathies; Colonel Isaac Barré, who had served in North America under James Wolfe[108] and others between 1757 and 1760, and had kept up a regular correspondence with friends there ever since; John Huske,[109] who had been born in Portsmouth, New Hampshire; Richard Jackson,[110] colonial agent for Connecticut, Pennsylvania, and Massachusetts; Barlow Trecothick, who had been born and educated in Boston; and Thomas Pownall,[111] who over a period of some sixteen years had held various administrative positions in America, including the governorship of Massachusetts Bay. Although these men did not support all the Americans' claims, they did work together for the repeal of the Townshend duties, and they attempted to bring the case for their friends to the attention of Parliament as fully as possible.

The Rockinghams and Grenvilles, on the other hand, did almost nothing of substance. Moreover, an outsider who had no idea of their past positions could conceivably have listened in on most of the debates and failed to see much to distinguish one from the other. There were occasions when it was impossible to cover up completely the differences that separated them as a result of previous actions. From time to time, Burke succumbed to the temptation to defend the repeal of the Stamp Act, forcing Grenville to speak out against him.[112] On the days when the Pennsylvania,[113] Massachusetts Bay,[114] and New York[115] petitions against the Townshend duties were presented to the Commons, the Rockinghams argued that they should at least be given a hearing, while Grenville was forced to support the majority in rejecting them outright as denials of Parliament's supremacy. For the most part, however, the two groups were able to act in concert by responding to the affair in a totally negative and nebulous manner; that is, they constantly deprecated the government's measures (or at least created the impression that they were doing so) but avoided putting forth any concrete proposals of their own.

Although the Rockinghams had decided at their meeting in early November not to bring up the subject of America, they nevertheless did so, probably because they realized that if they proceeded properly, common ground between them and the Grenvilles might be found. On 8 November, Dowdeswell proposed an amendment to the address "to assure his Majesty that this House will take into their immediate consideration what steps have been taken for maintaining peace and good order in his Majesty's Colonies in North America, for establishing, and confirming his Majesty's Government there, and procuring obedience to the laws."[116] Coming from a party that was known for its conciliatory views, these words sounded arbitrary. But if they were meant as a concession to Grenville, Dowdeswell must have been well satisfied. Grenville not only voiced his full support for the principle of the motion, but he demonstrated his willingness to stray from his former intransigent path when, at one point, he began to sound like a champion of American rights. The colonists had "a right to every privilege of British Subjects," he said: "I disapprove of the dissolution of their assemblies, no Corporation is bound to obey any order signified by a Secretary of State, further than they are directed by the laws of the land."[117] Phillip Lawson has noticed the change in Grenville's attitude at this stage and has explained it by saying that in the later years of his life, Grenville developed "a measure of sympathy" for the Americans' "constitutional and economic plight."[118] The problem with this explanation is that it does not give adequate consideration to the fluctuating political circumstances with which Grenville and his supporters felt they had to deal, particularly the need to have a working relationship with the Rockinghams.

After Dowdeswell's motion was rejected, the two parties reverted to a policy of avoidance. From this point on, neither took the initiative again. They chose merely to respond with ambivalence to the proposals and actions of the government and the small group of people who genuinely wished to do something to help the colonists. In the House of Lords on 15 December, Lord Hillsborough moved eight resolutions censuring the conduct of the people of Boston during the previous months in what he deemed to be an attack on Parliament's right to tax them. The Duke of Bedford proposed an address to the king pledging the House's support for all measures taken to enforce the laws and the supremacy of Parliament in the colonies, and requesting that the trials of all treasonable offences be transferred to England. These motions passed without divisions, and as one observer remarked, "Nobody much objected but the Duke of Richmond, and he was not very clear."[119] Lord Shelburne, who had recently resigned in conjunction with Chatham and who had previously also been known as a defender of American liberties, "spoke rather darkly, that he thought the resolutions, if meant to be general, ineffectual, if levelled only at Boston not improper." Lord Temple "declared he thought them all nugatory – a paper war with the colonies – and then went out of the House."[120] When these measures were first discussed in the Lower House,[121] Sir George Savile presented a petition against them from William Bollan,[122] the agent for the Massachusetts assembly. On that day, when the Commons concurred in the measures,[123] Dowdeswell and Burke coordinated their efforts with Grenville in attacking them as rash, speculative, and ineffectual. The two parties were so successful in keeping their comments general and negative that they were reported to be "entirely united."[124]

Despite all this, the Rockinghams did little to aid those who were sincerely sympathetic towards the colonists. In fact, partly to maintain their new-found friendship with Grenville, the leading members of the party used their influence to try to suppress motions of repeal, arguing that these would not be successful and might simply excite more hostility towards the Americans.[125] In April, when a resolution for repeal was submitted by Thomas Pownall, Burke was so equivocal in debate that it was difficult to ascertain whether he was for it or against it. "If the question stood to repeal, or enforce," he said, "I have no doubt to repeal. We can't repeal it this Session, it is a complicated, commercial system. Whether when you can not repeal it, you should agitate it ... I never thought America should be beat backwards, & forwards on the Tennis ball of faction. To propose plans of Government from this side of the House is not wise in general."[126] On this same occasion, Grenville refused to give an opinion either way, merely reverting to what by then had become his habitual expedient of assailing the ministers for failing to come up with a constructive policy. Pownall's motion was rejected without a division.

When Rockingham and his colleagues had repealed the Stamp Act in 1766, they had at the same time sponsored the Declaratory Act,[127] which stated that the king in Parliament had the power "to make laws and statutes of sufficient force and validity to bind the colonies and people of America *in all cases whatsoever.*"[128] Their actions were motivated in part by expediency. Repeal was designed to save British trade from the threat of nonimportation and to keep the merchants happy; and the Declaratory Act was intended to satisfy public demand that the supremacy of Parliament would be upheld. One should not be too cynical about this. There is no doubt that the party leaders believed in treating the Americans tenderly while at the same time upholding the supremacy of the mother country. This was a central theme that Burke repeated in all his major speeches on the conflict, including his noted speech on American taxation in 1774 and his two speeches on conciliation with the colonies in 1775.[129] If the Rockinghams are to be faulted, it should not be for deserting their principles but for failing at critical stages in the conflict to seek realistic long-term solutions. As the crisis mounted, they were preoccupied or hampered by other concerns. Fear of public criticism, growing anti-American sentiments in England, the opposition alliance, and very possibly their day-to-day lives in the country all combined to divert their attention from trying to find a means of improving colonial relations. In a sense, theirs was a non-policy policy. It was both firmness and leniency, and thus it was neither. The party's stand in 1769 was even fuzzier than it had been three years earlier. Then, the leading members had at least done something, whereas now they were willing to do virtually nothing at all. In a letter of May 1769, Rockingham came as close as anyone could to spelling out the party's position. There is little in it that suggests either foresightedness or a profound understanding of the problem. There is, however, a hint of some of the political constraints he felt. He wrote:

If you was now amongst us you would find our Sentiments on the Subject of America, just the same as when You left us. We still abide by that Opinion that the Idea of making America a *Revenue Mine* is absurd ... No actual Motion was made for the Repeal & indeed I tryd all I could & perhaps was very Instrumental in Preventing its being moved. My reasons were that it was Evident ... that the attempt to repeal it, would not be attended with the least chance of Success, but that it would only afford an opportunity of many violent & hot Speeches on the Subject of North American disobedience & that the report of those Speeches going to America wou'd only tend to add fresh Fuel to the Fire ... I much wish that the Colonies wou'd contain themselves & not break out into fresh Violences ... A contrary Conduct ... furnishes ... such arguments to the Passions of Man, that it makes it difficult for the Voice of Reason to be heard. I imagine some late appearance of G[eorge] G[renville] acting in a Sort of Concert with our Friends, must be to a degree a Matter of Surprise & must Occasion Various Speculation. – It may to be proper to remark – that he adopts many of our Points – not *us* his & it may also be to be remarked, that his Language & C, of late has softened upon the Subject of ... America.[130]

Rockingham had reason to concern himself with what the Americans thought when they read reports of the debates. In February, Joseph Harrison[131] had written from Boston, giving him an idea of how the oscillations of both the major opposition parties were being received. The Sons of Liberty, he said, were at first pleased "from the minutes that have been printed of Mr. Burke's and Mr George Grenville's Speech's" in the debates about the address. "The latter ... they say has changed sides, and from being an Enemy is now become their Friend. All this is found on their finding fault with Lord Hillsborough for ordering the Assembly to be dissolved." However, after reflecting on some of their other actions, said Harrison, "the more sensible have abated much of their Confidence in the Friendship of those Two Gentlemen; and now begin to think that tho' they have opposed the Ministry, they will condemn the Measures of the Colonies in general and of this Town and Province in particular."[132]

What eventually saved the Rockinghams and their allies from the imperial question was not their ambiguousness or their inactivity, but pure luck. It came in the form of another controversy, which emerged as the session progressed and which eventually drew so much public attention that it pushed even the conflict with the colonies off centre stage. The new issue was that surrounding the celebrated demagogue John Wilkes. In contrast to the American problem, it proved most useful for the Rockinghams and for all their allies. Indeed, the Wilkes affair emerged as the one great question through which a totally united and relatively popular attack could be made on the administration. At the same time, it displayed a potential to do more for the reconstruction of a united, broadly based court Whig party under Rockingham's leadership than anything that had preceded it.

In 1765 a grand jury in Middlesex had declared John Wilkes guilty of printing the "Essay on Woman" and of printing and republishing number 45 of the *North Briton*, whereupon Wilkes had fled to France to avoid punishment.[133] In January 1768 he returned to England and immediately set about the task of casting himself back into the limelight in English domestic affairs. Although still an outlaw, he contested two elections for a seat in the House of Commons, winning the second for the county of Middlesex. Then he surrendered, with considerable fanfare, to the Court of King's Bench, where he was sentenced to twenty-two months in prison and a fine of £1,000.[134] But instead of sitting quietly in jail and serving out his sentence, Wilkes proceeded to take steps that were calculated to provoke the ministry. These made it impossible for the government to ignore him and eventually made him a martyr for a cause which even many people who had little sympathy for him personally found difficult not to support.

On 14 November he had his friend Sir Joseph Mawbey[135] present a petition to the House of Commons charging or implicating several members of the government and judicial establishment, including Lord Chief Justice Mansfield,[136] with having used unjust and illegal measures to prosecute him between 1763 and 1765. If there is any doubt that Wilkes was intending to force the government to extremities, the step he took in response to the famous massacre of St George's Fields would seem to clear it up. On 10 May 1768 a number of people had been killed in a confrontation between the military and a huge "mob" that had gathered in a show of support for Wilkes outside the King's Bench prison. Previously, Lord Weymouth,[137] one of the secretaries of state, had sent a set of instructions to the Surrey magistrates entreating them to call out the military if necessary to cope with riots in the city, which had become widespread during the spring, mainly as a result of the high price of provisions. Wilkes procured a copy of these instructions and had it published in *St. James's Chronicle* of 10 December, prefaced with an introductory note implying that the recent killings were the work of an arbitrary and tyrannical government intent on imposing its rule on the English people by force. Willing or not, the Grafton government felt obliged to retaliate.[138] The authorship of the introduction to Weymouth's letter was established in the House of Lords and declared an "insolent, scandalous, and seditious Libel."[139] On 2 February 1769 the House of Commons concurred,[140] and the following day Wilkes was expelled from the House.[141]

The Rockinghams initially displayed little inclination to become heavily involved in the affair. In the early 1760s they had supported Wilkes against the government, and since their own term of office they had been paying him an annual stipend, ostensibly to prevent him from becoming their enemy.[142] Yet from their point of view, the relationship had always been an uneasy one because of the low esteem in which Wilkes was held by the political classes. More than anything else, he was seen as an agitator who had gone to unacceptable extremes in the *North Briton* and the "Essay on Woman." Thus, the prospect of being publicly connected with him had never seemed very attractive. In 1768 it seemed less so than ever, because on top of everything else, Wilkes had become associated with violence. When, formerly, he had fought the Grenville administration, the mobs had occasionally got out of hand in London; but after his return there was so much rioting in the city that even the older politicians could remember nothing like it.[143] The fact that most of the disturbances would have taken place even if Wilkes had not existed, and that many of the people who joined the crowds at different times and used the words "Wilkes and Liberty" were really driven by economic hardships, did not prevent him from being seen as the king of disorder and mob rule.[144]

On the other hand, the Rockinghams' earlier support for Wilkes and their current role as an opposition party largely prevented them from taking the government's side. Therefore, they voted in the minority, but before 3 February they did so cautiously and unobtrusively, and for the most part they were silent in the debates. Wilkes's expulsion, however, changed everything. Few people appear to have believed that it could be justified on the basis of sound constitutional principle. The ministry's actions suddenly seemed so high-handed that Wilkes's character began to look relatively less problematic. At this stage, therefore, the Rockinghams and all the other leading opposition spokesmen began to assail Grafton and his ministers with more gusto. They argued that it was unfair to take away a member's seat on the basis of accumulated crimes, that the House was unjustly punishing Wilkes a second time for his number 45 of the *North Briton* and the "Essay on Woman," and that the expulsion set a dangerous precedent for using the House of Commons as the instrument of ministerial vengeance. The major reason for the new-found vitality on the opposition side, however, appears to have been a general recognition that this was about to become a popular issue. As Professor Rea has so convincingly demonstrated, the antiministerial press in London took up the cause of the freeholders of Middlesex with much enthusiasm.[145] No one failed to recognize that public opinion was going to be a powerful factor. When voicing their disapproval in the Commons, most politicians expressed great fears of the "popular clamours," which in these tumultuous times would connect the case of John Wilkes with the cause of liberty. "Such a conduct as this will inflame the minds of the people against this Parliament," one of the Cavendishes warned. "If this Parliament do not give the last stroke to the liberty of the people, they will give a handle to a future House of Commons to do it."[146]

Over the course of the remainder of the session, the freeholders of Middlesex returned Wilkes three more times, and the Commons majority moved on to the dubious expedient of incapacitating him and then declaring Henry Laws Luttrell[147] duly elected, though Luttrell had received far fewer votes.[148] Each measure seemed to strengthen the charges of illegality. "That the people should not choose their own representative is a saying that *Shakes* the constitution," Burke asserted.[149] By the end of the session, the Rockinghams were working with London antiministerialists such as James Townsend,[150] John Glynn,[151] and William Beckford, and with Isaac Barré and all the rest of the Chatham politicians. Chatham himself was rumoured to be convalescing and on the verge of making a return to political life.[152] This must have seemed potentially an excellent opportunity for him to restore himself in the city, where he had once been so popular.

It was also most encouraging that the Rockinghams and Grenvilles were able to strengthen their ties significantly. Before the expulsion, Grenville had not been able to side with his allies consistently. Since it had been his administration that had originally sanctioned or carried out much of the treatment Wilkes was complaining about, his following found it necessary to vote with the government a good deal early on. At the expulsion, however, it was appropriate to make a complete about-face. After predicting that Wilkes would be re-elected and warning of the "storm" that might follow, Grenville joined forces wholeheartedly with the Rockinghams.[153] In February, Dowdeswell and Grenville began to coordinate their efforts in the Commons, and they got along famously. The two were, in fact, well suited to each other. Both approached political matters in a straightforward if rather ineloquent manner; both were recognized masters of affairs of finance; and both were generally were at their best when dealing with questions that required little subtlety, a lot of knowledge, and a businesslike attitude. The Middlesex election was not such a question, but it brought them together more than at any time in the past and gave them real hope that some important victories could be achieved against the Grafton ministry in the future. Moreover, when an opportunity to put their particular qualities to work did arise, it gave them the collaborative experience they needed to respond singularly and efficiently.

In February, the king sent a message to the House of Commons asking for some £500,000 to cover the arrears on the civil list.[154] This enabled the opposition parties to demonstrate that their current unanimity could be extended to the long-standing problem of favouritism. Dowdeswell had earlier been preparing for this day by drawing up motions which it was hoped would force "the Administration to lay the civil list debt before Parliament – specifying the particular Records."[155] He and Grenville got together to discuss these and were able to "agree perfectly"[156] on tactics. When the king's message came on the twenty-eighth, Dowdeswell moved for papers that would show "the particulars for which these sums were risen to so high an amount"[157] and for records that would demonstrate "the precise time … the debts were incurred."[158] Grenville seconded him and then actively supported him in debate. Both men claimed they wanted to prove that their respective governments had not been the cause of the arrears. They were, of course, implying that the costs had resulted from bribery, corruption, and an expansion of crown patronage since the rise of Bute. Unfortunately, this motion was defeated by a vote of 164 to 89. Dowdeswell and Grenville also attempted to obstruct the payment of the arrears until an inquiry could be conducted into the cause of the debts.[159] When they failed, they were forced to give up the fight until the next parliamentary session.[160]

In general, in the movement towards an alliance between the Rockinghams and Grenvilles, there was one very distinct anomaly that requires explanation. It was during this period that they attacked each other rather spiritedly in two widely circulated publications. The first to appear was William Knox's *The Present State of the Nation*. Knox not only stated the necessity of a firm American policy and propagated ideas such as the imposition of a land tax on the colonists, but he sought to justify all the policies that had been taken up during Grenville's administration and, by implication, he criticized the Rockinghams for departing from them. As has been seen, this work was written during a period when Grenville was interested in underlining his suitability for office. Ironically, the pamphlet was published just a few weeks before he was drawn into the union movement.

Immediately after *The Present State of the Nation* appeared, Burke, with crucial imput from Dowdeswell and possibly others,[161] began to plan a reply. Such an outspoken attack on the party could not go unanswered merely for the sake of political convenience. In February, just as the parties began to fortify their relationship in the Commons, the *Observations on a Late State of the Nation* was published. The authors pulled no punches. They took up each point made by the Grenvilles and offered a refutation in a clear, coherent, and apparently logical manner. They made no mistake of their disdain for everything the Grenvilles had stood for and of their belief that the Rockinghams were the antithesis of them in almost every respect. However, in one important way this pamphlet reflected political exigencies. There can be little doubt that ultimately it was meant to promote unity. Indeed, even the Rockinghams' insistence on their superiority can be seen as an a direct attempt to attain one of Dowdeswell's most important conditions for coalition. Moreover, the piece was brought to a conclusion with a direct plea for an amalgamation of all parties that were prepared to join in the construction of a broad and comprehensive ministry:

It is … false, that the idea of an united administration carries with it that of a proscription of any other party. It does indeed imply the necessity of having the great strong holds of government in well-united hands, in order to secure the predominance of right and uniform principles; of having the capital offices of deliberation and execution in those who can deliberate with mutual confidence, and who will execute what is resolved with firmness and fidelity … No system of that kind can be formed, which will not leave room fully sufficient for healing coalitions.[162]

The work also stressed that the one major cause on which the party would be willing to unite with others was the defeat of those who had promoted division within the highest councils of state:

It is a serious affair, this studied disunion in government. In cases where union is most consulted in the constitution of a ministry, and where persons are best disposed to promote it, differences, from the various ideas of men, will arise; and, from their passions will often ferment into violent heats, so as greatly to disorder all public business. What must be the consequence, when the very distemper is made the basis of the constitution; and the original weakness of human nature is still further enfeebled by art and contrivance?[163]

By the spring of 1769, the Rockingham leaders were thinking seriously of the prospects for a union that would include not only themselves and the Grenvilles but nearly everyone in opposition. On 9 May, the day after the adjournment, they and a number of the Grenvilles, Chathams, city radicals, plus a few independents who had supported them over the Middlesex election, attended a dinner at the Thatched House Tavern, at Dowdeswell's invitation,[164] to demonstrate solidarity. A few days later, Rockingham voiced the hope that "all the subdivisions of the minority will be consolidated into one grand constitutional party."[165] Over the following year, the Rockingham's main preoccupation was the reconstruction of a new court Whig connection, whose broad base of support would be in the House of Commons, whose central principle and objective would be the elimination of favouritism in government, and whose popular polemic would be the Middlesex election.

CHAPTER THREE

The Petitioning and Union Movements during the Parliamentary Recess of 1769

If there was ever any chance for the Rockinghams to create a grand Whig union, it was in the months between May 1769 and the end of the 1770 session of Parliament. In this period all the opposition parties fought on the same side over important issues, including the Middlesex election and that old stand-by, favouritism in government. Moreover, they worked together to foster and promote a nationwide campaign of protest against the actions of the House of Commons with respect to Wilkes. In the context of the debate over party that is currently engaging the attention of historians, what is interesting is how little progress they actually made. While the connections involved certainly cooperated at times and even claimed publicly that they had achieved complete unanimity, they never managed to break down the important differences that separated them. There are several factors that one could point to in explaining this, including divergent principles, dissimilar objectives, and lack of success in Parliament. What they demonstrate, however, is that the personal followings of the 1760s, as scholars such as Paul Langford and Ian Christie have recognized, had become too firmly entrenched to be eclipsed overnight by the kind of political alignment that had existed in previous reigns.[1] Quite simply, this was the age of multiparty politics. The opposition groups were not going to revive a long-dead Whig nexus or a national dichotomy based on a Whig-versus-court (or Whig-versus-Tory) struggle.

Between May 1769 and January 1770, the Rockinghams helped keep the Middlesex election issue alive. Their efforts now were turned to two fronts. The first involved the press. Over the summer they published two pamphlets that laid out what were thought to be the most salient arguments against the actions of the majority. One was written by William Dowdeswell[2] and the other by Sir William

Meredith,[3] MP for Liverpool, who at this stage was a Rockingham supporter. Rockingham himself, a few other leading members of the party, and Grenville's friend Alexander Wedderburn took some part in planning or criticizing both.[4]

These pamphlets demonstrate that what the members of the opposition really objected to was not the initial expulsion but the fact "that a Resolution of the House of Commons declaring one of its Members *incapable by Law*, could constitute such a legal Incapacity as annihilated the Votes of the Freeholders."[5] The argument was that the Commons majority did not have a valid precedent for pronouncing Wilkes incapable of sitting in the House (and, in effect, for disfranchising the Middlesex electors).[6] While it was admitted that a person might be disqualified on the grounds of criminal conduct, it was insisted that no general rule had been established in such cases and that an Act of Parliament was therefore requisite. By proceeding against Wilkes on its own authority, the House had usurped a legislative power that should not have been exercised without the official concurrence of the king and the House of Lords.

The fact that the opposition spokesmen had largely dropped their attack over the expulsion would seem to indicate that the constitutional issue with respect to it was not as clear cut, even in their own minds, as they had wanted to believe on 3 February. All along, their primary reason for dissenting had been the belief that the House was liable to find itself in conflict with the nationwide electorate. Much emphasis continued to be placed on the rights of the freeholders. Meredith, indeed, rather overstated the case when he wrote that "the Right of voting being the Essence of the Freehold you may as well take away the Freehold itself, as the Right of voting ."[7]

The Rockingham party also gave its support to the much-touted petitioning campaign, which undertook to persuade the crown to override the recent actions of the House of Commons. In scrutinizing the Rockinghams' activities in this campaign, one is impressed by two basic facts. First, the leading members of the party undeniably took a relatively keen interest in it. This particular summer and autumn recess stands out from most others during their opposition career in that the marquis, Dowdeswell, Portland, the Cavendishes, and others, who in normal circumstances shunned involvement in strictly political matters when Parliament was not sitting, were able (albeit with some telling lapses) to maintain at least a modicum of interest and involvement throughout. This fact, along with their reasoning in the process of discussing, designing, and ultimately producing various drafts of the *Thoughts*, reflects their enthusiasm for the re-establishment of a broadly based court Whig party.

The second noteworthy characteristic of the Rockinghams' performance was its ineffectiveness. George Rudé has stressed the importance of the leadership provided by the parliamentary opposition in
general in organizing and propagating the movement across the
country.[8] To some extent he is correct. However, it should be said that
he has given the Rockinghams too much credit by suggesting that the
party somehow managed to exaggerate feelings in the nation over the
Middlesex election.[9] John Brewer has estimated that the number of
signatures gathered, though large, actually "tends to understate
rather than exaggerate Wilkite support."[10] He considers the support
to have been more substantial than Professor Rudé does, and he notes
that there was considerable sympathy in many localities that never
actually presented petitions.[11] I agree, though I believe that most of
the support was for the electors of Middlesex rather than for John
Wilkes. It is equally apparent that Rockingham and his friends can be
held somewhat to blame for the fact that support for the cause was
understated. They failed quite badly to give the campaign the leadership and direction they might have provided, largely because at crucial moments they acted like country gentlemen rather than like
organized, professional political strategists.

The petitioning movement was described in detail by Professor
Rudé many years ago.[12] From May 1769 to April 1770, addresses to
the crown praying for redress of the wrongs inflicted on the freeholders of Middlesex, and either explicitly or implicitly urging the dissolution of Parliament, were signed by a relatively large percentage of
the electors in some fifteen counties and a dozen towns and cities
across England. The 60,000 freeholders who signed these documents
accounted for more than one-quarter of the total English electorate
and far outnumbered those who supported the loyal addresses to the
king, which were procured partly in the hope of counteracting the petitions. Unfortunately (from the opposition point of view), the overall
effect was disappointing. Before Parliament reconvened, it was
widely believed that the vast majority of the signatories were not of
the politically significant echelons of society (the wealthier propertied
classes for the most part held aloof)[13] and that the petitions were in
many cases a product of the direct leadership provided by unscrupulous and frighteningly radical London politicians in parts of the
country where their influence was substantial.

One of the first lapses in the Rockinghams' attention occurred immediately after the parliamentary session ended, and it allowed the
London politicians to take over the initiative for a critical period. Before the beginning of the summer, the party leaders had led the attack, and in doing so they had managed to restrain the extremist

tendencies of their more radical allies. After proposing a coalition in this business at the Thatched House Tavern, however, the party, much to Burke's exasperation, "broke up without any plan of action for the Summer,"[14] and the marquis and his friends returned to their homes in the country. Left on their own, the London politicians, in their determination to excite as much bitterness as possible, began to act immediately. By 24 April they had the first petition to the crown – that for Middlesex – ready for presentation.[15] Its tone was extremely inclement by eighteenth-century standards. It complained not only about the recent action of the House of Commons but also about a whole list of grievances, ranging from the suppression of freedom of the press to the mismanagement of the American colonies.[16] In June the London petition was drawn up by men from the same set, with a similar though shorter list of grievances.[17] And the following month, Bristol, where the radical element was also strong, produced an address that followed the example of both its predecessors.[18]

The national movement of protest thus started badly for the Rockinghams and for that part of the parliamentary opposition whose major concern was to gain the respect of the "men of weight and character" throughout the country.[19] As the campaign spread during the remainder of the year, numerous large landholders refused to support it, because they were afraid they might be connected publicly with the radicals and their hypercritical stand. Moreover, because of widespread fears of the influence of the crown, they proved reluctant to take up the objective of calling on the king to interfere with measures that had been sanctioned by the House of Commons. In a letter written that September, one of the Grenvilles[20] informed his leader of the lack of progress which the petition was making in his county. There are few better testimonies, first, to the considerable propertied support for the cause of the freeholders of Middlesex and, second, to the general failure of the opposition to enlist the full force of that support:

I fear the idea must be laid aside, as, whatever may be the inclinations of the freeholders at large, too many Gentlemen express their disapprobation of the measure for it to be carry'd through with an Eclat that would give Credit & weight to it. All Ranks of men, except those immediately connected with the Ministers, express their abhorrence of them & of their conduct but many even amongst the warmest of these, cannot be induc'd to see the expediency of applying to the Crown, & obstinately persist in blending what is in Fact the cause of the Freeholders of England, with that of Mr. Wilkes.[21]

It is probable that the Rockinghams' campaign would not have involved petitioning the king if they had taken the lead themselves.

They understood how distasteful it was to country opinion, in particular, to have the crown intercede with the elected voice of the nation. In September, Sir George Savile told Rockingham, "I have in my eye ... that objection to petitioning the King for dissolution vis., that it is against the stream of the Constitution to call on the Crown for help against the House of Commons, and that trying to lessen the power of the House of Commons is always lessening liberty."[22] In the same month, Sir Anthony Abdy informed the marquis that he was "not for the Crown's ever interfering with the House of Commons if I can prevent it, as I think Ch[arle]s 1st. offended the constitution more by such intermeddling where he had no business, than by any thing else he did."[23] It is likely that if the members of the party's central core had remained in control, they would have employed the convention of instructions to local MPs (which Rockingham favoured) or resolutions, or petitions to Parliament, (which many important men in Yorkshire appear to have preferred).[24] But the party did not really agree to do anything until September, when Rockingham, after much hesitation, finally began to move in his home county.

Rockingham's tardiness was a manifestation of more than indolence. To a considerable degree, it resulted from the nature of his influence in the county. His dominance in Yorkshire depended largely on his ability to maintain the good will of the local gentry. For this reason, he constantly attempted to avoid creating the impression that he was imposing his personal will, and he was always anxious to make sure that a policy was supported by the propertied classes before he adopted it. In 1769 he felt that he could not do anything to voice local discontent over the Middlesex election until he was certain that such an action would be widely approved. As early as June, he realized that there was "a desire in this County that something should be done,"[25] but he was not convinced that the desire was strong enough to warrant a petition. He therefore decided first to get the sheriff and grand jury of Yorkshire to express support for his party's recent parliamentary stand by writing a letter of thanks to the county's MPs,[26] Savile and Edwin Lascelles.[27] The letter was agreed upon and signed at the assizes in York on 14 July.[28] But even after this, the marquis's and the county's progress towards adopting a petition was very gradual. In September, Rockingham described the process to Burke in words that demonstrate how agonizingly slow political action could be under his direction:

The plain Narrative is – that on the Monday – a gentleman came to me and wished me to approve that an advertisement should be inserted in the next day's paper – to desire a County Meeting might be held on the Friday in that week ...

I told the persons who were eager ... to try to find – if there was a general inclination sufficient to authorize a number of gentlemen to apply to the High Sheriff for a County Meeting ... and that ... I would neither moderate their Zeal nor foment it, and should leave the determination ... according to their discretion ...

In my conversation with several in the course of the week I declined expressing any wish one way or the other – saying that in truth, my conduct in politicks was of an active Nature, and that tho' I did not care what might be said by the ministers &c ... yet I would not give any Handle in Yorkshire – for Yorkshiremen to say that my politicks had led them beyond their intentions – or that I checked their well founded Ardour.[29]

Clearly, Rockingham's role at this stage was more one of directing the flow of opinion in the county than of leading or fomenting it. If anything, he actually held the inclinations of his "warm" friends in check instead of exploiting them. Rockingham's attitude was very similar to that of his most influencial independent country friend, Savile, who also refused to take an active part in prodding the county to action. As always, Savile insisted that whatever was done must represent the will of his constituents. When there was "doubt whether a County Meeting should be called – [he] insisted, that he was not a proper judge – that if the County in general thought that wrong had been done to freeholders &c – It was in their option to take notice of it or not – that if a meeting was called He should attend – (as he said) *below the Bar* – that he might be asked whether he had or had not joined in doing *the wrong."*[30]

Finally, forty gentlemen agreed to ask the sheriff to call a meeting of the county. Among them were several of Rockingham's friends, including Nathaniel Cholmley,[31] MP for Boroughbridge, and Edwin Lascelles, MP for Yorkshire. However, Lord John Cavendish, who sat for the borough of York, was not among them, and neither was Rockingham's good friend Beilby Thompson,[32] who represented Hedon; nor, of course, was Savile.[33] The sheriff agreed to call the meeting, and it was set for 27 September.

After the decision to hold the meeting was made, Rockingham took care to see that it was advertised in the county newspapers, and he even suggested that handbills be distributed to the freeholders.[34] While he wanted to ensure that the gathering would be well attended, he was still not convinced that he should lend his support to petitioning the king for the dissolution of Parliament. "In my letter ... to Burke," he told Dowdeswell, "I said, one objection ... arose here from 'the where' that mode was first set. I should, indeed, have added not only 'the where' but 'the what' that petition was: for in truth the farrago included in that petition was of much detriment ... though in the very essential matter ... well founded."[35]

Rockingham's eventual decision to endorse the movement was the result of several factors, but the most important appears to have been a letter of 5 September in which Dowdeswell, who by then had become involved in Worcestershire, told the marquis in no uncertain terms of the importance of Yorkshire joining forces with the other counties:

I know but one case in which an instruction might be properly applied: and that is, where bad Members stand in need of being told of their faults and instructed to attend no more. But this not being your case in Yorkshire, I hope to hear that the idea ... is laid aside.

If the sense of Yorkshire should be instructing I wish to know what their Members are to do, if the Ministry should move a censure on petitions to the King against the acts of either house of parliament. Are they to differ from their Constituents, or their Friends in the House? Are they to stay away, or give their Friends a faint support?

Let Me say a word to you and our Friends as Politicians. Can We wish for any better event of an intemperate act of this Administration than a dissolution of this Parliament? If the time should come hereafter when You might wish to advise such a measure, will it not be fortunate that You have said from the first that nothing but dissolution can be a perfect cure for the desperate evil, and that the opinion You then give is not an expedient for the day, but yt same opinion which you had ever held.

Let me speak to You as good Men. Is anything so likely to cure the shamefull venality & prostitution of Parliament, as sudden dissolution known to be the consequence of their own corrupt proceedings?

I am aware of the objection to petitioning the King against either house: but unless We take parliament as they are in fact, and not as they are on paper We shall never be a match for our Adversaries. This however is not always done, but when their conduct has been such as to set the nation against them the opportunity is fair, & ought not to be mist. Nothing is wanting in the present case but to call Men & things by their proper name. The provocation will justify the irregularity: and When We have learnt what parliament is & what has been its conduct, We shall learn to get the better of the reverence due to it in its purer state, & present our petitions without much remorse.[36]

Dowdeswell's reasoning helps illustrate the gradual evolution of the Rockinghams' constitutional philosophy. He was arguing that it was correct to call on the king to intervene because the Commons had proved so venal that it had failed in its duty to uphold the will of the electorate. It had prostituted itself, presumably by selling out to the ministry for places and pensions under the crown, and it had to be disciplined. By 1773, their lack of success would encourage the Rockinghams to believe that the influence of the crown had grown to the point where the members of the House of Commons – and, indeed, the people themselves – could never withstand it. It was this conviction that prompted them eventually to embrace "economical reform." Thus, in 1769, they were being encouraged to focus on the problem that ultimately turned them into advocates of constitutional amendment. Clearly, on the other hand, they had not yet reached the stage where they thought the problem was nearly that severe. At this point they could still imagine themselves reassuming power, and as they were about to demonstrate in the *Thoughts*, they expected to employ the influence of the crown, as their court Whig predecessors had done, "in supporting the Ministers of State, and in carrying on the public business according to their opinions."[37] It was appropriate for Dowdeswell to argue, therefore, not that there was anything wrong with the system but that this was a particularly evil House of Commons, which on this particular occasion had acted very irregularly. What was needed was not a reduction of crown patronage but dissolution (and therefore a new election), which would bring forth a morally more advanced set of MPs, who would do the right thing with respect to the freeholders of Middlesex.

It is difficult to tell whether Dowdeswell would have so strongly advocated petitioning the crown if it had been up to his party to decide on the suitable convention in the beginning. Even if he had opted for such a course, he would probably have been willing to give it up once he heard the objections of Savile, Abdy, and others. His prime consideration, however, appears to have been that this form of action should be taken up everywhere in order to preserve the appearance of a united denunciation of the Commons' actions. By the time he wrote to Rockingham, the counties of Surrey, Wiltshire, Worcestershire (his home county), and Buckinghamshire had all produced petitions, which were much more respectful in tone than those of Middlesex, Bristol, and London, and which kept to the single point of the Middlesex election.[38] In Dowdeswell's view, it was most important that Yorkshire should do the same.

Burke had been attempting for some months to get his leader to join in the campaign, partly "because it carries more the air of uniformity and concurrence."[39] On 10 September, Abdy also wrote, stating that after observing the support in Surrey, he had suddenly become reconciled to the idea.[40] This helped the marquis finally make the decision to proceed. The Yorkshire petition was drawn up in meetings between Rockingham, Wedderburn, Savile, Lord John Cavendish, and a few principal gentlemen of the county.[41] It was revised by Dowdeswell.[42] It followed the example set by the more moderate petitions and kept to the single point of the Middlesex election. It also explicitly requested the dissolution of Parliament.[43]

When the county meeting was held at York on the twenty-seventh, a large number attended – Cavendish estimated that there were seven or eight hundred – including "almost all the Gentlemen of fortune of the County, except those who were known to be against it."[44] Savile (who, like Abdy, had suddenly warmed to this course), George Armytage,[45] another of Rockingham's friends, and Wedderburn voiced their support for a petition to the crown. Only three opposed the idea.[46] This would seem to indicate that Rockingham could have used his authority much earlier and obtained positive results. However, he felt that the gentry would *like the Appearance* of its being their own Act"[47] and therefore stayed away from the meeting.

After the petition was agreed on, it was important to get it distributed to the freeholders, signed, and presented to the king as quickly as possible so that it would appear to be a spontaneous outburst of public opinion. Jerome Dring, Rockingham's man of business in York, set to work immediately and had copies made and forwarded to men of influence all over the county so that they could procure signatures.[48] From this point on, however, there were constant delays because of organizational deficiencies. No committee was formed at or after the county meeting to deal with unforeseen problems. Men who were asked to obtain signatures failed to exert themselves, and the question of who should pay distribution costs obstructed progress considerably.[49] There was also the problem that in some areas people were rather lukewarm, but the fact that some 11,000 of the 20,000 freeholders in the county eventually signed the petition suggests this was not the main problem.[50]

Plainly, Rockingham and Sir George Savile, with all their influence among the gentry, could have done much to expedite the process of collecting signatures. Even after Rockingham heard the complaints of Dring and others about the inactivity of those who were supposed to be pursuing the matter, he did not take any very decisive action; he merely allowed Dring to let his displeasure be known.[51] Savile, when approached, refused outright to advance the process; he clearly felt that if people were not willing to go out of their way to sign the petition, it could not be looked on as a manifestation of their feelings and therefore was hardly worthwhile. "I really can take no part," he said, "in things so much out of my way as the management of the Petition & all the subsequent steps & consequences ... I can hardly believe that my sentiments can be mistaken ... I say my *sentiments & opinion* in contra-distinction to the making it a matter of obligation and a canvassing or voting match. The evil is small if there wants such means to *procure* complaints."[52] As a result, the campaign dragged on and on, and the lists of signatures were not complete until late December or early January.[53]

The lack of resolution displayed by Rockingham and his friends was a crucial factor, not only because it allowed the London politicians to take and to some extent keep the initiative, but because it largely nullified the effects which the entrance of Yorkshire might otherwise have had. The county was considered prestigious because of its size and population. Its involvement would have given the petitioning movement a substantial boost if it had moved quickly, efficiently, and with an appearance of spontaneity. Yorkshire was one of only a few counties in which a relatively high percentage of the larger property owners were supportive,[54] and if they had been able to demonstrate their sentiments even by September or October, they might have had a powerful influence on people elsewhere. As it turned out, the very long period taken to settle and sign the document gave ministerial writers in London a chance to represent the movement as the work of a few politicians who were connected with the London radicals.[55] In early December, Alexander Wedderburn warned Rockingham of the ill effects of delay. The ministry, he said, had "employed every means to represent ... [our petition] as the act of a small number of factious people. They have had the field to themselves for some time both in the Newspapers & in Conversation, and they have so far succeeded that it is very much believed here [in London] that the number of those who have signed is not considerable."[56]

Wedderburn's words point to another area in which Rockingham failed to exploit the resources available to him. He does not appear to have made any very extensive attempts to refute the damaging and unfounded rumours. The 11,000 signatures were impressive indeed. They amounted to more than one-sixth of the total number of signatures on the various petitions. Rockingham could have had some of his more prolific friends – notably, Burke – employ the newspapers to demonstrate to the nation that there was in fact a good deal more enthusiasm in Yorkshire than government writers were willing to allow. But Rockingham was relatively unconcerned about such matters. He believed that, when the petition was finally presented, people would see that it was well supported. The loss of political advantage in the meantime seems to have worried him very little. What really mattered to Rockingham was that the movement should be conducted with dignity. On 23 December he told Dowdeswell that the business had "gone on well, the Yorkshire Petition notwithstanding ... The *Inattention of many who were* anxious for a Petition and all the false reports &c – will at length prove to have been very amply & very creditably sign'd & I hope will be very respectably I (should I say respectfully) presented."[57]

Rockingham was totally successful in one respect only. He made it very obvious to the nation that he was not attempting to foment the people. However, it is extremely doubtful that this brought any positive results. The ministers and their writers were quick to point out that the propertied classes generally did not participate,[58] and the fact that the marquis was not very active was held as evidence to substantiate this theory. John Robinson[59] told a friend in November, "The Yorkshire petition I hear is signed by about 10,000 but chiefly the lower sort of freeholders – it is said Lord Rockingham *at* his own Table publicly talks against the Petition and condemns it."[60]

Except in the case of Burke and to some extent Dowdeswell, the performance of the influential Rockinghams in other parts of the country was much like that of their leader. In Surrey, which joined the fight as early as June, several party supporters were involved. Yet it is evident that had it not been for the efforts of Sir Joseph Mawbey, who was a friend and political ally of the Rockinghams but was known better as a Wilkite and a radical, nothing at all would have been done.[61] Although Rockingham's friends Sir George Colebrooke[62] and Robert Clayton[63] attended meetings arranged by Mawbey[64] and were on the committee appointed to draw up the petition, they both argued for instructions to local MPs and eventually acquiesced under pressure. Sir Anthony Abdy, the most influential of Rockingham's supporters in Surrey, declined to take any part in the affair. After he had witnessed the antics of Mawbey and Henry Bellas, another well-known Wilkite, he very nearly declined even to provide his signature.[65] Later, although his attitude changed, he expended little energy in support of the petition. When Essex, where he was also very influential, decided to take up the cause, he again played the role of a follower. After a meeting was advertised in the papers, he reported: "The Leaders in this Matter I know not or what steps are to be taken I have not heard."[66] He did, however, propose to attend the meeting and find out.

The Cavendishes in Derbyshire were probably less inclined to take part than any of the Rockinghams. Early in the summer, Lord John Cavendish made it clear to his friends that he thought the party should "have nothing to do with any thing of this sort," and he was thoroughly disgusted when he heard of the involvement of the London politicians in Surrey.[67] In July, instead of urging his county to take action, he prepared to prevent the men who were anxious to do something from going too far.[68] Ultimately, he decided to go along with the measure only when he learned that Rockingham himself had agreed to do so.

The Duke of Portland's response was much like that of the Cavendishes. In Cumberland he exerted himself only after Yorkshire had made a move, and even then he progressed very slowly. The Cumberland petition was not presented until 6 April 1770.[69] In Portland's home county, Nottingham, he, Savile, (who owned large estates there), and Frederick Montagu[70] discussed the possibility of promoting the measure, but nothing came of it.[71] Portland and Savile appear to have left everything to Montagu, who was probably right when he suggested that if Savile in particular would take a very active part, a respectable number of signatures would be forthcoming.[72] Savile had stated in September that since he was merely a freeholder in Nottingham and not an MP, he had no scruples about being more aggressive.[73] However, he probably found the county only lukewarm and drew the line at stirring things up when the people themselves were not enthusiastic.

In Worcestershire, Dowdeswell's actions were less reserved. He had no qualms about petitioning the crown, and after the county began to join in he made his position clear.[74] It does appear, however, that even he allowed other men to lead in the beginning and that this did some damage. One observer described the origins of the Worcestershire petition as follows: it "was first proposed by a skatter-brained fellow, Holland Cooksey,[75] (who is chairman to the disgrace of the County) at the sessions, a meeting was afterward advertised at the Assizes which, nothing being then done, was adjourned to the next week; It was again accordingly proposed and signed by a few Gentlemen, (after being corrected by Mr. Dowdeswell) and by some freeholders, but I have understood from time to time that it has been received but coldly by the major part of the County."[76] Later, Dowdeswell complained to Rockingham of poor management in the circulation and noted that Wilkes's character and the "injudicious list of grievances" in the first petitions had made many gentlemen averse to taking action.[77]

It would be possible to demonstrate the failings of many of the Rockinghams. The Duke of Richmond, for instance, refused to animate his friends in Sussex on the grounds that he was afraid of appearing factious,[78] and Sir William Meredith had to be spurred into action by the freeholders in Liverpool after attempting to impede those who were eager.[79] Among the important members of the party, only Burke demonstrated the kind of activity that was needed to turn the movement into a successful political manoeuvre. He had much faith in the power of this type of public agitation. In his own county, Buckinghamshire, he did all he could to promote the measure, though he had to await the lead of the Grenvilles, who pretty well dominated local politics.[80] The fact that the Grenvilles hesitated until they were sure that Rockingham had taken action was a clear manifestation to him of his party's failings.[81] In October he wrote to Charles O'Hara[82] and commented on the irresolution of many of his leaders both with respect to the petitioning movement and generally. His words are interesting in that they show how different in temperament Burke was from the other members of the party and how, in his own mind, he was able to admire even those of their characteristics that he found frustrating. The passage also helps us comprehend some of Burke's feelings about the union movement. As will be seen, he alone among the party's central core had serious misgivings.

We are diffident, scrupulous, timid, and slow in coming to a resolution; But when once we have engaged, we are not only much in earnest and very direct in our proceeding, but sufficiently bold and active in our Conduct. As for our Allies [particularly the Grenvilles] their manner is quite different; they resolve early and with boldness; but in the prosecution of business, they are never fair and direct; they have a thousand under plots and oblique views ... and they frequently dissipate and lose their publick object ... You know how much I felt from the slowness and irresolution of some of our best friends. Even to this moment, there are some ... who cannot be prevailed upon to take that lead, which is natural to their situation and necessary to their Consequence. But in the main, things are flowing into the right channel; and will go, I hope, down an Easy declivity for the future.[83]

If Rockingham's supporters (other than Burke) had been able to move aggressively in their respective spheres of influence, some of the ill effects of the marquis's own equivocation and inefficiency might have been overcome. In Surrey, for instance, Abdy could, with effort, have so overshadowed the radical element as to make its involvement almost unnoticeable, and in many parts of the country other members of the connection could have done much to establish the upper-class support and the illusion of spontaneity that was so obviously lacking. As things stood, the public remained relatively unimpressed. Horace Walpole summed up the situation accurately in December when he observed that the petitions had "contracted an air of ridicule from the ridiculous undertakers that have been forced to parade into indifferent counties to supply the place of all the gentlemen, who have disdained to appear and countenance them."[84]

The attitude of the propertied classes to the petitioning movement should not be taken as evidence that they approved of the Commons' handling of the Middlesex election issue. The independent members of the House were probably fairly representative of this element throughout the country, and in January 1770 almost half of the independents in the Lower House continued to support the opposition.[85] As has been seen, many aspects of the campaign were distasteful to country gentlemen in particular, and as Burke discovered in Buckinghamshire, many "who voted with us in the House of Commons" held aloof.[86] If the Rockinghams had taken over the leadership in the beginning, restrained the London radicals, adopted some other mode than petitioning the crown, and generally moved with vigour and efficiency, they might very well have received a great deal more nonpartisan support and, along with it, public credibility.

The repercussions of the Rockinghams' approach were to be seen during the 1770 session of Parliament. Meanwhile, one other political movement that was to affect future events – the opposition alliance begun during the previous session – was being nurtured. It had taken on a whole new complexion on 7 July when Lord Chatham made an appearance at the king's levee in London to announce his return to public life.

Although it was widely acknowledged that Chatham had failed miserably in handling the reins of power during his days as the leader of the administration and although his following in Parliament was and had always been very small,[87] he was still considered a force to be reckoned with. Because a number of his friends held relatively important positions in the present ministry, he was thought to have the power to effect resignations that would bring down the government or at least put it in a very difficult position.[88] Even more significant was the fact that Chatham had managed over the years to retain the aura of personal strength that he had cultivated when leading the country through the Seven Years' War. In the spring of 1769, as the Middlesex election issue came to the fore and as the riots broke out again in London, rumours of Chatham's recovery had been circulating and people had begun to watch for his return.[89] It is a testimony to the public confidence in him that when he did appear, almost everyone expected him to be asked to step back into power to re-establish order.[90]

Chatham's return brought new life to the union movement. However, this initially caused the Rockinghams more anxiety than satisfaction, largely because he became the dominant force and began to seem a real threat to their pretensions. When Chatham attended the levee on 7 July, he was interviewed personally by George III. During the interview he informed the king that he was unhappy with much that had been done during his absence and particularly with the way the Middlesex election had been handled, and he left little doubt that he intended to make a stand against the government's actions.[91] While this was the first reliable indication the king and his ministers had received of Chatham's intentions, it is evident that he had already made his decision when he resigned in October 1768. It had been about that time that he had begun to work to establish unity among the parties in opposition. He had contacted and developed an amicable relationship with Lord Temple (who was his brother-in-law, but from whom he had been estranged politically and socially since 1766),[92] and he then used Temple to approach the latter's brother, Grenville. Grenville appears to have believed that Chatham could be extremely helpful in furthering his designs to force his way into office, and for this reason he responded readily. Over the summer of 1769 he and Chatham exchanged visits, and when everything "passed extremely well between them,"[93] the family reunion looked to be complete.

Chatham realized that his forces and Grenville's needed bolstering in the House of Commons. Consequently, after his recovery, he also began to make overtures to the Rockinghams; but because of their distrust of him, the game was a very delicate one. He had to start slowly and cautiously. He made his first move in late July or early August when he invited his neighbour, the Rockinghams' friend Barlow Trecothick, to pay him a visit, during which he seemed to compliment the party.[94] Later, in October, Chatham sent communications to Sir Charles Saunders and Admiral Keppel, who had served under him during the Seven Years' War, paying his respects and implying that they should visit him.[95] This they failed to do only because Rockingham did not wish to give the impression "that they and all the world were flocking to *Redivivus*."[96] These initial openings were indirect, but Chatham was becoming much more outspoken and forceful by November. In three different contacts with members of the party,[97] he demonstrated superb insight in playing on its leaders' designs for a great Whig revival:

He said that he was now Domestically happy, but public affairs were too Black to give any body comfort – That the conduct of some persons in administration had much surprised him that he knows not what infatuation has produced such a situation of affairs. He ... is a body and soul united to L[or]d

Rockingham and Sir Geo[rge] Savile in ... [the Middlesex election issue], that he thinks Sir Geo[rge] the most Virtuous character in this country, and bows to his constitutional, as well as his private integrity; that he will go hand in hand with L[or]d Rockingham's party, who are, and who have proved themselves to be the only True Whigs in this Country.[98]

While the Rockinghams were thus being courted by their old enemy prior to the 1770 session of Parliament, they were also being approached by the Grenvilles in a manner that seems to reflect Chatham's influence. The alliance of the two groups had improved to some degree during the petitioning campaign, when Burke worked in conjunction with the Grenvilles in Buckinghamshire and when Rockingham and his friends worked with Wedderburn in Yorkshire. However, from the Grenville side, the most overt attempts to bring about a deeper understanding were made about the same time as Chatham's overtures. In late November, when Burke followed up an earlier invitation to visit Temple, the latter apparently "expressed the most earnest desire of the union of all Parties into one; wished that all memory of past animosities might be worn away; and stated very strongly ... the hopes which the Court built on the supposed impossibility of such an union."[99] When Burke insisted that "no union could be formed of an Effect or Credit, which was not compacted upon this great principle, 'that the King's men should be utterly destroyed as a Corps,'" Temple apparently "assented very heartily."

The reaction of the Rockinghams to the advances of Chatham and the Grenvilles demonstrates their determination at all cost to see that no one should challenge their primacy. Before Chatham had arrived on the scene, they had shown a good deal of genuine interest in the possibility of union once they had realized that Grenville was not going to be asked to join or form an administration. But Chatham's recovery and his merger with the Grenvilles made them feel insecure. Now they believed that he was likely to be the first to be called to office[100] and would therefore be difficult to control, and they were afraid that he and the Grenvilles as a single force might have an exaggerated sense of their own importance. In October, after hearing of Chatham's earlier more cautious approaches, Rockingham told Burke:

It is so improbable that I think it is next to impossible that the *three* Brothers and us can form a conjunct administration. *They* doubtless would have great pretensions – from their age – Habits of Business – talents of speech – &c &c ...

Many circumstances evidently point out that the idea at Court is ... that they think of trying to throw the new arrangement into Lord Chatham's Hands ...

The reconciliation of Lord Temple and G: Grenville with Lord Chatham I attribute to no other speculation.[101]

Rockingham was mainly afraid of Chatham now, but he did not give up hope that Grenville might still be of use, primarily because of his relative weakness. He continued:

In many respects amongst the three Brothers I think G: Grenville the best for us. The use of him in the House of Commons, would be of service, and I think notwithstanding his character of obstinacy &c – He would sacrifice *some-things*, to be really and confidentially united with us. His present situation makes it eligible for him and the particular circumstance of the present great inveteracy towards him – *in all the Bute Party* – and the *personal ill-footing he is and has long been on in the closet* – all coincide to make him the more safe for us.[102]

The marquis appears to have concluded that "the three Brothers" would not be able to form a strong ministry on their own because of their narrow base in the House of Commons and that therefore the court might eventually turn to him. In that situation, he thought it likely that Grenville would be willing to leave Chatham and take up the Rockingham banner. It was because of his desire to keep the possibility of a merger with Grenville in sight, and because he shared the opinion of some of his friends that the appearance of unity would be extremely useful in the battle against the court, that Rockingham decided to play along with both of his allies at this stage. With respect to Chatham, he advised Burke to be cautious. However, he also told him to mention the Corsican affair to friends, implying that a concerted attack on the administration might be made on that issue. Chatham's specialty had been foreign affairs ever since the Seven Years' War, and Rockingham was obviously attempting to act as amicably as he felt he could in the circumstances.

Thus, by the end of 1769, some progress towards the construction of a reconstituted Whig party had been made, and some had been lost. The Rockinghams, Grenvilles, and some of the Chathams had shown that they could work together in the petitioning movement, and Chatham had given indications that he was interested in cooperating in something more ambitious. No one would have estimated, on the other hand, that success was on the horizon. Chatham's entry had in a way been a setback. While he had been out of the picture, the Rockingham camp had been able to see itself assimilating his following along with the Grenvilles. Now, however, both the Rockinghams' allies seemed intimidating. The marquis and his friends had relished a union for some years, but as the largest Whig following in Parliament (and, in their own minds, the only true successors of the old Whig oligarchy), they had proved unwilling to treat other parties as equals.[103] Indications from the others that they were prepared to go "hand in hand" with them were not really what they wanted. They would have far preferred to hear their allies say that they were willing to accept their leadership, to seek their direction, or to become part of their following. This, of course, was hoping for too much. Grenville and Chatham had both held the highest political office in the land. As time would show, they, and especially the latter, had no intention of being as weak as the Rockinghams would like them to be or as acquiescent.

CHAPTER FOUR

The Union Movement in the Parliamentary Session of 1770

Between early November and the commencement of the session on 9 January 1770, there was very little contact between the three major opposition parties. Despite exhortations from both Burke and Dowdeswell,[1] Rockingham was unable to get up to London until 1 January. Lord Chatham was still experiencing occasional fits of his old nemesis, the gout, and therefore was unable to be very active. And the attention of both Temple and Grenville was consumed by the illness and sudden death of Grenville's wife in early December.[2] Consequently, the union movement stagnated and virtually no planning for the session was done until a meeting at the Thatched House Tavern on the day before Parliament reconvened.[3] Following the meeting, however, the opposition parties publicly displayed a greater degree of unanimity than they had previously shown. While they had a popular issue on which to take a stand and were able to keep the battle in Parliament reasonably close, they managed to overcome any fears or jealousies they harboured towards one another. Incredibly, during this period, Rockingham seems to have allowed himself to be convinced, for the first time, that his two main allies were ready to amalgamate with his following and give him the pre-eminence he craved. This would prove short-sighted of him, and one might well argue that past experiences should have kept the dangers of relying on Chatham, in particular, planted firmly in the forefront of his thoughts.[4] The explanation seems to be that he was unjustifiably swayed by the image of himself at the head of a new, broadly based, court Whig party.

On the opening day, Dowdeswell in the Commons and Chatham in the Lords, after making special reference to the freeholders of Middlesex, moved amendments to the address, requesting an inquiry into domestic "discontents."[5] Both motions were defeated by substantial majorities, and when Rockingham moved that the Lords assemble on the tenth so that he could introduce important business, he was beaten by 203 votes to 36. But the day was not without redeeming features. The opposition connections in both Houses were able to maintain their united front, and some of Chatham's key supporters in the government – including Lord Chancellor Camden,[6] the Marquis of Granby,[7] and John Dunning[8] – proved loyal to their leader and sided with the minority.

A major test of strength in the Commons came on 31 January, when Dowdeswell proposed a resolution which stated that "by the Law of the Land, and the known law and usage of parliament, no person, eligible by common right, can be incapacitated by Vote or Resolution of this House, but by Act of parliament only."[9] Previously, several Chathams had resigned from the establishment or had been dismissed after withdrawing their support for the government.[10] They included Camden, Granby, and James Grenville;[11] three lords of the bedchamber, Manchester, Coventry, and Willoughby de Broke;[12] the master of the horse, the Duke of Beaufort;[13] the groom of the stole, Lord Huntingdon;[14] the solicitor general, John Dunning; the attorney general to the Queen, Richard Hussey;[15] and two members of the Admiralty board, Sir George Yonge[16] and Sir Percy Brett.[17] Such desertions at a time when the government appeared to be faltering might have been expected to set off a large-scale revolt of placemen who hoped to placate the opposition parties. However, now the revolt was only partial, and Dowdeswell's motion was defeated by 226 votes to 180.[18]

Three days later the Duke of Grafton resigned because of the heat of the battle, but almost everyone else continued to hold firm,[19] and in the more capable hands of North, the ministry began to fight back. On the thirty-first, Dowdeswell's motion that a resolution of the House of Commons could not create a law was defeated by only forty votes.[20] But on 19 February, when Sir William Meredith proposed a resolution censuring the ministry, he lost by sixty-nine.[21] By the middle of February, the government was clearly out of danger, for the moment at least. Moreover, the Rockinghams must have found it disconcerting that they had failed to retain the support of some valuable friends on whom they had earlier believed they could count. The most important of these were the Yorkes. This family had been influential in British politics for many decades and had been extremely important in giving the Rockinghams the appearance of kinship with the Whigs of the past. Now they began what amounted to the last desertion by a great court family from the Whig party as it struggled to cope with the difficult game of opposition. There were three Yorkes in Parliament – Lord Hardwicke[22] in the House of Lords and Charles[23] and John Yorke[24] in the House of Commons.[25] These men were the sons of the late Earl of Hardwicke,[26] who had been the Duke of Newcastle's oldest and closest friend. After their father's death, they had remained for the most part on good terms with the Rockinghams, and Charles had been attorney general in the administration of 1765–66. However, Charles's lifelong ambition had been to become lord chancellor, and this had always been more important to the three brothers than loyalty to the Rockingham cause. They had therefore, on occasion, balked at supporting measures that might provoke enmity in the Closet. One such measure had been the petitioning movement. "I do not admire ... nor see the good end of such," Charles said at one point, "but ruin to the whole Government in the ignorance, the violence, the vindictive and selfish passions of the great."[27]

In early January, when it became evident to the king and Grafton that Camden would have to be removed from the chancellorship, they asked Charles if he would be willing to fill the vacancy.[28] He at first declined, partly it seems because of Rockingham's blandishments, but after interviews with the king on the sixteenth and seventeenth, during which "severe pressure" was brought to bear, he finally accepted.[29] The decision was very difficult. Charles had doubts because of the fluctuating state of affairs, and his anxiety was increased by Rockingham and Hardwicke, who attempted to persuade him that since "he had told everyone of his resolution to decline," it was "a disgrace to change & allow himself to be pressured" into it.[30] Charles was apparently in a very "distressed & nervous condition" on the evening of the seventeenth.[31] He did not sleep all night, and on the following day he became gravely ill. Whether this was caused or made worse by his anxiety over the appointment is impossible to say, but it resulted in his death two days later. Thereafter, the Yorkes were to have little to do with the Rockingham party. Hardwicke may have felt considerable remorse for having helped magnify his brother's distress, and Charles's wife believed she had reason to complain about Rockingham's behaviour.[32] In the early seventies, Hardwicke and John Yorke gradually made their peace with the court and then became regular supporters of Lord North.

The Rockinghams' inability to topple North in early 1770 was an important factor in convincing them to take a country-party posture against the influence of the crown. They and their allies seemed to have everything in their favour. They had moved against the government in concert; they had been able to effect a series of resignations; and they had had a popular issue with which to fight. All this helped them believe that the members of the House of Commons must be so beholden to the ministry that they had become permanently impervious to the will of the nation.[33] There was a variety of reasons other than crown patronage, however, why they were not victorious in early 1770. The first was that the petitioning movement failed either to strike fear in the hearts of the administration and its supporters or to persuade a large majority of the independent gentlemen in the Commons of the justness of the Middlesex freeholders' cause. There can be little doubt that the Rockinghams were in some respects responsible for this failure.

The second reason was a display of resolution and fortitude by George III himself. The events of January must have been very trying for the king. He was faced with a number of defections, including that of his chancellor and his first lord of the Treasury, and he could not have relished the possibility of being forced to bow to a revival of the Whig oligarchy that he had so detested in his father's reign.[34] Yet he at no time showed signs of panic. He held firm and was unwavering in his support of the men who were willing to struggle on. The "King's resolution is visible," it was said, "to support his Ministry, and men will either acquiesce or return to the ordinary parliamentary Arts of Opposition."[35] Early 1770 marked an important milestone in George III's life. He proved that he was able to cast off the insecurity that had so pervaded his personality in the earlier years of the reign, when he had been unable to fulfil the responsibilities of office without leaning on men such as Bute, the Duke of Cumberland, and Chatham. As John Brooke has told us, he "succeeded to the throne with less experience of life than any of his predecessors for over a hundred years." He had been forced to serve "his apprenticeship to kingcraft after, not before," his ascension.[36] Now he stepped forth as the true head of the executive, and victory seems to have done much to boost his confidence.[37]

The final reason for the failure of the opposition was the emergence of Lord North as first lord of the Treasury. Grafton resigned on the twenty-seventh, leaving the administration in an extremely precarious state. It was expected that this would have a serious effect and that the government would almost certainly be defeated on Dowdeswell's motion of the thirty-first. However, North immediately took up the duties of his office, displaying a determination and ability that had seemed so lacking in the ministry over the past four years, and received acclaim from almost everyone who was not closely connected with the Rockinghams and their allies. "The great danger," wrote David Hume, "was the Effect of the Pannic, and ... [North] checkt the Pannic by his Declaration, that he would never resign, and whilst his breath was in his body that he would support the King's faithful Servants, and the Dignity of Parliament against faction and Conspiracy. [His] ...

is reckond the most spirited Conduct that any man has held since the Revolution, and he is extolld to the Skies."[38]

Until mid-March, the most encouraging aspect of the session, from the opposition's point of view, was the degree to which the Rockinghams, Chathams, Grenvilles, and city radicals were able to maintain a united front. The Rockinghams had started working rather guardedly with the other parties. The marquis at first remained particularly suspicious of Chatham and was afraid that he would attempt to take over the leadership of the alliance.[39] In the first two weeks of the session, however, he and several friends in the House of Lords began to plan operations with Temple, who was working under Chatham's direction.[40] Then, on 22 January, Chatham made his second appearance in the House, and he backed Rockingham's motion to take into consideration the state of the nation. "I consider my seconding his lordship's motion," he said, "and I would wish it to be considered by others, as a public demonstration of that cordial union, which, I am happy to affirm, subsists between us; of my attachment to those principles which he has so well defended, and of my respect for his person … The friends of this country will, I doubt not, hear with pleasure, that the noble Lord and his friends are united with me and mine upon a principle which, I trust, will make our union indissoluble."[41]

For his part, the marquis began to develop more trust in Chatham and to enjoy the thought of being the leader of an even more broadly based constitutional party than he had originally envisaged. He kept up his correspondence far more scrupulously and became active in arranging meetings and discussions in order to concert measures in the House of Lords.[42] In that assembly a dramatic change came over Rockingham, which may well have had its roots in the union movement; he at last came to grips with his innate fear of speaking before public audiences. Since he was anxious to demonstrate that he had the capacity to lead the motley opposition alliance, he had to compete with his new friends in the House, particularly the impetuous and often domineering Chatham, who seldom failed to speak out. Thus, Rockingham forced himself to break silence.[43] When Parliament adjourned in May, Burke was able to observe that the marquis had "spoken so often this Session, that he may be said to be now among the regular Speakers – a matter of infinite consequence to himself and to all of us."[44]

It is symptomatic of the leading opposition politicians' desire to strengthen their relationship that they again took pains to agitate the one broad issue of the time that went beyond the Middlesex election and on which they were united in opinion. Rockingham first brought it up during his state-of-the-nation motion in mid-January when he charged that the present unhappy condition of affairs, and the universal discontent of the people, did not arise from any immediate temporary cause, but had grown upon us by degrees, from the moment of his Majesty's accession to the throne. That the persons, to whom his Majesty then confided [specifically Bute], had introduced a total change in the old system of English government – that they had adopted a maxim, which must prove fatal to the liberties of this country viz. "That the royal prerogative alone was sufficient to support government, to whatever hands the administration should be committed"; and he could trace the operation of this principle through every act of government since the accession, in which those persons could be supposed to have any influence.[45]

The expectation of victory in early 1770 had, it would seem, enabled the marquis, like Dowdeswell, to continue to view politics from the top down. When he spoke disapprovingly of the "royal prerogative" determining the "hands" into which governments should be committed, he was thinking above all of how, during his own administration, "Bute and the lady" had gained control of the king and turned the court party against him. Now he could still visualize his reconstituted Whig connection being in a position to establish a new administration, and he was determined that it would not have this problem. He did not advocate new constraints on the royal prerogative. He wanted instead to ensure (presumably in consultation with the king) that it would not fall into the hands of non-ministers. Once that was done, the "old system of English government" – one in which the ministers enjoyed substantial control over the influence of a compliant crown – would be restored.

On 2 March Chatham, in uncharacteristic humility, made it clear that he agreed fully with the charge that meddlers had been given too much power in the present reign. He

pronounced that since the King's accession there had been no ... [independent] Minister ... in this country; that there was a *secret influence* ... which governed and impeded everything, and was greater than the King. Everything [he said] ... in Council or in Parliament ... was defeated by the faction of the secret influence. He himself, he said, had been duped and deceived by it; and though it was a hard thing to say of himself, confessed he had been a fool and a changeling.[46]

In the Lower House, Dowdeswell and Grenville combined their efforts to focus attention on the problem of secret influence by reviving the question of the arrears in the civil list. In this session, it was Grenville who took the initiative. On 28 February he moved for an account of all civil list expenses "which were incurred, or became due, between 5th of January 1769 and the 5th of January 1770."[47] Two weeks later, Dowdeswell submitted a resolution calling for accounts that showed the expenses added to the civil list by each of the administrations since the rise of Bute.[48] The government at first opposed this, but when Bute's son, Lord Mountstuart,[49] stated that he wished to have a report of his father's expenditures so "that his Conduct should be vindicated,"[50] the motion was allowed to pass. Grenville then observed that this "deference to Lord Mountstuart's request proved his father's actual influence, and ... Lord North's servility to him."[51]

For the time being, Rockingham's "grand constitutional party" had demonstrated sufficient coherence to give hope for the future, despite its failure to defeat the ministry. However, in March, hope clearly began to fade as a result of certain actions of the radical London politicians with whom the major opposition connections had become increasingly involved. On the fourteenth, the City of London, under the leadership of Lord Mayor Beckford and the Common Council, where the radical element was now very strong, presented a remonstrance to the crown complaining that nothing had been done to redress the grievances outlined in the petitions.[52] This was not the first remonstrance of 1770, but it was by far the most exceptionable. In language and tone it was very violent, and its circuitous but unmistakable comparison of the king's actions to those of James II seemed directly to threaten revolution.[53]

On the following day, Thomas Clavering,[54] an independent country gentleman who had previously voted with the minority on the Middlesex election question, attacked the remonstrance in the Commons and moved for an address to the king asking that it be laid before the House along with the king's reply.[55] The House "was full of resentment, and at eleven at night the Address was carried by 271 to 108: a vast majority in the present circumstances, and composed ... of many who abandoned the Opposition."[56] On the nineteenth and twentieth, respectively, Clavering successfully proposed a resolution of censure against the measure[57] and a counteracting loyal address to the king.[58]

The London remonstrance came at a time when public reaction against such excesses was already acute. In the early months of 1770, the disapproval of social unrest was not primarily directed at physical violence, as it had been in 1768 and 1769, for the mob uprisings had mostly abated. Now people were horrified at the harangues in the newspapers by opposition and city spokesmen, who claimed to be concerned about the rights of freeholders. The first of these to make a substantial impression had been a letter of 19 December 1769 from Junius to the king, which was printed in the *Public Advertiser* and then reprinted in all the newspapers "not dedicated to the ministry."[59] Junius had been impudent enough to advise the king on the proper policy to take respecting Wilkes, and he warned of a possibile insurrection. His letter did wonders for newspaper sales in London, and in the early months of 1770 it inspired numerous similar outrages against the government, Lord Bute, the queen mother, and the royal family in general. At one point it was observed that papers "to which the *North Britons* were milk and honey, have been published in terms too gross to repeat. *The Whisperer*, and the *Parliamentary Spy* ... Every blank wall at this end of the town is scribbled with the words, impeach the King's Mother; and, in truth ... her person is in danger."[60]

The remonstrance thus seemed to be the culmination of the current audaciousness in the city, and many felt that North and his colleagues displayed a great deal of patience in not seeking retribution.[61] The men who were most horrified were of course those whose fixed or landed property gave them the greatest stake in tranquillity.[62] Naturally, their views were directly reflected in the House of Commons and this hurt the opposition badly. The Rockinghams, Chathams, and Grenvilles appeared in some measure to be responsible. They had sided with the radicals in the Wilkes affair from the beginning; they had participated with them in the petitioning movement; and most recently, they had publicly demonstrated solidarity with them by attending both the meeting at the Thatched House in January and a ball at the Mansion House in February organized by Beckford.[63] "The violence, I may say madness, of the opposition," it was reported, "have done administration as much good as all their own sagacity. A man may wish to see a house altered or cleansed, who does not wish to see it blown up."[64] From the time the Commons took its stand against the remonstrance, the opposition began to decline seriously.

In the first place, it began to fare less well in the divisions. On 2 April, when Dowdeswell and Grenville proposed a motion for an address to the king to request that he direct that his expenses be kept within the income "of His Majesty's said revenue,"[65] they were defeated by 208 votes to 75. In the second place, the alliance in general began to show some new and dangerous signs of discord. Initially, tension began to develop between the Rockinghams and the radicals. The Rockinghams had allowed themselves to become involved with the latter probably because they recognized the propaganda value of widespread city approval and of favourable media support, and because they felt that they could be a moderating influence. Now, however, their allies were getting out of hand, and the marquis and his friends became more inhibited. When the remonstrance was debated in the Commons, Burke and Dowdeswell opposed Clavering's motions on the grounds that the people had a right to petition the crown. However, they noticeably declined to countenance the language used in the remonstrance,[66] and Lord John Cavendish "owned ... [it] had gone too far."[67] The London politicians were hoping at this time to start a remonstrating campaign comparable to the petitioning movement of the previous year. They had produced a remonstrance on behalf of Westminster in January[68] and were about to present another.[69] They expected the support of the established connections in opposition and were angered when the Rockinghams declined to come out unequivocally on their side.[70] On 12 January, when a second banquet for the opposition was held at the Mansion House,[71] only a last-minute intervention by Chatham prevented the Londoners from confronting the Rockinghams at the gathering.[72] A few days later, Chatham's friend John Sawbridge[73] prevented London politicians from denouncing the Rockinghams publicly.[74]

If it had not been for Chatham, there is little doubt that these two sections of the opposition would have split irrevocably at this time. Chatham played a very difficult game. In order to prevent the complete alienation of the radicals, he decided to take up their cause in the House of Lords with renewed vigour and to attempt to coax the Rockinghams to join him. After consultations with the marquis and his friends, he submitted a bill in the Upper House that would have reversed the "Adjudications ... whereby, John Wilkes ... has been adjudged incapable of being elected a Member to serve in the present Parliament." Then he proposed a resolution censuring the king's answer to the London remonstrance.[75] On 14 May he introduced a motion for an address to the king requesting the dissolution of Parliament because of discontent at home and abroad.[76] Chatham also largely wrote the second London remonstrance, giving it a much more moderate tone than the first.[77]

All of this endeared Chatham to the radicals, but it imposed some inauspicious strains on his relationship with the Rockinghams. When he approached Rockingham with his plan to reverse the Common's adjudications respecting Wilkes, the marquis argued for a narrower bill that would simply declare what the powers of the House of Commons were in expulsion cases and would not mention incapacities.[78] The matter had to be debated at a meeting at Rockingham's residence before Chatham got his way.[79] The Rockinghams apparently were less than delighted about yielding. In the Lords they did not speak when Chatham submitted his motion, though they joined him in signing a protest when it was defeated.[80] The marquis also balked at the resolution for the dissolution of Parliament. He tried to quash the idea altogether and only relented when Chatham reluctantly accepted certain modifications.[81]

Rockingham's reaction does not appear to have been based on political expediency. Many MPs had become extremely tired of the Middlesex election by this time and were anxious to see the matter dropped. As Walpole would latter report, the affair had been "heated and heated so often over, that there is scarce a spark of fire left."[82] Yet the modifications Rockingham argued for evince, if anything, a desire to press the issue further. He agreed to the motion for dissolution only after Chatham had consented to insert the words "that under the late violation of the rights of the electors of England in the election for Middlesex still unredressed,"[83] so that no mistake could be made about the specific purpose. What seems to have been foremost in his mind was the fear that had plagued him throughout the union movement; he was feeling threatened by one of his allies. Chatham was suddenly taking the initiative far too much – as if he were no longer content to recognize the Rockinghams' right to lead. In demanding that he conform to certain stipulations, the marquis was attempting to reassert a proper balance. Evidence does not suggest that he was yet on the verge of giving up his aspirations for the united ministry. He merely appears to have felt it necessary on this one occasion to demonstrate that his own wishes had to be taken into consideration. On other matters, he continued to work amicably with the aristocrats in both the other major connections, and he appears to have developed a feeling of security from the knowledge that Chatham was on his side in the House of Lords.[84]

In this sitting, the Rockinghams' desire to maintain unanimity with the other groups in opposition was also visible in their actions with respect to America. When all the Townshend duties except that on tea were repealed via a bill submitted by Lord North,[85] the party spokesmen for the most part avoided the issue. Neither Burke nor Dowdeswell participated in the debates of 5 March when North introduced his bill, and although they and some of their friends supported motions by Pownall and Trecothick that the tea duty also be abandoned, none of them was at all vociferous. While their timidity was partly a result of public opinion and their fear of encouraging the Americans to further acts of disobedience, there can be little doubt that the desire to act in concert with Grenville was also an influence. Whenever the American question was revived during the session and people such as Burke, Dowdeswell, Grenville, and Wedderburn felt that they could not remain silent, they tended to revert to the expedient of attacking the administration for having no consistent policy either of firmness or leniency.[86] The Rockinghams took the initiative on only one consequential occasion. In May, Burke in the Commons and Richmond in the Lords submitted a set of eight resolutions denouncing the government's American policy over the previous three years.[87] These resolutions were "strangely refined and obscure."[88] They made no policy statement whatever; and when speaking in support of them, neither Burke nor Rockingham did much to clarify the party's position. Burke later commented that "Lord Rockingham ... spoke very much at large, and with great ability" in support of the resolutions, "and with great dexterity, so as not to give the least Offence to the opposite sentiments of some of the Allies."[89]

It is only through an understanding of the Rockinghams' sense of responsibility for broadening the base of the Whig party, not only in 1770 but generally over the years since 1767, that Burke's celebrated pamphlet, *Thoughts on the Cause of the Present Discontents*, which was published in April, can be placed in its proper political and historical context.[90] Burke had begun planning the *Thoughts* sometime in the summer of 1769. In the party correspondence, the first mention of it was made by Rockingham in his letter of 15 October in which he told Burke of his hope that Grenville might be won away from Chatham and "would sacrifice *somethings* to be really confidently united with us." He wrote:

I am exceeding anxious, that the Pamphlet which you shewed me in such forwardness – when you was here – should make its appearance as early as possible. In all respects – now is the time – I wish it read by all the members of Parliament – and by all the politicians in town and country prior to the meeting of Parliament. I think it would take universally, and tend to form and to unite a party upon real and well founded principles – which would in the end prevail and re'establish order and Government in this country.[91]

There seems little doubt that Rockingham hoped the work could do something to further the cause of a merger with Grenville and that this would help bring a new broadly based Whig party back into office. He apparently believed that the government would fall in the coming session as a result of the opposition's onslaught over the Middlesex election issue. When he spoke of re-establishing "order and Government," he must have been referring to the possibility of his party taking over the reins of power. It is safe to say that he would not have credited any other set of men with the capacity to resolve the country's current problems. He was not, however, suddenly so taken with the idea of a return to power that he was prepared to forget Dowdeswell's strictures of July 1767 and his connection's commitment to the prerequisite of union. Therefore, he clung to the hope that Grenville could be had.

Interestingly, the one person in the following who did not share Rockingham's optimism was Burke. Although, for the sake of the petitioning movement, he worked amicably with Thomas Whately, Lord Temple, and others, Burke was very doubtful about the possibility of a permanent coalition with the Grenvilles. Like his leader, he believed that the present government would fall in 1770. However, he felt sure that any attempt to form a broad and comprehensive ministry would fail as it had in 1767, because the pretensions of his party's newly united allies would be too high. Even George Grenville, he told Rockingham, "is no longer ... a disengaged individual; but one of the Triumvirate; to whom by the way, he brings all the following they possess."[92] Burke was convinced that Grenville, Temple, and Chatham would never allow the Rockinghams pre-eminence, and he could argue that they would not prove faithful to the principle of resistance to the Bute system. Consequently, he wanted to justify, "to our friends and to the world, the refusal, which is inevitable, of what will be thought very advantageous Offers. This can only be done by shewing the ground upon which the Party stands; and how different its constitution, as well as the persons who compose it are from the Bedfords, and Grenvilles, and other knots, who are combined for no publick purpose; but only as a means of furthering with joint strength, their private and individual advantage."[93] In retrospect, it can be seen that Burke was being realistic. It is difficult to imagine how Chatham and George Grenville, both of whom had held the highest office in the land, would ever have allowed Rockingham to make all the decisions about the men and measures that were necessary for the formation of an administration.

It had been intended that the *Thoughts* would be published before the session. But in November, when Burke sent him a copy of what he had then accomplished, Rockingham was experiencing one of his bouts of inertia and was unable to get around to criticizing it for some weeks. His consequent tardiness in sending the copy on to Savile, Portland, Dowdeswell and others delayed publication considerably.[94] The delay was not, however, totally untoward. It gave all the important members of the party a chance to read the manuscript over and offer criticisms, and it enabled them to make it more representative of their feelings after having worked closely with Chatham, as well as Grenville and Temple. As a result, Rockingham's desire to further the cause of union, rather than Burke's desire to elevate the Rockinghams above all their allies, became the paramount objective.[95] The original draft that Burke had forwarded to his leader had contained a number of charges and insinuations against the other groups in opposition.[96] These were deleted before April. A "General Union – of the Whole is necessary to save the Whole," the marquis was later to announce, the "System recommended in the Pamphlet ... is in fact no other than pointing out how necessary it is – that Honest men should now Unite – in order to save this Country from the Power of a System – which has been established in great Part on the Foundation of dividing and subdividing all Parties & all connexions."[97]

If the Rockinghams' particular conception of union is kept in mind, it becomes clear when examining the *Thoughts* that this statement is fundamentally appropriate. There are two central theses developed. The first is that the country's problems are all connected to the weaknesses that the system of favouritism has created in successive ministries since 1760. The second is that the solution is for all good men first to unite under the Rockinghams and then to re-establish the kind of strong and enduring administration that had existed before George III ascended the throne. In order to build his first argument, Burke attempts, in the first three-quarters or so of the work, to demonstrate how an "unnatural infusion of a *system of Favouritism*" into a constitution "which in a great part ... is popular," has effectively destroyed the government process.[98] To do this he relies heavily on the theme of disunity; "disconnexion and confusion," he claims, "in offices, in parties, in families, in Parliament, in the nation, prevail beyond the disorders of any former time."[99] He alleges that in 1760 a cabal of secret advisers set out to create two types of division in government. The first was that of "*the Court from the Ministry*," which was to be accomplished by establishing the "*double cabinet*";[100] "two systems of Administration were to be formed; one which should be in the real secret and confidence; the other merely ostensible, to perform the official and executory duties of Government. The latter were alone to be responsible; whilst the real advisers, who enjoyed all the power, were effectually removed from all danger."[101] The cabal wished to usurp ministerial power without having to worry about the problem of responsibility to the House of Commons. In order to enable it to stand in defiance of the party leaders who formed the ostensible portion of the double cabinet, its members sought to extend this division as far as possible. They were also, therefore, to have a party of their own "*to be formed in favour of the Court against the Ministry*."[102] Their following was to consist of the corps of "Kings friends" – the men who looked to the crown alone for leadership and preferment, or those who held the lower court offices that normally did not change hands on the formation of each new administration.

The history of the reign as related in the *Thoughts* is essentially the story of how this scheme prevailed. In general, its success depended more than anything else on the cabal's ability to create the second type of division – that of the "public men." To ensure that they would overcome the parliamentary forces that might try to stand in their way, the favourites attempted "gradually, but not slowly, to destroy every thing of strength which did not derive its principal nourishment from the immediate pleasure of the Court."[103] They first turned against William Pitt and pushed him out of office, and then they brought down the old Whigs. Thus, they divested the government of "the *two only securities for the importance of the people; power arising from popularity; and power arising from connexion.*"[104] Having accomplished this, they proceeded to do everything possible "to disunite every party, and even every family, that *no concert, order, or effect, might appear in any future opposition.*"[105] To make this point, Burke describes a number of their methods. He argues that "whilst they are terrifying the great and opulent with the horrors of mob-government, they are by other managers attempting ... to alarm the people with a phantom of tyranny in the Nobles" and thereby "sowing jealousies amongst the different orders of the State, and ... disjointing the natural strength of the kingdom."[106] He also describes the "*Rota* in the Court," through which the cabal brings a group of politicians into office, draws the "rotten members" from it by offering them preferments, and ensures that "the party goes out much thinner than it came in; and is only reduced in strength by its temporary possession of power."[107] While a ministry holds office, the leaders of the court use various means to ensure that it does not have the unity to resist them. For example, they like to have it composed of "two parties at least; which, whilst they are tearing one another to pieces, are both competitors for the favour and protection of the Cabal."[108]

These are only a few of the methods cited. The important point is that this section of the pamphlet is largely a lament about disunity. There is little in it that could be described as new and profound. As has been demonstrated, it had been widely accepted in the 1760s that the favourite thrived on discord among the politicians. Burke merely reiterated this theory. He was the first author, at least of a major work, to delineate the idea of a double cabinet. However, in so doing, he really only contributed a certain amount of sophistry to current doctrines. Conor Cruise O'Brien is correct in his estimation that concern about a group of secret advisers who had gained access to the king was very real in the late eighteenth century.[109] It had been accepted that Bute did not work alone in promoting his aims but that he had surrounded himself with a number of his "creatures" and was working with them to usurp all executive power. It was a natural progression to call these "ministers behind the curtain" a second cabinet. No one had previously defined the court party so clearly or made the explicit distinction between it and the ministerial party. However, all anti-Bute writers and politicians believed that the favourite had formed a following in Parliament and that it was composed primarily of men who were competing for permanent offices, pensions, and so on under the crown.

Burke departs directly from most earlier writers only in his refusal to bring personalities into the fight. He insists that it is the "system, and not any individual person who acts in it, that is truly dangerous."[110] While others had attacked favouritism in a general sense, on principle, they had ultimately been attempting to strike a blow at Lord Bute. The system was his, and therefore he was the main culprit. In 1770, however, it was well known that Bute had been in Italy since early in the previous year. Burke, like many politicians, now realized that Bute communicated "very little in a direct manner with the greater part of our men of business,"[111] and he was coming to the conclusion that the "System is got into firmer and abler hands."[112] It was therefore convenient for him to change the emphasis. Moreover, Dowdeswell, the brains behind Rockingham policy, had been insisting at least since July 1767 that the "public misfortunes" were not a manifestation of "the influence of particular persons but ... [of] the prevalence of a political principle."[113] When Dowdeswell took a line, it was normally adhered to by the other members of the party.

The last quarter of the *Thoughts* discusses what should be done to extricate the kingdom from the rule of the cabal. Two answers are provided. The first is simply "*the interposition of the body of the people itself.*"[114] Burke calls on the people to watch their representatives in the House of Commons closely and make sure that they are not supporting administrations that are subservient to the cabal. How he expects them to interpose with men who do not conduct themselves in the proper manner is not totally clear. However, he seems to be referring to traditional conventions by which MPs could be pressurized from outside – for instance, with instructions, messages of thanks, or petitions. He does not stress this mode very strongly. He merely states that by "such means something may be done."[115]

Burke offers his second solution to the problem with much more conviction. It is that all the public men and all parliamentary groups opposed to the current court system should unite in a new, broadly based ministry. If one regards the first three-quarters or so of the *Thoughts* as a reiteration of the standard belief that the favourite and his associates thrived on the discord they were able to create among their enemies, it is difficult to see how passages such as the following can be viewed as anything but an attempt – such as had so often been made by the Rockinghams and other parties in the past – to end it through a coalition, first in opposition and then in office.

It is not every conjucture which calls with equal force upon the activity of honest men; but critical exigences now and then arise; and I am mistaken, if this be not one of them. Men will see the necessity of honest combination; but they may see it when it is too late. They may embody, when it will be ruinous to themselves, and of no advantage to the country; when, for want of such a timely union as may enable them to oppose in favour of the laws, with the laws on their side, they may, at length, find themselves under the necessity of conspiring, instead of consulting. The law, for which they stand, may become a weapon in the hands of its bitterest enemies; and they will be cast, at length, into that miserable alternative, between slavery and civil confusion, which no good man can look upon without horror; an alternative in which it is impossible he should take either part, with a conscience perfectly at repose. To keep that situation of guilt and remorse at the utmost distance, is, therefore, our first obligation. Early activity may prevent late and fruitless violence. As yet we work in the light. The scheme of the enemies of public tranquility has disarranged, it has not destroyed us.

If the reader believes that there really exists such a Faction as I have described; a Faction ruling by the private inclinations of a Court, against the general sense of the people ... he will believe also, that nothing but a firm combination of public men against this body, and that, too, supported by the hearty concurrence of the people at large, can possibly get the better of it.[116]

Historians have argued that the *Thoughts* is anything but a call for a general union. They have, for instance, seen statements such as this merely as a reflection of a desire to unify the Rockingham connection; as evidence, they have pointed to Burke's endeavour to demonstrate that his party is more meritorious than all the rest.[117] Such an endeavour is indeed evident. However, anyone who understands the Rockinghams' conditions for uniting forces with the other groups in Parliament should recognize Burke's eulogies as a bid to give credence to one of the most important of these conditions – his party's superiority. The Rockinghams had always maintained that they would never coalesce with their allies on the basis of equality, and for this reason Burke had to be very careful. On the one hand, to make union possible, he had to demonstrate that his party deserved pre-eminence. On the other, in order not to disrupt the union movement, he had to refrain from making declarations that were likely to be resented by the other parties. Therefore, while dwelling on the

Rockinghams' virtues, he was careful not to attack the Chathams and Grenvilles in any direct sense.

The other aspect of this work which might be held as evidence that Burke was not attempting to promote unity is his famous justification of party. Some historians – with loud applause from Conor Cruise O'Brien – have praised this as a rather prophetic anticipation of the modern party system,[118] and certainly Burke does present a refutation of some predominant ideals. Throughout the eighteenth century, most politicians admired independence and wished to be looked on as men who were free of the bias of party pursuits and who disinterestedly decided all questions of public interest on their merits. Burke pronounces emphatically against this value. He attacks the phrase "Not men, but measures,"[119] which Chatham had espoused with so much self-righteousness when forming his ministry in 1766, and he goes so far as to imply that a refusal to act in a connection is equivalent to neglect. He holds that if men have just principles, they are obligated to act in concert with other men in order to work effectively towards bringing those principles to bear on government and public policy:

It is not enough, in a situation of trust in the commonwealth, that a man means well to his country; it is not enough that in his single person he never did an evil act, but always voted according to his conscience, and even harangued against every design which he apprehended to be prejudicial to the interests of his country. This innoxious and ineffectual character, that seems formed upon a plan of apology and disculpation, falls miserably short of the mark of public duty ... When the public man omits to put himself in a situation of doing his duty with effect, it is an omission that frustrates the purposes of his trust almost as much as if he had formally betrayed it.[120]

Burke unquestionably was suggesting that party has a permanent and important role to play in the constitution.[121] However, we give him more credit than he deserves when we imply that he was attempting to sanction parties in general and the system of the future. His eyes were on the past. His purpose was very much like that which Lord Bolingbroke had pursued in his celebrated *Dissertation upon Parties* some thirty-five years earlier.[122] Bolingbroke had attempted to form one great alliance composed of everyone outside government and supported by the nation at large. It was not to be one of several parties but a party to end all parties and the disunity they seemed to cause. Burke also was attempting to establish one great party. He, like Bolingbroke, was reacting against division and disunity – not hoping to create them. However, what Burke was attempting to establish was not a party to end all parties but a party to end all parties except one – his own. When he said that he wished to demonstrate the difference between the Rockingham connection and "the Bedfords and Grenvilles, and other knots," he was in fact saying that only his own group was worthy of the title of party. Several months after publication, the Duke of Richmond stated this belief clearly when he told Chatham that "the larger our party was the better it would answer to our idea of What a party should be, but we look'd upon ourselves as the only party at present subsisting."[123] It does not seem to have occurred to Burke that more than one justifiable party could possibly exist. He viewed politics as a continual struggle between good and evil, and he appears to have believed that the good elements would naturally want to come together: "When bad men combine, the good must associate; else they will fall, one by one, an unpitied sacrifice in a contemptible struggle."[124] Burke wanted to demonstrate that the Rockinghams' allies could honourably unite under their banner in pursuit of the political system that had been abandoned in the present reign. Anyone who feels that he was ahead of his time might compare his ideas to those of a pamphleteer who seems genuinely to have been visualizing a system more like that of later centuries. In 1765 that person had written:

Parties produce changes, and we expect them as the natural effect of a natural cause, nor do we desire to be without parties to create changes. I do not mean parties in *principle*, which are distress and ruin, but parties in *opinion*, in friendship, connection and attachments. Parties of that sort are but ventilators to fan the constitution, and purify administration. They over turn one another by superiority of strength excellence of system, or advantage in abilities; and while these things hold the balance of power, opposition will itself be a means of safety, and an instrument of the public good. The contest will both regulate and estimate the contenders: and the rise and fall of Ministry, in such a case, will most probably be for the true interest of the nation, as those will prevail who have the most influence, that is stand best by their country, are ablest to serve her and adopt the most approved measures.[125]

The year 1770 was a significant one for the Rockinghams' development. Rockingham himself emerged as a somewhat more confident and articulate leader, and, through Burke's *Thoughts*, his following publicly defined itself as a party with a platform of opposition to the current court system. The year was important for another reason, too. It saw the central core of the connection take a step towards the development of the country-party platform which, in the later years of the American Revolution, would enable it to design the "economical reform" package. This step was encompassed in the bill that Dowdeswell presented to the Commons on 12 February for the disfranchisement of revenue officers in national elections.[126] The reason the Rockinghams came up with this measure during the 1770 session of Parliament is the same as that which caused the propertied classes as a whole to give impetus to the movement for reform. In view of the growing antipathy among the wealthier echelons of society towards the radical element, it would seem logical to expect the cause of political reform to have been substantially quashed. In fact, just the opposite was the case. From January to May, a number of reform propositions were introduced and debated in Parliament, and in some material instances they received the approval of one or both Houses. All of them were at least partly the product of the Middlesex election controversy – though some were more directly and more obviously related to it than others.

The first came from Chatham. In January, during a speech in the Lords, he suggested that the best way to improve the political system in Great Britain would be "to permit every county to elect one member more [to the Commons], in addition to its present representation."[127] This, he suggested, would increase the size of the independent country element to counterbalance the growing force of corruption. Chatham offered this merely as a recommendation, and he did not try to formalize it in any way. In February, one other proposal that originated with the opposition was drawn up in bill form. It was submitted to the Lower House on the fifth. Its purpose was to regulate the consequences of expulsion by declaring that it implied incapacitation only in cases where certain specified crimes had been committed. Although the bill was introduced by Henry Herbert,[128] an independent member who had voted with the opposition in the Middlesex election issue, the Rockinghams were among those who had taken a hand in it.[129] North and his colleagues declined to oppose the bill outright, but they eventually filled it so full of amendments that "it was impossible for the framers of it to know their own Bill." They therefore "very prudently embraced the first opportunity of withdrawing it."[130]

Two reforms considered during the session became law. The first was contained in George Grenville's bill in March–April to reform the trials of election petitions in the House of Commons. It established an important change in the political system by transferring the examination of election petitions to committees chosen by lot. This did much to ensure that, in future, controverted elections such as that for Middlesex would not be resolved by party votes. Although all the opposition members supported the bill, its success was not generally considered a defeat for Lord North. In the first place, North did not throw the full weight of government decisively against it. In the words of William Burke,[131] he "trifled and hesitated to the last, and at the last absurdly decided to oppose it on the third reading."[132] More-over, it was made clear that many independent members who supported the measure did not consider their votes a demonstration of their general attitude towards the administration. On 30 March Sir William Bagot,[133] a highly independent Tory country gentleman though a friend of North,

in a set speech ... answered for the Tories, and took that opportunity of acting with opposition to abuse and vilify them as an interested faction, who aimed through the Sides of the Constitution, to wound the Ministry; and character-ized the Tories as the body who disinterestedly supported Government ... and gave it as one of his Inducements to support the Bill, that it was likely to bring more Tories into the House, and to prevent so many Lawyers and Mer-chants, and so much Eloquence from finding place in the house.[134]

The other successful measure was secured by a bill designed by George Onslow, a government man.[135] It placed new and stricter lim-its on the extent to which one could be protected from legal prosecu-tion by privilege of Parliament. It provided that while MPs would continue to enjoy immunity from arrest and imprisonment for some offences, no action in any court of law would be stayed by reason of privilege. This helped alleviate the hardships perpetually suffered by debtors, for instance, who were constantly obstructed in their efforts to obtain legal sanction for their claims against men who held seats in the House of Commons. The bill "passed easily through the Com-mons,"[136] but apparently many who might otherwise have opposed it declined to do so in the belief that "it would be rejected in the other House."[137] However, in the Lords, the government's chief spokes-man, Lord Mansfield,[138] gave it his full approval and it was allowed to pass.

The only reform measure that North and his colleagues came out earnestly against was Dowdeswell's bill for disqualifying revenue officers from voting in national elections. The administration's objec-tion could not really be said to have been based on the fact that the bill represented a very extreme attack on the status quo.[139] It was aimed at the lower "Excise and Customs house officers,"[140] who were dispersed throughout the country and whose influence in elections was rather limited. Paradoxically, it was the conservative type of ap-proach that would have been popular among country Tories in the reigns of Queen Anne and the first two Hanoverians. One reason

why the government took an unequivocal stand against Dowdeswell's bill was that it was submitted early in the session, when
North had just taken over from Grafton and was still endeavouring to
convince himself and the public that he had the political strength to
resist the opposition's attacks. At that stage, he could not afford to
give the Rockinghams a chance to succeed with a blatantly antiministerial proposition.

Notwithstanding this failure, it is apparent that politicians in general displayed an unusual propensity to consider reform measures.
Even the latter bill received relatively strong support in the Commons. It was approved by 188 votes and defeated by only 75. This
would seem to indicate that the Rockinghams attained independent
support that was comparable to that which had been forthcoming on
some of the closer divisions in January. In order to explain the growth
of a reform mentality, it is necessary to look through the eyes both of
those who had voted against Wilkes and those who had voted with
him. The attitude of Wilkes's adversaries was influenced considerably by criticism evoked by the highly polemical Middlesex election
issue. All the accusations of venality and corruption currently being
hurled at the majority by the London press in particular produced a
desire among many members of the majority to demonstrate that
they were not as iniquitous as charged. When speaking of Grenville's
measure and the privilege of Parliament legislation, Horace Walpole
estimated that the "scandal deservedly thrown on members for their
corruption and servility, and their dread of losing their future elections from their unpopularity, made such impression on most of them
that ... they concurred in two most wholesome acts."[141]

If the court and its supporters were influenced by the Middlesex
election issue, the opposition was too. Among those who had opposed the administration, the main pressure for constitutional change
actually came from the groups of London politicians whose leaders
had been transforming a bias for traditional country reform measures
into a distinct political program even before Wilkes was expelled
from the House of Commons.[142] The Wilkes affair not only helped to
strengthen antiministerial feeling; it also enforced the conviction that
the system of government was in need of alteration – that it was unable to reflect the will of the people at large because of the strength of
crown and executive influence in the House of Commons. As a consequence, Londoners began to promote with renewed vigour long-
standing country-party usages such as shorter Parliaments, place
bills, and oaths against bribery in elections, and they even began to
contemplate methods for effecting a more equitable system of representation in the nation as a whole. This in turn placed pressure on the

established groups in Parliament. They themselves had done much of late to propagate the theory that the House of Commons had acted in opposition to the will of the people. In view of the aspirations of their more radical associates, the established groups found it necessary to demonstrate their sincerity. It is no coincidence that the measures respectively proposed by Dowdeswell, Grenville, and Chatham were all in some measure aimed at securing a greater degree of independence in the Lower House.

In view of their continuing efforts to broaden and strengthen the Whig party, it is apparent that the desire to find common ground with others was much more important to the Rockinghams than any concern for constitutional amendment. The marquis and his friends saw their bill largely as a compromise. At this stage in their career, they were still too defensive towards the constitution, which they felt their court Whig ancestors had built and flourished under, to accept material alterations to the system of government. They appear to have had an instinctive distaste even for the more limited measures which in previous reigns had regularly been advanced to curtail the power of the oligarchy.[143] On the other hand, their past involvement in highly emotive matters, such as the campaign for the repeal of the Stamp Act and the Wilkes episode, had made them well aware of the potential force of public opinion in the city. The disfranchisement of revenue officers was a means of ensuring that they would avoid making enemies among interests in London who might turn the wheels of the press against them. It enabled them to offer a relatively benign measure to reduce Crown patronage and thus indicate to the radicals – and of course to Chatham, who was closely linked with a number of them – that the party did not reject the idea of change altogether. The Rockinghams had first submitted their measure for consideration in the House of Commons two years earlier, when Dowdeswell had offered it as an alternative to prevent a split between his party and city spokesmen over Beckford's bill to make MPs swear that they had not bribed their electors.[144] That the party leaders were primarily thinking in terms of compromise rather than meaningful alteration is demonstrated by the fact that at the same time as they were preparing their bill in 1770, they took pains in the *Thoughts* to point out that there was nothing wrong with the influence of the crown as such. It was fine to use it, as the Whig oligarchy had understood, "in supporting the Ministers of State, and in carrying on the public business according to their opinions."[145] The problem was not that crown patronage had grown too great but that, in the hands of the cabal, it had become a means of "enfeebling the regular executory power."[146] What the Rockinghams really wanted was not so much to change the system as to oust Bute and his supporters. They were prepared to embrace the "disqualification of a particular description of Revenue Officers from seats in Parliament; or, perhaps, of all the lower sorts of them from votes in elections"[147] only because such a measure, as they themselves were quick to point out, was very moderate and would affect "only the inconsiderable."

Precisely because all the opposition groups were able for the time being to compromise and cover up their differences, the political polarization resulting from the Middlesex election issue in 1770 did briefly provide something that looked like a two-party alignment in Parliament. On one side, the administration and the independent members who had voted against Wilkes rallied around Lord North. On the other side, the Chathams, Grenvilles, and city radicals seemed to be rallying to Rockingham's call for a "broad and comprehensive" plan. The division lists demonstrate that they at times also received the support of a relatively large percentage of the independent members in the House of Commons. But by the end of the session, an astute observer could have forecast that the dichotomy was not going to last, if for no other reason than that the opposition was not going to be able to achieve its former strength and cohesion. Its independent support was already rapidly departing, and its various political followings were having increasing difficulty keeping their differences in check.

CHAPTER FIVE

The Growth of Disunity
in Opposition, May 1770
to February 1771

For the Rockinghams to make the transition from a court Whig party to something approaching a typical eighteenth-century country opposition point of view, they had to acquire three important insights. First, they needed to understand that they were not in the near future going to have to live up to their responsibility of resurrecting the court Whig oligarchy. Second, they were going to have to see ministerial strength rather than ministerial weakness as the greatest threat to the nation at large. And third, like all country-party politicians, they had to view this strength as a product of the advantage that ministers had as a result of the patronage of the crown. By the parliamentary recess of 1770, Burke in particular was emitting signs that he was beginning to learn these lessons. In late May he outlined his feelings regarding the situation in the Lower House:

Undoubtedly no House of Commons was ever less in dread of an administration. They see plainly, that they are totally out of a condition to punish; and that their fund of reward is almost too large for the claimants; so that they are not afraid every now and then to contradict the Leaders; and they know that the ordinary services will entitle them to a full share of emollument. This is the Case in all general questions ... but when the question is such as may involve the fortune of the Ministry, or affect their interest in any degree, they support them with the utmost ardour and resolution. The Majority does not act as subject to the Ministry, but as a Sort of an *Ally* which has a strong and common Interest.[1]

To Burke, the failure of the opposition to emerge victorious in the previous session must have seemed especially disheartening. In the *Thoughts* he had offered the hope that a "firm combination of public men against" the court faction "and that, too, supported by the hearty concurrence of the people at large" would defeat the forces of evil. "As yet we work in the light," he had said. "The scheme of the enemies of public tranquillity has disarranged, it has not destroyed us."[2] The events of the session, however, seemed to indicate that his hopes were misguided. Despite the fact that a grand alliance of sorts in opposition was achieved, at least over the Middlesex election issue, and that it received significant support outside Parliament, the opposition did not manage to defeat the government on a single division. The unavoidable conclusion was that the *Thoughts* itself was out of date even at the time of publication, because the problems were more deeply rooted than just the division and disunity which Bute and his friends had been able to create. In attempting to find another explanation, Burke could not bring himself to point to any failings of his own party. He needed something else, and he was naturally inclined to focus on the one factor about which most opposition interests in the eighteenth century at one time or another concerned themselves – the leverage the ministers had in the House of Commons from the offices, pensions, and contracts they controlled.

In the months ahead, others, including most of the leading members of the Rockingham party, began to adopt Burke's reasoning. In the spring and summer of 1770, men in virtually all segments of the alliance were showing the effects of losing the battle against the ministry. Lord Temple, for instance, believed that "Parliamentary minority or opposition is now scarce even a Name."[3] By September, he was "much disgusted with the Publick," indeed, "with the whole world."[4] The Duke of Manchester, who was on good but not intimate terms with both Rockingham and Chatham, complained in October about the "languid inattention to the measures of the Court [which] seems this summer to have seized the nation."[5] In the same month, Lord George Germain,[6] who was more a Grenville man than anything else but was not firmly committed to any one party, observed that he could "see no prospect of any good arising from opposition."[7]

At least partly because of the general decline in spirits, the relations between the various sectors of the opposition had worsened dangerously over the summer. As might be expected, the largest crack in the façade of union developed between the Rockinghams and the London radicals. Ironically, it was opened up just at the time when, on paper, the Rockinghams' status in the city had reached an all-time peak as a result both of coincidence and some careful planning by the marquis and others.

The first apparent improvement in the party's position resulted from the election for the two sheriffs' offices in Middlesex in July. The successful candidates were the Rockingham MPs William Baker, Jr,[8]

and his close friend Joseph Martin.[9] Rockingham, Lord John Cavendish, and Sir Anthony Abdy had done a great deal to persuade both
men to run in the election.[10] The fact that both Beckford and James
Townsend promoted them would seem to indicate that Chatham had
been successful in keeping the strains between his city friends and his
moderate allies in check to this point.[11] The Rockinghams also had
the full approval of John Wilkes, who had been released from jail on
27 April and was soon to become the most powerful man in city politics. After Baker and Martin were elected,[12] Wilkes reported: "Everything goes on according to my most sanguine wishes. The two new
Sheriffs are Rockingham men."[13]

While the Rockinghams were pleased with this election, they must
have been thrilled with the one for the office of lord mayor of London, which was contested because of the death of William Beckford
on 21 June.[14] Rockingham had earlier convinced Barlow Trecothick,
who had been second in the previous contest, that he should run
again when Beckford's term ended.[15] Later events demonstrate that if
Trecothick been forced to wait until September, when the office was
usually contested, he would not have been successful. Now he won
with little difficulty and again to the satisfaction of Wilkes, who personally "accompanied him to the commissioners of the great seal,
amid the acclamations of the people the whole way."[16]

All of this looked good to the Rockingham central core. However,
it is clear that at the time when Beckford, Townsend, and Wilkes
were giving the party their support, the animosities that had developed during the previous session were already resurfacing. The first
point of disagreement was the *Thoughts on the Cause of the Present
Discontents*. It was published in late April 1770 and went through
"three editions … in the course of a few weeks."[17] However, it
appears to have taken two to three months before its effects on the
alliance became fully manifest. The first evidence of the reception it
was to get in London is seen in an extremely hostile review written
by the noted radical historian and publicist, Catherine Macaulay,[18]
about mid-May. It was Burke's partisan panegyric of the aristocracy and his refusal to laud measures of reform which she found
obnoxious.

Whilst the obvious intent of this pernicious work is to expose the dangerous
designs of a profligate junto of courtiers, supported by the mere authority of
the crown, against the liberties of the constitution; it likewise endeavours to
mislead the people on the subject of the more complicated and specious,
though no less dangerous manoeuvres of Aristocractic faction and party,
founded on and supported by the corrupt principle of self-interest; and also

to guard against the possible consequence of an effectual reformation in the vitiated parts of our constitution and government.[19]

Opposition spokesmen in London publicly attacked the *Thoughts* on other grounds as well. For instance, the gentle manner in which Lord Bute was treated naturally received fairly widespread condemnation from the section of British society that had been most responsible for defaming him.[20]

Burke was indignant at the radicals' response. In August he told Richard Shackleton[21] that the "party which is most displeased, is a rotten subdivision of a Faction amongst ourselves, who have done us infinite mischief by the violence, rashness, and often wickedness of their measures, I mean the Bill of rights people[22] but who have thought proper at length to do us I hope a service, by declaring open War upon all our connection."[23] Although the *Thoughts* was certainly disruptive, Burke's statement exaggerates its effects. In the first place, there is little doubt that the pamphlet merely contributed to the conflict that would have broken out anyway between the two groups over the question of reform. In July the reform movement gathered strength in London as Richard Oliver,[24] an influential Wilkite, succeeded to Beckford's seat in the House of Commons. One of his first commitments was for "shortening the duration of Parliament" and implementing "an effective not a nugatory place and pension bill" and "an adequate and true representation throughout the Kingdom."[25] In later years, the Rockinghams were to become moderate reformers themselves, after they had waged the fight against the influence of the Crown long enough to be persuaded that specific measures could be adopted to curtail it. Dowdeswell's measure of the previous session seems to indicate that, as a compromise, they may already have been willing to accept a very limited place and pension bill. However, throughout their career, they were never to lose their court Whiggish respect for the existing system and conventions of government.[26] Consequently, they never embraced a total exclusion of placemen and pensioners from the House of Commons or plans to alter Parliament and the system of representation.[27]

Moreover, by August (when Burke wrote the above letter), the process of alienation had been speeded up as a result of the remonstrating campaign. Between May and November, a third remonstrance was procured from the City of London[28] and one each from Newcastle-upon-Tyne,[29] Surrey,[30] Kent,[31] and Westminster.[32] All of these complained (in somewhat milder and more "decent" tones than the one from London in March) that nothing had been done to secure the rights of the electors of Middlesex. However, the campaign did not catch on. Outside London, most people had had enough of the Wilkes affair. It was particularly exasperating to the radicals, therefore, that the Rockinghams with their relatively large influence in the counties did not throw their weight onto the scale.

Rockingham did in fact consider it. There was some discontent in Yorkshire over the king's refusal to heed the petitions of 1769. Furthermore, a few of the marquis's friends, including the Duke of Richmond,[33] Sir George Armytage,[34] Alexander Wedderburn,[35] and especially Burke, wanted him to take action in the county. "The people ... felt upon this, but upon no other Ground of our opposition," the latter argued. "We never have had, and we never shall have a matter every way so well calculated to engage them; and if the spirit which was excited upon this occasion were sufferd to flatten and evaporate, you would find it difficult to collect it again, when you might have the greatest occasion for it."[36] In August some "ten or a dozen"[37] gentlemen in Yorkshire, including Sir George Savile, discovered at the York races that there was a general desire that something should be done, and they approached their sheriff to request a county meeting.[38] When the sheriff refused, a gathering was advertised in the local papers on behalf of twenty-eight gentlemen, including such well-known Rockingham supporters as Stephen Croft,[39] Lord John Cavendish, William Weddell, and Nathaniel Cholmley.[40] At the meeting, Rockingham discovered that a few "very Warm People," led by Charles Turner, were "eager for a Remonstrance." However, they seemed to represent only a very small minority, and it was equally clear to him "that the real general Sense of the County"[41] was against it. Savile declined to promote the measure and Lord John Cavendish spoke out strongly against it. Instead of agreeing on a remonstrance, the men who attended adopted a letter to local MPs, thanking them for their stand on behalf of the rights of electors and imputing the failure of the petition to the "arts and management of those who have no other means of justifying their own misconduct to their Sovereign, than by misrepresenting the desires and affections of a loyal people."[42]

Thus, although the county expressed its displeasure at the king's neglect, the Rockinghams did not give their support to the remonstrances, and consequently ill humour towards the marquis and his friends in London was heightened. If Rockingham believed that the new-found influence of Trecothick, Baker, and Martin would offset animosities towards his party and keep the opposition alliance in tact, he was disappointed. From June until November, when Trecothick's term of office ended, a number of factors combined to render these three men almost as repugnant to the radicals as the leading

Rockinghams were. In the first place, the mere fact of their involvement with the Rockinghams did them considerable harm. On 28 September the two sheriffs were apparently "very coldly received" when they were sworn in at the Guildhall, because they were considered "more the partisans of the Rockingham Faction than the Friends of Liberty."[43]

Trecothick, Baker, and Martin also suffered serious difficulties because, like the party they associated with, they proved too moderate to satisfy many in the city. In the case of Trecothick, holding as he did the central political office in London, this was particularly important. Almost immediately after his election, he attracted criticism because of his refusal to support the radicals in their stand with respect to the Falkland Islands conflict.[44] In the autumn and winter of 1770, this conflict ignited an international crisis that nearly embroiled Britain in a war with Spain.

The Falkland Islands had been granted to Spain and France by the Treaty of Utrecht in 1713 and had been recognized as the property of the former since 1767, when France relinquished her claims. But in 1763 the British had established a very small colony or outpost at Port Egmont, on the major western island in the group, and they refused to give it up until Spain agreed to pay the Manila Ransom.[45] The resulting dispute between the two countries nearly spread beyond the bounds of diplomacy in 1770, because of two naval incidents that resulted in the ejection of the British from Port Egmont by Spanish forces acting under the instructions of Governor Bucarrelli of Buenos Aires.

The evacuation of Port Egmont was known in England in early September. Almost immediately the administration entered into negotiations with the Spanish in an effort to obtain reparations. Although the governments on both sides appear to have wished to avoid a military conflict, it was hard for them honourably to compromise their respective points of view, and misunderstandings and diplomatic blunders caused all sorts of difficulties. It took until 22 January the following year for them to agree on a peaceful solution. In the interim, the crisis had some serious repercussions on London politics. Although North and most of his colleagues worked for conciliation from the beginning,[46] they had to prepare the country for war in case it proved unavoidable. This required putting the much-hated press-gangs to work in order to bring the navy up to maximum strength. Trecothick was formally requested by the lords of the Admiralty to give official backing to the warrants in the city. Knowing that these would enrage both the working class of London and the radicals, he initially resisted.[47] However, since Trecothick shared the predominant feeling among the propertied classes that nothing should obstruct the progress of the government's naval preparations at such a critical time, he eventually acquiesced.[48]

The problem was that John Wilkes and a number of opposition leaders from the city were not affected by similar scruples, and they did everything they could to disrupt the conscription process. By October, incidents such as the following were being recorded in the newspapers: "John Shine a journeyman barber, impressed as a seaman, by virtue of a warrant from the Lords of the Admiralty, and backed by the Lord Mayor, was brought before John Wilkes, Esq; the sitting Alderman at Guildhall; when the Alderman adjudged the impressing illegal, and ordered Shine to be discharged."[49] Inevitably, the rift between the lord mayor and the radicals was widened.[50] Trecothick left office at the end of 1770, having done the Rockinghams more harm than good, and by November the alienation of the radicals was more or less complete. This need not have been a very serious problem in the short term. The radicals represented only a very small force (some four or five politicians) in the House of Commons. However, their dissatisfaction continued to impose strains on the Rockinghams' friendship with Chatham, and this threatened to be most serious.

At the beginning of the summer, Chatham had continued to do everything in his power to keep the motley opposition alliance together by restraining the extremist tendencies of his radical friends'. On 14 May the Common Council of London voted him the thanks of the city for his efforts on behalf of the rights of the electors and publicly referred to his supposed support for shorter Parliaments and a "more full and equal representation."[51] No doubt realizing that many of his moderate friends would not condone such measures, Chatham sent a reply in which he politely stated that he could not "recommend triennial Parliaments as a remedy against that canker in the constitution, venality in elections."[52] This delighted the Rockinghams[53] and in fact appears to have drawn them closer to him. However, Chatham was still anxious to do something to satisfy the radicals' desire for aggressive action, and he probably also felt a need to revive the sinking spirits of such people as Lord Temple. He therefore collaborated with John Sawbridge and John Calcraft in promoting the Kent remonstrance,[54] and he also attempted to convince the marquis and his friends to take action in their own spheres of influence.[55] When it became clear to him that the party would not be moved, he was annoyed.[56]

Chatham seems to have kept his dissatisfaction in check when dealing directly with the Rockinghams over the summer and early autumn, and no open quarrels developed. On the surface this is somewhat surprising. The decline of the opposition had no doubt been as discouraging to him as to anyone, and both in temperament and outlook he was far less suited to the Rockinghams than to the aggressiveness of the radicals. Furthermore, it is evident that he felt personally wronged by the *Thoughts on the Cause of the Present Discontents*. He did not mention it in his communications with the party until mid-November, but it is clear that he disliked it. "A pamphlet of last year," he told Rockingham, "however well intended I find has done much hurt to the cause. In the wide and extensive public the *whole* alone can save the *whole* against the desperate designs of the court. Let us, for God's sake, employ our efforts to remove all just obstacles to a true public-spirited union of *all* who will not be slaves."[57] Primarily what he objected to was the exaltation of the Rockinghams. Although Burke had treated Chatham with respect, he had insinuated that only the marquis and his friends had carried on the great Whig traditions in the current reign and that they alone had consistently stood in defiance of the court cabal. A few months later, when the opposition alliance was breaking down over another issue, Chatham was to complain directly of the injustice done to him. "He was the oldest Whig in England & he could not now submit to be call'd only an *ally* of the Whigs. He was a Whig."[58]

The Rockinghams had attempted in the *Thoughts* to promote unity, but Chatham, like the radicals, understandably viewed their panegyrics primarily as an open declaration of their superiority. The pamphlet angered him not only because it damaged the union movement but because it seemed to pose a threat to his own political status. He had approached the marquis with much deference, particularly in late 1769 and early 1770, and in attempting to achieve pragmatic political ends, he had eulogized the Rockinghams. However, he does not appear ever to have intended to become their inferior on a permanent basis. In fact, evidence suggests that he was somewhat jealous of the marquis's claims to the leadership of the Whigs. He hoped to join the party largely as a means of becoming its leader in a new administration. At the same time as he complained to Richmond about the treatment he received in the *Thoughts*, he told him:

That He thought a great defect in our Party was disposing before hand of the Treasury for your Lordship [Rockingham], as a *sine qua non*. That this was making a man the object of the Party and of the opposition. That for His part He could never subscribe to that: He did not mean to say that He had the smallest objection to Your being in that office ... If ... His Majesty thought of putting you there he should have much pleasure in seeing it. But if the King put all other things to rights & only wished that office for another man equally proper. He did not see why all should break for the single object of Your having that particular office.[59]

The problem was that Chatham's pretensions were as high as the Rockinghams'. He wished to work hand in hand with them, but as at other times in his career, he wanted to have control. All this points to the futility of the union movement as a long-term proposition. It is difficult to imagine how two parties such as these – each intent on gaining ascendancy over the other – could ever have formed an administration together. The *Thoughts on the Cause of the Present Discontents* did not make this much less likely. It merely helped bring out a little more quickly the tensions that almost certainly would have developed.

The fact that Chatham did not even mention Burke's pamphlet until November seems to corroborate the supposition that he intentionally used restraint. There may have been two reasons for this. Firstly, it appears that Rockingham was briefly involved in some sort of bargaining with the government for offices. He made a rather uncharacteristic (considering the time of year) visit to London in late July, and later Lord Hardwicke was informed that "an offer was made to ... [him] of three Great Offices (the Chamberlain staff one) for himself & two Friends ... but he rejected it."[60] Walpole may have been correct in his assumption that the overtures were initiated by Mansfield, who was married to Rockingham's aunt and had remained on good terms with him since the 1750s, when he had acted as his political mentor.[61] Whatever the case, it is apparent that the negotiations were extended to include Chatham. He, too, made a journey to London at this time, and he met with the marquis,[62] who evidently later reported that he had been "in great health & spirits & full of affected surprise at least, that they had *heard* nothing. He had seen (so they had both) old Tilbury, but Tom had nothing to say to either."[63] Tom Tilbury was a sobriquet of the Earl of Northington, who after holding high office in the sixties[64] had taken on the role of mediator between the king and those politicians with whom he wished to discuss government appointments.[65]

To Chatham, as long as any negotiations involving both himself and Rockingham were being conducted, it must have seemed opportune to avoid disagreements if at all possible. Moreover, between June and November, his connections with the London politicians suddenly grew somewhat tenuous. In the first place, his influence was greatly weakened by the death of William Beckford. Beckford had been the only politician in the city who had achieved enough eminence to make Chatham's views widely influential, and he had been the one man capable of keeping the city opposition together. Soon after his death, the radicals began to split into two hostile camps of which Chatham's people were the weaker. Exactly when the break started is not clear, but it seems to have been well advanced by September. It was during that month that the second mayoral election of the year was held and James Townsend, John Sawbridge, and their friends did everything in their power to prevent the election of Brass Crosby, who ran with the support of Richard Oliver. On the thirteenth someone informed Calcraft: "All Measures to set Alderman Crosby aside in the City are in Vain ... The City is changed from what it was Six Months ago. A little Junto of Mr. Oliver's Friends now manage everything ... I am confident L[or]d Chatham's and Lord Temple's friends would never have had one moment's uneasiness in the City affairs, if the City had been looked after in the proper Season, by the proper Person."[66] Chatham had returned to active politics in 1769 intent on developing a very broadly based opposition alliance. Now, part of that alliance seemed to be slipping from his grasp and he became more determined to hold onto what remained, at least for the time being. He was not therefore prepared to risk alienating his moderate allies by confronting them directly on current points of possible conflict.

Such was the state of affairs before the outbreak of the Falkland Islands crisis in September. This affair had a dual effect on Chatham's relationship with the Rockinghams. On the one hand, it strengthened it by giving the parties common ground on which to stand in their fight against North. This is not to say that their points of view were exactly the same. Chatham was concerned primarily because the crisis seemed to have the potential to usher him back into power. It was well known that North and his colleagues were attempting to resolve the dispute diplomatically, but many people believed that they would fail and would eventually be forced to call on the former hero of the Seven Years' War to take over the administration.[67] Chatham and his followers were naturally anxious to accept this theory. When Calcraft first learned of the ejection of the British from Port Egmont, he informed his leader: "The only Comfort that can be derived is from the Hope of a thorough conviction at St. James, how impossible 'tis to Treat with Foreign Powers, unless Your Lordship will Re Establish Government and once more Save this Distracted Country from Destruction."[68] Calcraft might have saved his ink. Chatham had already come to the same conclusion. Indeed, as early as July, when the first news of trouble had reached England and before anyone knew of the forced evacuation, he had displayed some premature enthusiasm in deducing that "tho' war is not declar'd yet ... we are in fact at war."[69]

Before the session, however, Chatham could not be certain that the conflict would escalate, no matter how much he wanted it to; and even if it did, he could not be sure that the king, who had had reason to feel ill used by him since 1769, would consent to take him in. Therefore, it was necessary to work with all his allies – particularly the Rockinghams, with their relatively large following in Parliament – in order to agitate the issue from the opposition side. In this objective, Rockingham must have seemed a very usable partner. He made it clear that he was most anxious to arouse public interest.[70] His concern arose primarily from the fact that during the previous session, his party had submitted a motion in the House of Lords for an increase in the number of seamen in the naval forces.[71] During the debate on the motion, the Duke of Richmond had taken a leading part and had even pointed out "the encroachments and dangers from France and Spain in Corsica and the East Indies and from the formidable Spanish fleet that seemed to threaten Jamaica."[72] The motion had been rejected, and since then the navy had deteriorated for a number of reasons, including a disastrous fire at Portsmouth dockyard.[73] At the outbreak of the Falkland Island crisis, Britain's sea forces seemed to be in a perilous state,[74] and Rockingham found himself in the enjoyable position of having been defeated by the government in attempting to do something about it. It was the perfect situation for displaying his moral superiority, especially to the opposition parties he so deperately wanted to lead, and he was quick to take advantage of it. "The motion we made in the end of last Session," he told Burke in September, "is a very untoward circumstance for the administration who refused it. The total want of confidence and the general dislike &c of the ministry, must bear strongly now upon them. The Sanctum Sanctorum of the Court System – must tremble."[75]

Just before the opening of Parliament on 13 November, Rockingham's enthusiasm was much in evidence. The Grenvilles were somewhat at a loose end. George Grenville had been suffering from a serious illness for some months and was now known to be dying. Rockingham therefore contacted his important followers and brought them into discussions concerning the coming session and the currently dominant issue.[76] He also established regular contact with Chatham and generally did his best to coordinate their efforts.[77] This was the high point of Rockingham's trust in his one-time political enemy. He could hardly have failed to realize how much the crisis might enhance Chatham's importance.[78] Yet he showed no trace of the fears and jealousies he had earlier experienced when his rivals seemed to have a good chance of being called to power. This attests to Chatham's success in convincing the marquis of his sincerity. Perhaps, too, it is indicative of Rockingham's concern for the rejuvenation of the Whigs. The desire to control a new broadly based party seems to have influenced him uncharacteristically to cling to the hope that his ally would be true to that same cause.

The Falkland Islands crisis, then, initially helped draw Rockingham and Chatham together. But there was one respect in which the effect of the issue on their relationship was less than totally beneficial. As the prospect of war increased, the possibility that Chatham would be called on to lead Great Britain through another major conflict tended to augment his sense of his own importance and make him difficult to deal with. At times he seemed unable to show Rockingham the deference he had shown him earlier or to put up with the characteristics of the party he disliked. Thus, his attitude in November was confused. At one moment he would be meeting with the marquis, discussing the crisis amicably, and reporting to his friends that his "esteem and confidence in his Lordships upright intentions grows from every conversation with him."[79] At another, he would be writing to the marquis in noticeably cool tones, lecturing him on the effects of the *Thoughts*, or, as on one occasion, criticizing the party publicly for its particularism.[80] This is one of the first indications of the difference between Chatham's priorities and Rockingham's. Since 1767, Rockingham had consistently been trying to effect a union of all the groups in opposition. His party had shown that it was prepared to repudiate power for this project. Chatham also had supported the alliance – at times very strongly. But his behaviour during the Falklands crisis suggests that he was inclined to lose his enthusiasm the moment the chance of rising to office on his own seemed good. Whereas Rockingham's major concern was the grand constitutional party, Chatham was emitting signs that office was his first priority and that party was merely a means to that end. To put it another way, in the union movement, Rockingham was trying to establish a great Whig connection that might or might not rise to power; Chatham wanted to form something that cynics would have called an "interested faction who aimed through the sides of the Constitution to wound the Ministry."[81]

Initially, Rockingham did not take exception to Chatham's behaviour (and in fact may not even have noticed it), but as the session progressed, Chatham's new-found self-esteem was to cause irreparable damage. The two parties began the parliamentary session on 13 November in a common assault on the government over the Falkland

Islands dispute.[82] In the Commons, Isaac Barré put forth his leader's point of view by assailing the ministers for not deeming the initial act of hostility "an effectual declaration of war";[83] and both Burke and Dowdeswell accused North of betraying "the interest and honour of Great Britain to our enemies abroad" by keeping the country "naked and defenseless."[84] Meanwhile, in the Lords, Rockingham made an emotional speech charging the administration with neglect.[85] No divisions were attempted in either House, partly because George Grenville died on that day and the majority of his friends did not attend.

The first test of strength came on 22 November, when Dowdeswell and Richmond moved for papers which they hoped would enable them to "prove the folly, or treachery of the King's servants, in not accepting of the augmentation of seamen proposed and urged by the Lords in opposition."[86] Despite the support of a number of the Grenvilles, the motion was lost by 225 to 101 in the Lower House and by 65 to 21 in the Upper House. The most remarkable event of the day was Chatham's speech in the Lords. He first openly displayed his desire to push the country into a war by denouncing the ministry for "so shamefully betray[ing] the King's honour, as to make it matter of negotiation whether his Majesty's possessions shall be restored to him or not."[87] Then he criticized the Rockinghams for what he believed to be their desire to form "an administration ... on an exclusive system of family connections or private friendships," and he attacked his city friends for opposing press warrants. Chatham's eyes seem to have been blinded with visions of personal glory. He believed that he had suddenly become necessary to the nation and that his links with the opposition were an impediment. Thus, he attempted to distance himself from all his friends. He had wanted to go hand in hand with the marquis and others so long as that was the most direct route to power. When it no longer seemed to be, he was prepared to desert them on a moment's notice and go it alone.

On that day the opposition entered a period of relatively consistent decline. The numbers voting against the ministry in the Commons on 22 November proved to be the largest on the controversy before the approval of the peace settlement in February 1771, and the third largest on any issue during the session. This was primarily a testimony to the ministry's success in convincing the public that it would be imprudent to push the nation immediately into a war over an unimportant group of islands or to allow politicians to advertise the poor state of the country's defences while negotiations were being conducted with the enemy.[88]

Over the Christmas recess, the peace agreement between the British and Spanish governments was settled, and a treaty was signed on

22 January 1771. When the convention was laid before Parliament on the twenty-fifth, Dowdeswell, Burke, Barré, Richmond, and Chatham pointed out that it merely provided for the restitution of Port Egmont and left Britain's right to the islands in considerable doubt.[89] The government yielded to motions for an inquiry but insisted that only papers pertaining to the dignity and not the sovereignty of the crown should be investigated. Motions calling for correspondence and papers concerning any intervention by France were easily rejected.

The ministry produced the promised papers on 4 February,[90] and the peace was approved by the Commons on the thirteenth[91] and by the Lords on the fourteenth.[92] Although the Rockinghams and Chathams retained an outward appearance of mutual respect during this period, the one basic difference in their attitudes is more noticeable. Rockingham had fallen seriously ill and therefore was not directly involved. However, he corresponded with Burke and Dowdeswell and with Richmond, who took over the leadership of the party in his absence. The policy they agreed on is best represented in a letter written by the marquis at the end of the month:

I am fully convinced that the publick in general *are* glad of *peace* and I am equally convinced that they *will be discontented* at the *mean* terms of the present conciliation.

I have no objection to sounding high – the dishonour this country has suffered, but I think the object should be to shew the defenceless state this country was in – in September and to shew how highly culpable the administration have been in having neglected taking earlier precautions.

That the very existence of this country had been endangered by their supine neglect. That their conduct had been the encouragement to Spain to venture to insult us. That the terms of this conciliation, were – like the Peace of Fontainbleau, acceptable to the Court System for their political convenience.[93]

When the other party leaders met in London a few days later, "all agreed in damning the Peace & finding great faults with the Whole Negotiation but in not starting anything that would tend to break it."[94]

Chatham's position was different because he had a much greater interest in seeing the nation pushed into war.[95] His actions after the signing of the convention suggest a last desperate effort to bring on a military conflict by demonstrating through questions to the judges in the House of Lords that the peace agreement was illegal.[96] Dowdeswell and Burke both tried to dissuade Chatham from this approach,[97] and when he attempted (unsuccessfully) to submit his questions, it was only with considerable reluctance that Richmond upheld him in debate.[98] It would appear that Rockingham was correct in his belief that there was public discontent over the terms of the peace. On 13 February (when the Commons approved the settlement), Dowdeswell moved to leave out of the three-part "Address of Thanks to the King" the two parts that expressed the House's approbation of the ministers' actions.[99] In the division, a number of the independent country gentlemen voted against the government, and the minority, though defeated by more than 100 votes, rose to 157.[100] This was about three times what it had been previously.[101]

In general, the Falkland Islands crisis was little less than a disaster for the opposition parties. Their attacks on the ministry between November and February were seen as poorly disguised attempts to provoke a war over "a morsel of rock"[102] just to make a change of administration necessary. For this, the public tended to turn against Chatham in particular. As Horace Walpole put it, "Though the nation might have called for the vigour of his spirited councils had war been declared, nobody was desirous of making war only to make him necessary."[103] To the degree that the Rockinghams seemed to be working with Chatham, they shared his discredit. Furthermore, in their attempts to prove the government's neglect, they were thought to be taking "the liberty of advertising our enemies of our deficiencies."[104] Here, the Rockinghams were even farther out of tune with the rest of the nation than Chatham. It was they who persisted in having information indicative of the inadequacy of the British navy laid before Parliament. In late November, Shelburne apparently realized the bad effects and told Chatham that it "can do no good and only tire the House."[105]

The Rockingham leaders well knew the power of public opinion. They had concerned themselves with it a great deal in such matters as Anglo-American policy; they had played it as well as they could over the Middlesex election; and they had attempted with their collective strength to marshall it in the *Thoughts*. However, they now allowed themselves to go against public opinion almost totally. The reason was that in this particular issue, their pervading desire to prove the justness of their policies and their own right to take the lead in a Whig coalition put them on a collision course with the pulse of the nation at large. There was no way the party could work towards its goal of broadening its following in the arena of high politics at Westminster without alienating most independent interests both inside and outside Parliament. In this instance, the Rockinghams seem not to have recognized the need to choose between the two objectives, but they would not make this mistake again. In future, they were to recognize that both the union movement and the hope for parliamentary victory were lost causes. Thus, they tended to disregard political advantage in an effort to build credit with the public at large. This would allow them to exhibit their country-party values as never before.

The significance of the episode in tipping the scales in the House of Commons towards the ministry is illustrated in Peter Thomas's estimate that Lord North emerged from the affair "a true Prime Minister."[106] Few people failed to realize how destructive it was to the minority:

Never was there in the history of this country an opposition so formidable as the present was last winter, in the space of twelve months so broken, melted down, and discomfited as this has been [it was noted in late January]. Never was there a more sudden and total change of sentiment than appears at present with regard to the Opposition, who seem to have effectively convinced the impartial world that they were equally, at least, destitute of principle. with those they opposed, and had no manner of intention to serve the public, but merely to aggrandize themselves.[107]

Along with popularity, the opposition lost personnel. Once it was realized that there would be no war, many of the more active politicians – knowing now that Chatham was not going to be able to bring them into power after all, and seeing the disrepute into which he and Rockingham had fallen – gave up the game altogether. Of these, the most noteworthy were George Grenville's former supporters. Earl Temple, who had been disillusioned with politics since May, was seriously affected by his brother's death; he did not attend at all in November, and at the beginning of December he announced his retirement.[108] Released from the influence of their leaders, a number of the rest of the party began negotiating with the administration.[109] Many of them gave only token support to the opposition before officially deserting it in January. At about the time of the signing of the peace treaty, the Earl of Suffolk[110] was made lord privy seal,[111] Thomas Whately was appointed to the Board of Trade,[112] and Wedderburn accepted the office of solicitor general.[113] It was further agreed that others, including Lord Lyttleton and Lord Hyde,[114] were "to be first considered whenever any places suitable for them became vacant."[115] Hyde thereafter became a regular government supporter, whereas Lyttleton,[116] like Temple, for the most part retired.[117] In February there were apparently some seventeen Grenvilles left in opposition in the Lower House.[118] They included Robert Clive[119] and a number of his friends in the East India Company, as well as Henry Seymour,[120] Lord George

Germain, and Thomas Townshend, Jr.[121] After early 1771 most of the Grenvilles in opposition slowly drifted apart,[122] and Clive's group went over to the court in March 1772.[123]

The loss of the Grenvilles was undoubtedly distressing to Rockingham and Chatham. However, other signs of wavering in the opposition ranks must have been even more perplexing to Chatham. In January a number of his personal friends broke rank. On 1 February Richmond informed Rockingham that Lord Northumberland,[124] who had gone into opposition in conjunction with Chatham in 1770, was "very unsteady" and that Lord Huntingdon, who had resigned his place as groom of the stole at that time, "will ... be for the Peace."[125] Neither signed a protest against the Spanish convention which the Rockinghams submitted in the Lords on 14 February,[126] and thereafter they appear to have given up opposition altogether. There was also a noticeable change in Chatham's old friend Lord Camden at this time. Camden had been displeased with his mentor since the end of the previous session, apparently because of his failure to heed certain advice with respect to the motion in May for the dissolution of Parliament.[127] In the early weeks of the sitting he did not attend the Lords with any regularity;[128] and after the Christmas holidays, although he continued to take the opposition side in Parliament, he made it known that he considered himself "a single man, detached from all party, & Connection, even Lord Chatham."[129]

The Rockinghams themselves did not experience a comparable disaffection. However, one noted politician, the Earl of Dartmouth,[130] who had supported them off and on since 1765 though he had never been particularly faithful, began to break completely with them as the peace was being signed. After 22 January, Richmond reported to Rockingham with "much regret" that he believed they had lost him.[131] In fact, Dartmouth would never act with the party again. In the summer of 1772 he joined the North cabinet as secretary of state for the colonies. Another former Rockingham, Sir William Meredith, also separated from the party around this time, although the Falkland Islands crisis appears to have been a minor consideration. Meredith had been dissatisfied with the Rockinghams for some years. It was their country gentlemanly ways he disliked most. Back in 1768 he had told Portland: "I firmly am of Opinion, Ld. Rockinghams Friends may do Themselves great honor & redeem their Country. Not by mounting once in a Session on some particular Question, but by a constant active systematick conduct; and, the first they should be to lay aside that go-cart [the attack on Bute and the court system], in which they have been so often drawn by persons, who meant to overturn them, or at best cared only for Themselves."[132] In April 1771,

Burke was to tell Charles O'Hara that "from the beginning of the Session, Meredith has quitted our party."[133] So he seems to have come to his decision before this issue had brought the Rockinghams any real discredit. However, there can be little doubt that the first three months of the session did nothing to encourage him to change his mind. The loss of Meredith was serious. He had first joined the Rockinghams during Grenville's administration and had become a valuable asset to the party in the House of Commons, where he spoke regularly and rose to some eminence. Over the next few years he was to form "a little light squadron of his own"[134] with some independent members of the House, and in 1774 he joined North as the comptroller of the household.

The Falkland Islands issue adversely affected the "broad and comprehensive" alliance not only because of what it did to its public credibility and Parliamentary strength but because of its effect on the ability of the Rockinghams and Chathams to act as a cohesive force. In the short term the issue did not prevent the two groups from working together, but it created an atmosphere of frustration and failure which, when combined with Chatham's periodically revived sense of self-esteem, helped cause a great deal of ill will over another issue that emerged at about the same time. In the end, this other matter was to erect a barrier between the two parties which they would never really overcome.

CHAPTER SIX

The Elimination of the Union Movement in the Spring and Summer of 1771

The dispute with Spain over the Falkland Islands did much to help the Rockinghams make the adjustment from a court Whig to country opposition perspective. From the beginning of his career, Rockingham's central objective had virtually always been the establishment of strong, stable, and enduring government. His and the party's stand against Bute and the system of favouritism had been based on the ministerial weakness and instability they had wrought in the 1760s as successive government's rotated in and out of office. His attempts to construct a new, broadly based party in opposition had been aimed in part at the formation of the kind of government over which the court Whigs had presided in the past. However, on witnessing the formidable decline of the Whig party's fortunes during the 1770–71 session, the marquis, like Burke, began to suspect that the major problem for Britain was not weak government but an unduly powerful one. As he realized just how firm North's base of support was in the House of Commons, he began to identify, more than at any time previously, with the problems of opposition and to turn his attention to the forces that tended to give government an unfair advantage. This in turn encouraged him to focus (again, as Burke was doing) on the age-old problem of government corruption and the influence of the crown. It is no coincidence that by early 1771 the marquis was beginning to sound like many of the country spokesmen who in decades gone by had regularly defied his court Whig ancestors:

I fear indeed the future struggles of the people in defence of their Constitutional Rights will grow weaker and weaker.

It is much too probable that the power and influence of the Crown will increase rapidly. We live at the period when for the first time since the Revolution, the power and influence of the Crown is held out, as the main and chief and only support of Government. If we ... do not exert now, we may accelerate the abject state to which the Constitution may be reduced.[1]

Two other important matters in the second half of the 1770–71 parliamentary session strengthened this line of reasoning in the minds of all the party leaders and, along with the Falkland Islands conflict, helped set firmly in motion a substantial realignment of Whig ideals.

While the dispute with Spain dominated public affairs from September to February, a domestic problem concerning the rights of juries was also drawing considerable attention. It originated in a legal battle between the crown and four newspaper publishers who had printed Junius's letter to the king in December 1769.[2] Over the summer of 1770 the attorney General, William De Grey,[3] started libel proceedings in the Court of King's Bench against the four men, and the subsequent trials revived a long-standing disagreement between Lord Mansfield and the King's Bench judges, on the one hand, and opposition lawyers and spokesmen mainly from the City of London, on the other, over the powers that juries had a right to exercise in trying libel cases. For the former side, the argument was set out by Lord Mansfield in July and used as the basis for all four trials: "If the jury find that the defendant published at all, they find the paper, as charged in the information" (i.e., guilty of publishing a "false scandalous and malicious libel"), "for that is their only enquiry."[4] In Mansfield's view, all the jury could do was decide whether the defendant had published the material in question. It was left to the judge to decide whether the material was meant as a libel and therefore whether the publisher had broken the law. Obviously, this maxim gave the magistrate, and therefore the crown, very considerable powers of censorship over the press.

The other side of the argument had been submitted in 1764 by Sergeant John Glynn[5] when, as counsel for one of the printers being tried for republishing the *North Briton*, he had told the jurors that they were the proper judges of both law and fact.[6] As the trials progressed in 1770, this maxim was reiterated over and over again in pamphlets, in the newspapers, and in the House of Commons by politicians anxious to portray themselves as the champions of the rights of juries as well as of the liberty of the press.[7] In the City of London emotions ran high indeed, in part because of Lord Mansfield's image. Resentment of him had been strong for some time because, as a lord chief justice, he had presided over the Court of King's Bench on so many occasions when Wilkes and other city spokesmen had been "persecuted."[8]

For the more respectable opposition politicians in Parliament, this issue, with all its popular overtones, held great possibilities. To the

Rockinghams, however, there was one major difficulty. Rockingham was Mansfield's friend and relative, and the marquis had little desire to join in the personal recrimination that became part and parcel of the stand taken by other groups. To Chatham, on the other hand, the question was much simpler. He had never been on good terms with Mansfield, partly because of his friendship with Lord Camden, one of Mansfield's principal competitors for high office in the legal profession.[9] Furthermore, the issue gained public attention in July, when Chatham was most anxious to regain credit with his London friends. Therefore, he early determined to take up the issue. [10]

It is very likely that Chatham knew of the Rockinghams' discomfort. Nonetheless, before Parliament reconvened, he began planning a bill to *declare* that juries had the right to determine both law and fact in libel cases.[11] Declaratory legislation would secure the juries' rights that were demanded by antiministerial opinion and would also do something to gratify people's animosity towards Mansfield. It would purportedly state what the law had been all along and would therefore indirectly censure those who had acted on contrary principles.

Partly because of Camden's disinclination to support him,[12] Chatham allowed the matter to ride for a time. But towards the end of November he became determined to make a stand, because of his attack on the city magistrates on the twenty-second.[13] This attack appears to have been the result of a momentary loss of temper in the heat of debate. As one observer put it, Chatham had been "moderate at first, but ye *Lyon* grew angry at last, & abused ye City for supposing Press Warrants to be *illegal*."[14] He soon regretted his rashness, and in order to placate their friends among the London radicals, he and Lord Shelburne decided to stir up something as soon as possible "regarding home grievances."[15]

On 5 December, Chatham moved a resolution in the Lords which stated that "the Capacity to be chosen a Representative of the Commons in Parliament ... is a Matter wherein the Jurisdiction of the House of Commons is not final or conclusive."[16] Then he attempted to find someone to champion declaratory legislation in the Commons. At first, Shelburne asked Charles Wolfran Cornwall,[17] a friend of both his own party and the Rockinghams, to propose a motion for an inquiry into the administration of justice at Westminster, which would have been aimed at examining and eventually censuring Mansfield's conduct. Cornwall declined, because he felt obligated to tell the Rockinghams of his intentions, and it was "his own very decided opinion, that any previous communication ... might lead to insuperable difficulties."[18] Then, at a meeting at Dowdeswell's London residence on 26 November, Cornwall and others were able to devise an alternative plan when they discovered that Constantine Phipps,[19] a somewhat independent friend of the opposition, intended to bring in a motion the following day for a bill to curtail the attorney general's power of filing information *ex officio*. The plan called for Cornwall to support the motion in debate but also to argue that a greater threat to liberty had been evidenced in the behaviour of some of the judges in the Court of King's Bench. Phipps's motion would then be changed to a request to the king for an inquiry.[20] The scheme failed completely. On the twenty-seventh, Phipps submitted his bill and Cornwall proposed the amendment, but all the Rockinghams were silent. Moreover, Phipps changed his mind during the debate and would not give up his motion. It was defeated by 85 votes.[21] Still Chatham and Shelburne refused to give up. Over the next few days, they contacted some of their friends in the law profession and persuaded them to agree to a separate motion for an inquiry into the administration of justice at Westminster. This was proposed by Sergeant Glynn on 6 December and was defeated by 187 votes to 76.[22]

When Chatham and his friends agitated this issue in November and December, they received plenty of evidence that it had the potential to alienate the Rockinghams. Leading members of that party voted with the minority in all the motions submitted in the Commons, but it was often all too clear that their attitude differed from those of the other opposition politicians because of their disinclination to join in the attacks on Mansfield. On 27 November, for instance, Burke, while agreeing that an inquiry was necessary, said he was certain that all the accusations against the judges were "false and groundless."[23] Much to Chatham's exasperation,[24] he also insinuated that juries themselves were inclined at times to become the tools of ministerial vengeance against apparent libellers. Chatham and Shelburne both became convinced that their allies were intent on "skreening" Mansfield from his many critics,[25] and for this reason they planned each of their moves in secrecy for the most part. Dowdeswell was the only Rockingham who had any prior warning of the scheme with regard to Constantine Phipps's motion, and none of the members of the party was sent any extensive communication regarding Glynn's motion.[26]

Chatham was apparently quite prepared to see the opposition alliance, which he had taken great pains to help construct, destroyed completely over the rights of juries. He continued to push forward even though he knew that the Rockinghams would not be able to agree to his ultimate aims, and at one point he told his friend Calcraft that "if Burke's picture of juries, and of that mode of justice ... be adopted, I will separate from so unorthodox a congregation."[27] It is

unlikely that Chatham's desire either to strike a blow at Lord Mansfield or to put things right with his friends in London would have influenced him to be so intransigent if he had still considered the union
movement as important as he had several months earlier. The main
reason for his sudden loss of concern about it appears to lie in the
Falkland Islands crisis. He and the Rockinghams were getting no-
where in propagating that affair in Parliament, and Chatham was
feeling extremely dissatisfied. When he informed Calcraft on 28 November that he was ready to break with his allies over the jury issue,
he also told him that matters were "hastening to some crises, in the
interior of the thing called Opposition." He added, "I think all is ru-
ined, and am determined to be found in my post when destruction
falls upon us."[28]

The Falkland Island crisis not only gave Chatham reason to feel
disillusioned with the regular game of opposition; it also made him
feel that the game was relatively unnecessary. In the period between
late November and early January, the government made some distinctly warlike moves,[29] and Chatham managed to convince himself
that a military confrontation was virtually a certainty.[30] As noted in
the previous chapter, this increased his confidence that he was about
to be called on to take over the government. Urged on by Calcraft,
who told him that the "country looks to your Lordship only for salva-
tion ... and [I] think numbers, in the present circumstance, by no
means the object,"[31] he became less able to compromise.

Meanwhile, the Rockinghams became just as determined as
Chatham to make a stand on behalf of the rights of juries. Rockingham appears to have been the force behind this decision. Smarting
from his recent disgrace over the Falkland Islands, he saw in the juries controversy an opportunity to regain some lost public credibility.
He could portray himself as the champion of liberty against a widely
recognized evil, which he was beginning to see as the major threat to
the constitution. In the letter in which he told Burke of his deep fears
of the influence of the crown, he estimated that every "Constitutional
Right may be consider'd to be held by the same tenure, which this
right in Juries seems now to be. Law and authority will construe *one
way*, and the people at large may construe *another*, the Right of election in the Middlesex Case, is not unlike it. The House of Commons
(as directed by the Crown's Ministers) hold one opinion the people at
large hold another. But in this case indeed they go further than the
Courts of Law, for they *enforce* their opinion *now*. The Courts of Law
only will."[32]

At this point, the marquis's perspective had shifted dramatically.
In the Falkland Islands issue, he had lost sight of national sentiments

while attempting to keep the opposition alliance together for the struggle at Westminster. Now, he was turning his back on the latter altogether. This was pivotal. In every single major issue the party was to face in the next several years, credibility outside Parliament was to take precedence over immediate strength within. A country-party type of desire to display undefiled virtue was to overshadow any court-party type of concern about political advantage at the centre.

The Rockinghams' determination in the juries question made it impossible for them to back down. On 10 December, Dowdeswell notified the House of Commons that after the Christmas recess he would be submitting legislation "to remove doubts and controversy" regarding the powers of juries.[33] However, the Rockinghams' approach was slightly different from Chatham's. They drew up an *enacting* bill to give juries the power to decide both law and fact for the future. This would not in any way censure Mansfield's past conduct. Irrespective of the party's motives, this was by far the most sensible solution. Even Camden admitted that "the weight of Authority as well as Numbers"[34] in the Upper House, of which all the law lords were members, supported Mansfield. Today, noted legal and constitutional historians agree that he was merely enforcing the law as it then stood (whether justly or otherwise).[35] Rockingham deduced that the bill would be rejected because of opposition from the court,[36] but he was confident that *in the future*, enacting legislation would have the greater chance of achieving "security to the Publick."[37]

The marquis soon realized that Chatham and the radicals were displeased with the measure.[38] But he did not seriously consider giving up. After a meeting of opposition politicians on 4 February broke up in a dispute between the two parties,[39] Dowdeswell showed some signs of wavering and Rockingham immediately intervened with the full weight of his authority. He wrote to Dowdeswell referring to "some alterations you would propose ... in order to accommodate," and then stated, "Accommodation does not appear to be reciprocally the Intention, & therefore I should think you should be more guarded least without obtaining any End, you should render Your own Bill more perplexed."[40] On the occasions when Rockingham spoke in such tones, even Dowdeswell could be moved. He immediately wrote back promising to stand firm and not "give up a little of ... [our] principle."[41] On 6 March, when Dowdeswell submitted the bill, the outcome was, as Burke described it, "disgraceful to opposition; and matter of no small Triumph to the Courtiers; who saw, (I believe a thing without parralel) the whole debate, a hot and long one, carried on wholly between the Members of the opposition. The Ministerial people looked on, as if they were in Boxes at the Opera."[42] The Rockinghams were humiliated by a vote of 218 to 72.

This was a fiasco for the two major parties left in opposition in 1771, because they allowed themselves to compete rather than cooperate in attempting to champion what they considered a popular cause. Rockingham saw the whole affair as a race for public approval. Repeatedly, he told his followers how important it was that they should pursue their measure "for the Sake of the Publick & for our own Credit."[43] "Lord Chatham," he insisted, "can not assent to *our friends* getting the credit with the publick which on this and all occasions they have deserved."[44] The Rockinghams' original decision to promulgate enacting rather than declaratory legislation was at least partly governed by their disinclination to censure Mansfield; but if they had merely wanted to protect their friend, they need not have done anything. Mansfield was in no real danger. The moves against him in the House of Commons had all failed, and no one was likely to try again. Moreover, the actual wording of the bill was so vague that no one could have used it to demonstrate that Mansfield had acted according to the law. Everything was omitted which "having the appearance of providing for the future only might seem to give something to the jury that it ought not to have had before."[45] No explicit or implicit claim to novelty was made. Later, Burke was completely justified when he pointed out that the bill "enacts, not that the jury *shall* have the *power*, but that they shall be *held and reputed in law and right competent* to try the whole matter laid in the information. The bill is directing to the judges concerning the opinion in law which they are known to hold upon this subject; and does not in the least imply that the jury were to derive a new right and power."[46] This entire episode again casts serious doubt on the possibility of there being a lasting union between Rockingham and Chatham even if they had succeeded in bringing down Lord North. Surely, if they could not agree on a procedure concerning an issue in which they were so close, they would never have been able to concur in anything as productive of party feeling as the distribution of offices in a new administration.

After this dispute, the cordiality between the Rockinghams and Chathams was not restored. "Since that time," Burke would write in April, "we have had no consultation with Lord Chatham. We have had no declaration of Enmity neither. But the matter rests in a kind of sullen discontent on both sides. It would have, I dare say, broken out into Something of more eclat by this, if we had not been hurried into action by other Events, which have coverd our mutual jealousy from the public."[47] The "other Events" were those surrounding the final major issue of the session, the printers' case. Its effects on the relations between the Rockinghams and Chatham were much as Burke here states. It tended to cover up animosities but did little to restore amicability. Its chief attraction to this study is that, like the rights of juries debate, it helps document the development of the Rockingham Whigs as a country opposition connection.

The printers' case began when Colonel George Onslow[48] successfully moved in February and March that eight men responsible for printing and publishing newspapers should attend the House of Commons and explain why they had been printing its debates and "misrepresenting the speeches."[49] Of the eight men ordered to attend, three appeared on 14 March[50] and were reprimanded after apologizing for their indiscretions. The other five evaded their summonses and became involved in a plot, which was apparently instigated by Robert Morris,[51] the former secretary of the Society for the Supporters of the Bill of Rights, John Wilkes, and other radicals. Its purpose was to provoke a confrontation between Parliament and the city.[52] The plot was extremely successful. Various methods were used by (or in the names of) some of the fugitive printers to insult the House and challenge its authority.[53] Eventually, two city magistrates, Richard Oliver and Brass Crosby,[54] who were also MPs, were tried before the House for refusing to honour its warrants of arrest. They were subsequently committed to the Tower of London for breach of the privileges of the House of Commons.[55] However, as Professor Thomas has observed, this was really a victory for the city. There, public demonstrations in support of the two magistrates were widespread, and there were outpourings in support of their actions from political voices of all colours. Never again would the House of Commons dare to take on the city over the reporting of parliamentary debates.

Thus, the implications were far-reaching, particularly in establishing the freedom of the press and the right of the people to know what their representatives were doing and saying in Parliament. The case also provided the Rockinghams with an opportunity to embrace a little more firmly their stance against strong government and the influence of the crown. It was these powers, and a plot to enlarge them, which spokesmen from all sectors of the opposition, both inside Parliament and outside, eventually blamed for forcing the Commons into the conflict in the first place. [56]

Initially, the issues were not as clear-cut as the party leaders would have liked, and they offered only nominal resistance.[57] But on 19 March the government, supported by a substantial majority, ruled that the mayor should be allowed counsel during his trial in the Commons only on those points that did "not controvert the privileges of this House."[58] This gave the Rockinghams an opportunity to oppose on constitutional grounds without directly supporting the magistrates' transgressions. Dowdeswell, Savile, and Burke immediately combined with Barlow Trecothick in arguing that "it would be impossible to plead the Lord Mayor's case without to some degree, controverting the privileges of the House."[59] And during the remainder of the contest, they moved directly behind the two city officials, on the grounds that these men were being punished without a proper opportunity to state their case.[60] This also created the requisite opportunity to lecture the members for turning their backs on liberty for the sake of places and pensions under the crown. "This H[ouse] used to be the great War Horse of this Country & to face & bear down all its Enemys," Burke claimed. "Its now become a meer blind servill Horse moving only in the regular track of the minister."[61] Lord John Cavendish told his fellow MPs that they "must one day or other abridge our privileges & throw some overboard to save the rest, the prerogative has been served so, but in its stead" this government "has made use of influence."[62] After the two magistrates were sent to the Tower, the marquis and his friends[63] publicly displayed sympathy by honouring them with a well-advertised visit.[64]

Politically, the case did the Rockinghams little good, though they did manage to gain some independent support in the Commons at various points. On motions against denying the magistrates counsel on all parts of their defence and against committing them to the Tower, the minorities fluctuated between 79 and 97 in a thin House. However, in the long run, the issue did nothing to restore the party's pre-Falkland Islands strength.[65] Although some of the country gentlemen refused to back the ministry in some measures, they supported it wholeheartedly in the desire to uphold the privileges and authority of Parliament. The Rockinghams did not attempt to deny the House's authority, but some of them voted against the administration throughout, and for this they must have received no thanks from nonpartisan members. They also received little thanks from the London radicals. Among this set, the fact that some of the Rockinghams voted in the minority throughout was offset by the fact that they refused to countenance either the magistrates' original actions or the generally immoderate behaviour of the city. At one point, the connection was criticized in the press by Junius because of a rumour that some of them had "said the City was too violent."[66]

The issue also did little to make amends with the Chathams. Once again, this was despite the fact that the Chathams' responses were very similar to those of the Rockinghams. Chatham, Barré, and Shelburne initially objected to the magistrates' provocations,[67] but as the trials in the Commons progressed, they joined the Rockinghams in opposition both to bringing the magistrates before the House and to punishing them.[68] There is no evidence, however, of any communication between the Rockinghams and Chathams over this issue, and immediately after it subsided their mutual enmity was as strong as before.

By the end of the 1771 session, the administration's adversaries were in a sad state. In London the moderates, represented by such people as Trecothick, Baker, and Martin, again found themselves alienated from the radicals. And the latter were again split into two hostile camps – one led by the Reverend John Horne[69] and the other by the celebrated and now dominant John Wilkes.[70] In Parliament many were dispirited in the extreme. Chatham, who had not attended since January, made a last attempt to revive the fight during the closing days of the session. In April his friends in London urged him to take a stand on behalf of reform measures such as triennial parliaments.[71] Ostensibly as a compromise, he considered bringing in a bill to add one additional representative to the House of Commons for each of the counties,[72] but when he found that the more moderate of his friends would not support him, he decided instead to submit another motion for the dissolution of Parliament. His attempts to get his friends to take an interest even in this moderate measure proved futile. Lord Temple confessed, "The general state of the Opposition, the implacable division in the City, which the demon of discord hath so plentifully scattered, have ... reduced me to a state of despondency for the public, which makes me think it almost unmanly to step again into any public transaction."[73]

On 25 April, Chatham also approached Rockingham[74] and was able to obtain a pledge of support. However, before he introduced the measure, his friend John Sawbridge submitted the first of his annual bills for shortening the duration of Parliament, and the Rockinghams joined the majority against it.[75] This dealt the final blow to the relationship between the Rockinghams and Chatham's city friends, and pressurized Chatham to make a final choice between two not very attractive alternatives. One was the affirmation of his friendship with a small group of radicals in the City of London, and the other was the preservation of the remnants of a now discredited, impotent, and somewhat distant parliamentary alliance. Chatham chose the former. On 1 May he introduced his resolution for the dissolution,[76] declared himself a convert to triennial parliaments, and then began another era of retirement, which was to last almost continuously until the late 1770s, when the misfortunes of the war with America were to bring back a glimmering of hope that this government might eventually be defeated.

Unquestionably, the party least affected by the drastic transforma-
tion of political fortunes in 1771 was the Rockinghams. It is true that
at times they had grown discouraged with the fight in Parliament.
Many of them missed most of the printers' debates, and at one point
during the prosecution of Crosby and Oliver, even Dowdeswell decided to attend "this matter no more, while the guilt or punishment
of Men not allowed the necessary means of defence was in agitation."[77] However, although they had little desire to face constant humiliation in divisions that placed them in minorities that were "not
sometimes above 7 or eight; and never above thirty,"[78] nevertheless,
none of the leading members of the party ever seems to have contemplated abandoning politics. Only Burke, who reported in April that
the "opposition is as much divided and deranged as the Ministry;
and nothing can be in a more distracted state than they stand in at
present,"[79] displayed any noticeable disappointment. Of the rest,
Rockingham was probably the least unhappy. Whereas Chatham,
during the ensuing recess, commented on the "deplorable state of affairs" and bitterly blamed his former allies for having "weakened
Whiggism and rendered national union on revolutionary principles
impossible,"[80] the marquis found contentment in euphonic declarations about his party. "I dont expect much satisfaction in the state of
politicks," he told Burke in December, "except that satisfaction which
I have now often experienced of finding all, the friends I love and Honour, much in the same sentiments and dispositions as they were in
when we last parted. I am not more now than hithertofore a convert
to the doctrine of *Measures* not *Men* and tho' the fruit is not always on
the tree, I shall chuse to continue to cultivate the vine rather than the
thorn in expectation of grapes."[81]

After the Falkland Islands crisis, the only reward any of the opposition connections could realistically hope to achieve in Parliament was
the thanks of one or more public sectors or interests for specific political stands, and the strengthening of their own party ties. For the
Rockinghams alone, this seems to have been enough to overcome the
trauma resulting from the fall to what seemed to be political insignificance. It was both for public recognition and party solidarity that they
made their rather theatrical visit to the Tower after the printers' affair
and that they refused to be dissuaded from their rights of juries legislation. One of the best indications of the Rockinghams' priorities was a
decision they had made in early 1771 to take up the old Middlesex
election issue at virtually every opportunity. As a consequence of this
decision, Dowdeswell, in consultation with Burke and Rockingham,
drew up a bill for "securing the rights of electors."[82] If passed, it would
have returned Wilkes's seat to him. Sir George Savile introduced the

bill in the Commons on 7 February,[83] but it was defeated by 167 to 103. (Savile submitted the same bill in every subsequent session until Wilkes finally took his seat again in 1774.) In the closing days of the session, the party leaders also devised a motion for presentation in the Lords which would have expunged from the journals a resolution of 2 February 1770 by which the members had stated their determination not to interfere with the Commons' actions with respect to the Middlesex election. It was presented by Richmond on 30 April and negatived after a long debate without a division.[84]

The party leaders could not have expected to gain any political advantage by rehashing this issue. They had been warned on a number of occasions that the members in both Houses were no more anxious to revive it now than they had been at the end of the 1770 session. This did not dampen their zeal, however, and they brought forward the motion in the Lords, despite advice such as that from an independent friend, who told Rockingham, "I ... shall be ready to attend, the House ... upon the old desperate subject of the Middlesex Election; It may be right to pursue our Enquiry into that Measure, so very exceptionable as it is, whenever there is an Opportunity; but I own I have not any Prospect but of being struck dumb at once by the old Weight of a dead Majority; the Ministry have been so triumphant over this point that I expect a Horse-laugh at the very mention of it."[85]

By the late spring of 1771, the marquis's viewpoint had changed dramatically from what it had been little more than a year earlier. In his mind, strong government had now become the major threat to the country rather than the potential saviour of it, and he was beginning to see his party as a regular advocate for those whose liberties were under attack. It seemed to him appropriate to bring together the rights of freeholders with those of juries because both had been sacrificed by ministers presiding over a subservient majority in the House of Commons. He saw himself now as an outsider, powerless to stop this process, and he wanted to be sure that his party would have the public recognition it deserved for being among the few who were prepared to shun place and pension in order to fight it. As early as February, he had told Dowdeswell, "I do not expect any great good being carried *into Effect* in *either House of Parliament* in these Times but what I think is very Material is, that our Friends should shew that in their Endeavours, the *Public Advantage* is their object. If we look back for some years ... past all measures which have either been for the security or advantage of the Publick have *originated* & [been] carried into effect by our Friends."[86] This deep-seated concern for the credibility of the party appears to have been the main preoccupation of all the leading Rockinghams even in the period 1769–70 when the union in opposition had seemed to offer them an excellent chance of rising to governmental power and office. They had shown what for them was a great deal of interest in the game of politics at that time; among other things, their contention in the *Thoughts* that it was their "purpose, to pursue every just method to put the men who hold their opinions into such a condition as may enable them to carry their common plans into execution, with all the power and authority of the State,"[87] demonstrates their anticipation that they would consent to form an administration. The relative ease with which the marquis and his friends accepted their political decline in 1771, however, seems to indicate that their earlier ardour had resulted more from a desire to restore the Whig party's former strength and influence than from the offices that might incidentally have resulted. Later, when it was evident that their hopes would not be fulfilled, they refused to feel totally dejected; although they could not expect for the time being to strengthen the party in numbers, they could still work to demonstrate its consistency and integrity to the public and to secure the bonds of mutual esteem and trust which would preserve it in its present form.

To the marquis's euphemisms might be added those of the Duke of Richmond, who in February 1772 told is leader: "We have long lost all hopes from numbers, character alone must support us and that will give us great inward satisfaction but never bring us into power. I confess I despair of that, but do not lament it for I do not think ... it is to be wished ... The utmost of my political wish is to prove the very sincere Friendship I have for you."[88] Similarly, the Duke of Portland commented: "The only hope of ever seeing the credit & character of this Country restord to its antient lustre consists according to my apprehension in a great measure in preserving the small remains of that Party to which we have steadily adhered, & of all the leading members of which [the marquis] most deservedly enjoy[s] the intire confidence."[89] In statements such as these one finds something of the essential quality that would enable the Rockinghams to relax in the role to which by nature and temperament they were best suited – that of a country-party opposition – and to survive many more years of more or less futile manoeuvring in relative political obscurity.

CHAPTER SEVEN

The Influence of the Crown and Religion, 1771–1772

During the summer and autumn of 1771 only in London, where the feuds between the two factions of radicals[1] and attacks by the latter on Trecothick, Baker, and Martin[2] continued to draw attention, did anything of much political interest occur. Elsewhere the nation lapsed into a calm such as had not been experienced for several years. The Rockinghams were able to return to their farms and enjoy the freedom of country life undisturbed by petitions, remonstrances, and the like. The marquis spent most of his time attending to business at Wentworth and following the racing circuit at Newmarket, Doncaster, and elsewhere. Meanwhile, he did not entirely lose contact with the more important members of the party. He entertained, visited, or met with most of them at least once.[3] However, his interests appear to have been more social than anything else, and, in general, he devoted very little time to politics. From a strictly political point of view, prospects for the coming session of Parliament looked anything but good, and towards the end of the year he and his friends considered the possibility of a total secession from Parliament. This would have given the party a form of protest against the government which did not require facing up to the frustrating and arduous task of regularly opposing an apparently unbeatable ministry.

Characteristically, the Rockinghams eventually agreed to something rather less extreme. As Burke later put it, they decided "to attend to circumstances, and to pitch only upon those, where the advantage of situation might supply the want of Numbers, or where, tho' without hope of Victory, you could not decline the combat without disgrace."[4] In other words, they would attend or secede, depending on whether an issue was likely to bring political advantage and public recognition. Rockingham appears to have decided that this justified delaying his move to London indefinitely. When

Dowdeswell arrived in the capital towards the end of December, he was disheartened to discover that his leader was still in Yorkshire and had sent no word of when he might be expected. On the twenty-fourth he dutifully wrote to remind the marquis of his responsibilities: "I do not wonder at your inclination to stay in the country, the season having been so remarkably fine. But business need be done: and it will be hurtful if your Lordship & your Friends are not in town some time before the meeting of parliament ... I know several Members who conjecture from what passes the first day upon the operations of the Session. Therefore, I think the Public interested that your Lordship & your Friends with you, should be here as soon as you can."[5] By this time, Dowdeswell may have realized that something worthy of the party's attentions was beginning to develop as a result of the recent and much-publicized marriage of the king's brother, the Duke of Cumberland.[6] Eventually, this marriage was single-handedly to shake the nation out of its present calm. It would also encourage the Rockinghams to embrace a country-party stance more fervently than ever before.

Cumberland had been married secretly in September, and the public had learned of it sometime in November, shortly after the king had been notified. The union evoked considerable comment because of Cumberland's choice of a bride. She was Mrs Anne Horton,[7] a widow whose father was an Irish peer, Simon Luttrell, Lord Irnham,[8] and whose brother was the same Henry Lawes Luttrell who had displaced John Wilkes in the House of Commons in 1769. Many people considered the marriage scandalous. For a prince and possible heir to the throne to wed a subject (and particularly one such as this) was astonishing. The king himself was horrified. In a letter to his oldest brother, the Duke of Gloucester,[9] on 9 November, he gave his reasons: "In a Country a prince marrying a subject is looked upon as dishonourable, in Germany children of such a marriage cannot succeed to any territories, but here, where the Crown is but too little respected it must be big with the greatest mischiefs. Civil wars would by such measures be again coming in this country, those of the Yorks and Lancasters were greatly owing to intermarriages with the nobility."[10]

Undoubtedly George III would have been even more disturbed if he had known that Gloucester, too, had recently entered into a rather morganatic marriage.[11] Recent research has demonstrated how difficult it was for eighteenth-century society to divest itself of some traditional standards and values.[12] The king's attitude reflected a Shakespearean view still adhered to by many people. Chaos would ensue, it was believed, if degree, priority, and place were disregarded and the "chain of being" broken. When Cumberland's marriage became public knowledge, letters appeared in the newspapers making allusions to Shakespeare's works. "Posterity may see the Royal Diadem torn from a Brunswick's Brow," they warned, "and the Spawn of a Luttrell, like a third Richard, usurp the Throne of these Realms."[13]

If most people in British society disliked Cumberland's marriage, not nearly as many approved of the measure that was brought forth, largely at the instigation of the king, to guard against such occurrences in future. The Royal Marriage Bill, when passed into law after being pushed with great difficulty through both Houses of Parliament in February and March 1772, gave the king new and extensive control over the marriage of members of the royal family. At a stroke, it became illegal for all the descendants of George II who were under the age of twenty-five (except for the children of princesses who had married into foreign families) to marry without the consent of the king. The descendants of George II who were over the age of twenty-five were excused from obtaining consent only if they gave a year's notice and if neither House of Parliament declared its disapprobation. The power given the king was generally considered excessive. The descendants of George II included a large number of people, and as the years went by, they would include a great many more. It was realized that the act could eventually give the king a new form of control over subjects who were far removed from the throne. So besides being considered unfair to the royal family, the act caused great concern because it represented a revival of the influence of the crown in its original and most direct form, prerogative.

Thus, while the bill was being considered in Parliament, a large portion of the nation, including many people who had been shocked at Cumberland's marriage, turned against it. Edward Gibbon[14] gave a fairly accurate description of the strength of public opinion when he observed in late March: "The attention of the Public is much engaged about the Marriage Bill ... I do not remember ever to have seen so general a concurrence of all ranks, parties and professions of men. Administration themselves are the reluctant executors, but the King will be obeyed, and the bill is universally considered as his, reduced into legal or rather illegal form by Mansfield and the Chancellor."[15] The people who opposed the Royal Marriage Bill can largely be divided into two categories. First, there were those who were against the legislation only because they considered it too extreme. Their attitude to the marriage had been antipathetic and they would, at least in principle, have been willing to consider a less extensive form of control over future marriages in the royal family. Secondly, there were those who in principle were against any bill of this nature. They represented the small minority in Great Britain who scoffed at their countrymen's fears of marriages between the royal family and British subjects. "While some People absurdly talk about the Necessity of allying our Blood Royal to the little Princelings of Germany (to the utter Exclusion of our own fair Country-women)," they argued, "let it be remembered, for the Honour of the English Name, that the glorious Elizabeth was Grand Daughter, on the Mother's Side, to a Merchant of London; and that the Revolution itself proceeded from a Marriage between the immortal William, and the Grand Daughter of Lord Clarendon."[16] This group was particularly strong in London, where the reform movement was gaining momentum and where many people were so alienated that they actually enjoyed the king's distress. In December, when Cumberland appeared publicly in the city, it was observed that "the Populace thronged about his chariot, as if the circumstances of his Marriage had made the most surprising alteration in his Person."[17]

For the most part, the Rockinghams fell into the first of these categories. This was demonstrated in a division that was forced in the House of Commons on 11 March. The point in question was whether the Speaker should leave the chair and therefore whether the House should consider the bill at all. In this division only the members who were against the principle of the bill, and not merely its more exceptionable provisions, voted in opposition. As a result, the government succeeded on the motion by the huge majority of 236.[18] A few of the Rockinghams joined the minority, including Sir George Savile, Sir William Meredith, the city radicals, and all the friends of Chatham and Shelburne,[19] but most members of the party followed the lead of William Dowdeswell, Burke, and the Cavendishes and voted with the administration.[20] They appear to have agreed with Burke, who had recently written: "With regard to the preventive Law, I am much for it; if I did not see infinite, and I should fear unsurmountable difficulties, in the manufacture of such a Law."[21] In principle, they did not disagree that some new controls or limitations were needed; they were concerned only about dangerous or unjust ramifications of specific measures.

For the duration of the controversy, the division of 11 March was the only one in which any of the Rockinghams sided with the government. Although they were generally more moderate in their approach than other opposition groups, the leaders of the party were as active as anyone in taking a stand against the provisions that were thought most objectionable. Once the implications of the measure were understood, the marquis, believing that he had a very popular issue, shook off his earlier apathy and took up the fight with a vitality that he had not displayed since the Middlesex election issue or the

Portland-Lowther conflict. He took great pains to get all his supporters to town,[22] and in February and early March, when the bill was in the Lords, he came forth as one of the three or four most frequent speakers on the opposition side, along with Richmond, Shelburne, and Camden, as well as Lyttleton and Temple, who came out of retirement specifically to voice their opinion. Rockingham attacked the bill on two general points, both of which concerned the extraordinary powers allotted to the crown. The first was the "Law Laid down in the Preamble that the controul of marriages in the Royal family was in the King"; the second was "the extent of the power given by this act to the King [since] in 6 or 7 Generations it might take in numbers who could not be looked on as inheritable to the Crown from their great remoteness."[23] Although the opposition members inevitably were beaten in the Upper House, some of the divisions were rather close, and it was noted that at times Rockingham and his allies were supported by "many who were with Government on other occasions, and even some who held employments."[24]

It was, of course, in the House of Commons that the government ran into the most serious difficulties. There, under Dowdeswell's capable leadership, the Rockinghams sided with the other opposition groups and with members of many and diverse political leanings, and "fought the matter inch by inch."[25] Before the bill was passed on 24 March, the administration came very close to defeat on several occasions and at one point experienced a defection in its own ranks of some thirty politicians, according to one estimate.[26] The defectors included Fletcher Norton,[27] the Speaker of the House; Richard Suton,[28] an under-secretary of state; Sir Lawrence Dundas,[29] governor of the Royal Bank of Scotland and a privy councillor; Henry Seymour Conway,[30] who had been secretary of state under both Rockingham and Chatham and was currently a colonel of the Royal Horse Guards and lieutenant-general of the Ordnance; and Charles Vane[31] and the two Walpoles,[32] who were normally regular government supporters. Norton appears to have led the defectors. He joined the opposition on 13 March when Dowdeswell moved to amend the preamble of the bill by leaving out the words "the Right of Controul in the Crown over all the Marriages of the Royal family."[33] Norton supported the motion by a clear enunciation of his fear of the increase in the power of the crown. He said that these words were "a bold assertion of a high Prerogative," and he charged that "to imagine" that the king's control "extends thro' all the descendants of the Royal family in the wide idea of families, is absurd, is Shocking, to every liberal mind."[34] The motion was defeated by only thirty-six votes, and from then until the bill passed, Norton remained in the minority.

To historians interested in the development of the Whig party in the eighteenth century, the most interesting defection from the administration's ranks was that of Charles James Fox – the man who, over the next decade, joined the Rockinghams on a permanent basis and eventually became their most dominating force. Fox resigned from his post as a lord of the Admiralty on 20 February 1772, partly because of his dislike of the Royal Marriage Bill. However, from his own explanation, it is clear that dissatisfaction with the treatment he had received from Lord North was equally important. "I should not have resigned at this moment," he informed a friend, "merely on account of my complaints against Lord North, if I had not determined to vote against this Royal Family Bill, which in place I should be ashamed of doing ... But it is also certain that the bill alone (if I had had no reason to complain of L[or]d N[orth]) would not have made me resign."[35] Fox was angered at North's failure to consult him about government measures, and at his refusal often even to acknowledge applications for favours that Fox had requested for himself and for his family, friends, and political supporters.[36] While the Royal Marriage Bill was in agitation in the Commons, Fox attacked it vehemently and often. However, there was little communication between him and the Rockinghams that directly foreshadowed their future relationship. Fox made it clear that this first flirtation with opposition would be a short one. He thought himself "very safe from going into opposition ... which is the only danger."[37] In January 1773 he rejoined the administration as a lord of the Treasury.

The efforts of the MPs who fought the Royal Marriage Bill were chiefly aimed at limiting the extent of the prerogative powers extended to the king. On 16 March, Dowdeswell introduced a motion that would have changed the age of the members of the royal family whose marriages were to need the sanction of the crown from twenty-five to twenty-one; and another motion that would have substituted the words "child, grandchild and presumptive heir of George the 2nd" for "descendants of George the 2nd."[38] The closest call for the administration came on 23 March, when Rose Fuller,[39] the member for Rye, who had supported the government on most issues since early 1770, moved to restrict the act to the king's lifetime. "It is imprudent for P[arliament] to make a perpetual bill w[ithou]t knowing what the effect will be," he argued. He added that it was "likewise very imprudent" not to ensure that from "time to time" the act would receive a "revue."[40] His amendment was rejected by just eighteen votes.[41]

For a society keenly aware of its seventeenth-century heritage and of the upheavals that were thought to have resulted from Stuart despotism, the word "prerogative" evoked a very emotive reaction.

People felt almost instinctively that it was something to be abhorred. Moreover, to such politicians as the Rockinghams, the apparent attempt to revive prerogative appeared to be part and parcel of the program promulgated by the court in recent years to expand the crown's influence. They were not opposed to giving the king the power to veto the prospective marriages of the few people who had a reasonable chance of ascending the throne; their opposition to the act was based on the fear that it could give the king a form of control over too many people. During a speech in the House of Lords, the marquis pointed out that in an important legal verdict some sixty-five years earlier, the judges had ruled that "care and approbation of marriage includes care of education, and care of education supposes custody of the person." Consequently, he said, "by this Bill, and the reasoning of the Judges ... the King might soon have many thousands of his subjects depending upon him, not only for leave to marry but even for the direction of their education."[42] The feeling, as Burke later stated, was that "the Crown will have from [this measure] ... an improper addition of not the best kind of strength; by creating an entire and slavish dependance upon [it] of a family that may become very numerous."[43] This additional strength it was believed would, like all sources of influence during the current reign, go straight to the support of the court.[44]

The opposition came even closer to defeating the government at times than it had done over the Middlesex election. Moreover, it is beyond doubt that a substantial number of independent members voted in opposition. Even in the minority of 11 March (the only division for which there is a list),[45] there were some ten country gentlemen who were genuinely independent (in the sense that they had no close connections with any of the established political groups, had succeeded in the previous election without financial backing other than their own, and had, throughout their careers, shown no interest in offices under the crown or central government). They included Sir Henry Hoghton,[46] MP for Preston; Sir Thomas Clavering,[47] MP for Durham County; George Jennings,[48] MP for St Germans, and Sir Matthew Ridley,[49] MP for Morpeth. If ten independent members voted against the very principle of the bill at this stage, it would seem logical to infer that they voted in the minority thereafter, and that in fact a number of others joined them against some of the more "obnoxious" provisions.

Considering that the opposition was composed at different times of such a broad spectrum of the Commons membership, the extremely significant question that arises is, Why was North not defeated in at least one or two divisions? On the surface, it looks as if later Whig historians were correct in their belief that the House had become completely subservient to the influence of the crown – that the court's control over it was so extensive that the government could win even when faced with the combined weight of opposition, independents, and a significant slice of its own regular following. There are, however, grounds to suspect that North's ultimate victory was a result of more than just the influence of the crown. In the first place, it is clear that he received some independent backing. This is borne out by extant accounts of the debates, which record speeches in support of the bill by people such as the Tory, William Bagot, who, though a personal friend of North, voted and acted with considerable independence in the House of Commons.[50] It is also borne out by two surveys conducted in early March by John Robinson, the joint secretary to the Treasury.[51] In both cases, Robinson attempted to forecast the way the voting in the Lower House would go. His estimates are by no means completely reliable, since he could not have been totally free of subjectivity in establishing his conclusions, but the second survey was based on the voting in the House of Commons during the first reading of the bill on 4 March, and it therefore represents more than educated guesswork.

Of the members Robinson believed the administration could count on, a number were independents. There were Tories such as Bagot, who had always been anxious to give his support to the government when his conscience permitted; and others such as Sir Edward Blackett,[52] who had voted with the opposition over the Wilkes issue in January 1770 but had begun to support the government with some regularity after being shocked at the city remonstrance in March; and Edward Southwell,[53] who also had voted with the minority in January 1770 and then drawn away from opposition. Men such as these appear to have voted with the government because they were less afraid of the prospect of a revival of prerogative than of the dangers to society arising from intermarriages between the royal family and subjects of the realm. Bagot declared on 13 March that since it was impossible to draw a line defining prerogative, he, "as a commoner," thought it "safer to trust that line with the Crown than ... anywhere else."[54] Without this bill, he believed, "the younger children of the Crown would intermarry with the great families, and the regal and aristocratical powers would oppress the commoners."[55] There is no way of ascertaining exactly what percentage of the independent MPs voted with North throughout, but in view of the fact that even a number of placemen defected at various points and that there was strong feeling on the matter in the nation as a whole, it seems safe to conclude that the percentage was relatively small.

The most important reason for the bill's success was not so much any particular support as the irregular behaviour of many who at one point or another opposed it. When the affair was first considered in the Commons in early March, the total attendance figures usually ranged from 350 to 382. However, as the weeks went by and the House began to examine some of the more exceptionable clauses, the figures dropped considerably and at times fell below 200. During the second half of March, a number of men who constantly acted with the opposition commented on the problems they were having in keeping the minority steady. "I see plainly," an independent spokesman wrote on the twenty-first, "that no Business will keep an opposition together longer than a Single day. People will not attend repeatedly."[56] At about the same time Rockingham told Portland:

We got at least 12 to come to Town & to attend in Monday's debate, yet in the division we were only 160 instead of 164 – which we had been on Friday. Some staid away … & Seven or Eight of the Ministerial Gentry who had been on our Side on Friday – were with the Ministry on Monday … In the different divisions on very Strong Points in the Bill – about 208 – have voted against it … Many begin to feel a little tired & wish to reserve themselves for the 3d reading. I should think if the 208 – were all present … on the third reading – near – 190 – or perhaps more – must Vote ag[ains]t the Bill, if they wish to preserve any Consistency of Conduct.[57]

In the event, Rockingham must have been very disappointed. the 208 did not appear, and his friends were defeated by 54 votes despite the fact that the government could muster only 168. What appears to have happened is that many people who disliked this legislation felt uneasy about voting consistently against Lord North and therefore, after taking the opportunity to record their disapprobation, intentionally did not attend crucial divisions. This seems to have been true even of a number of independent members. By 1772, many of them had drawn close to North, partly because of the excesses of the opposition, and they probably felt it would be imprudent to help the Rockinghams and their allies discredit him. No one failed to realize that the Royal Marriage Bill was important to North's prestige – particularly with the king.[58] The bill had initially come to both Houses of Parliament with a special message from the crown urging its necessity, and the first lord of the Treasury did his utmost to enforce a strict obedience from the placemen in the House of Commons. In February, George III told him, "I have a right to expect a hearty Support from everyone in my Service and shall remember Defaulters."[59]

The Royal Marriage Bill was the only thing of much political significance debated during the 1772 sitting. The two other weighty matters centred on religion. These suggest little about strengths and
weaknesses of opposition and government. However, they are of interest here primarily because they help to confirm the absence of two-
party politics at Westminster. The House of Commons first turned its
attention to religion on 6 February, when Sir William Meredith presented a petition signed by 250 Church of England clerics, calling for
an end to the need to subscribe to the Thirty-nine Articles.[60] This was
largely the work of academics and divines from the University of
Cambridge. The intention was to obtain official recognition that the
Bible alone should be accepted as the basis of Christian belief.[61] The
petition was defeated by a vote of 217 to 71, but not before the objectives that underlay it were discussed thoroughly.

These objectives appealed to people who considered themselves
liberal in religious matters, and the minority, though small, was composed of most of the Rockinghams who attended, virtually all the
Chathams and city radicals, a few independents, and even some government supporters.[62] During the debates, Lord John Cavendish and
Sir George Savile enunciated typical attitudes on the petitioners' side.
Savile was the more assertive. It was time, he felt, to abolish the
Thirty-nine Articles, since the "Scriptures are the only rule to the
church of Christ, and adhering to the Scriptures in opposition to human inventions and corruptions is the first principle of Protestant-
ism."[63] Cavendish, on the other hand, while agreeing that many of
the articles were outdated, contradictory, and "absurd," voted for re-
ceiving the petition merely because he hoped that Parliament might
be able to see them modified.[64]

Those who opposed made little or no attempt to refute the principles of the other side. Instead, they made their stand on the indivisi-
bility of church and state. Articles of subscription, they urged, were
essential to the existence of an established religion without which society would sink into chaos. The most outspoken was Sir Roger Newdigate. How, he asked, could efficacy "be given to a system of religion
without some public form, some general standard of reference established as the basis for the alliance between church and state?" He virtually went so far as to argue that change of any sort in the liturgy of
the church was inadmissible because it would invalidate the Act of
Union.

One of the members of the Rockingham following who voted with
Newdigate was Burke, whose sentiments were "in opposition to the
opinions of nearly all my own party,"[65] Burke was, however, less cautious than Newdigate and the "high church" voice. The Act of Union,

he argued, had "not precluded the possibility of a change in either our civil or ecclesiastical establishments; nor is the King bound by his oath not to listen to the restitution of the purity of the gospel and primitive Christianity."[66] Burke conceded that the Thirty-nine Articles might be changed once a majority of the clergy desired it. However, he was as concerned as anyone about the harm that the rejection of the articles would do to the preferred position of the Church of England. At great length, he warned against the upheavals that might follow the abandonment of "some criterion of faith more brief, more precise and definite than the scripture for the regulation of the priesthood."

A second major debate on religion occurred as a result of a petition requesting that Protestant dissenting clergy and teachers in England be given relief from the Thirty-nine Articles, to which the Toleration Act compelled them to subscribe. The petition was presented on 3 April by Henry Hoghton, an independent country gentleman and himself a dissenter.[67] Because it gave MPs a chance to demonstrate their toleration, it received nearly unanimous approval in the House of Commons, and a bill to fulfil its requests was allowed to pass quickly and easily through three readings. The only real opposition came from Newdigate, Bagot, and a few others, who again believed that they were protecting the principle of establishment. Lord North was urged by the king to "oppose it in every stage, which will give you the applause of the established church."[68] But he discovered that the opposition were "all united in favour of it, and one half of the friends of Government will either stay away or vote with the Opposition."[69] Therefore, he prudently decided not to stand in its way. Burke again took an active part, but this time he disagreed with those who felt there was a potential threat to the church. He reminded the House that "the very principle of toleration is that you will tolerate, not those who agree with you in opinion, but those whose religious notions are totally different." Although the Dissenters' Relief Bill met little opposition in the House of Commons, it was defeated in the Lords by the combined weight of the administration, with the notable exception of Lord Mansfield (who was an advocate of relief)[70] and the Anglican hierarchy.[71] Hoghton submitted the bill again, in a slightly revised form, during the next session with the same results. The requested relief was finally granted in 1779.[72]

The debates on religion in 1772 demonstrate relative ideological uniformity at Westminster. In the national theatre, where Anglicans so vastly predominated, only a few opposed the twin pillars of mainstream philosophy: an established church, and toleration to the dissenting faiths that did not threaten it.[73] On the first bill, the positions of Newdigate, Burke, and Cavendish differed only in degree. They all believed that articles of faith were necessary to define the established religion and distinguish it from others. What divided them was simply the question of whether or not the Thirty-nine Articles should be changed and by what method. Although they voted on different sides, Burke and Cavendish were very close to each other on this. They were also closer to Newdigate and some of the Tories, who were unwilling to modify the articles, than they were to Savile and other Whigs, who were prepared to dispense with them.[74] The men in the latter group carried on the doctrines of "radical country Whigs" from earlier in the century.[75] They represented a small minority in propertied Anglican society who were prepared to separate church and state and see the end of establishment.[76]

On the other bill, Savile, Cavendish, Burke, the vast majority in opposition, and many in administration stood together. In this case, Newdigate and the high church Tories were in a small minority. They, presumably like the king, saw the extension of the principle of toleration as a potential threat to the mother church. The point of disagreement between them and the majority was not, however, substantive. Few if any in the House would have disclaimed toleration. All they were debating was whether it was propitious now to extend the principle. The majority believed it was. Twenty years later, however, many had lost their enthusiasm.[77] Their attitude was essentially the same as Burke's. Throughout the 1770s and into the 1780s, Burke took up the fight on behalf of religious minorities on several occasions. For instance, he actively support Savile's Catholic Relief Act in 1778 and the bill for the relief of dissenters in 1779.[78] However, the quest for better treatment of minorities was always secondary to his concern for the union between the Church of England and the state. Consequently, the fears for the established order which accompanied the French Revolution dampened his zeal.[79] He turned diametrically against measures for relief of nonconformist groups at home, because it seemed clear that they were bent on the destruction of all establishments – ecclesiastical and political alike.[80] There was no fundamental inconsistency here. In 1772 most Anglicans agreed that reform was acceptable only when it was compatible with the principle of union between church and state. It is logical that when reform no longer seemed compatible, they ceased to support it.

Recent scholarship has demonstrated that, in some borough constituencies, dissenters consistently tended to align their cause with Whigs before the American Revolution.[81] Thus, religion seems to have blended with and even solidified a traditional two-party competition. This was hardly the case in the House of Commons early in

George III's reign. There, relative homogeneity prevented a polarization from occurring, and lines between Whigs and Tories, administration and opposition, and personal followings were crossed with impunity. When divisions were taken, there had to be two sides with respect to a proposed piece of legislation. But rather than reflecting opposite views, the two sides represented various shades of opinion, most of which accepted both establishment and toleration. It took the cataclysmic events in France in 1789 and afterwards to change this situation, causing Burke and other conservative voices, both Whig and Tory, to rally to the Pitt administration.[82] Then, and only then, did religion help to produce the kind of cleavage in propertied society that could fuel two-party politics in Westminster.

In general, the debates on religion in 1772 were of little overall consequence to the fortunes of opposition. The fact that Burke and most of the other members of the Rockingham connection were on different sides at one point and were together at another did not affect their future relations. Because religion was not a heated party issue at this level, people were expected to voice their feelings as individuals. Rather than religion, it was the Royal Marriage Act that was to have an effect on the historical development of the Whig party.

Notwithstanding the actual explanation for their defeat, the Rockinghams saw this episode principally as confirmation of their belief that the influence of the crown had weighted the system too heavily in favour of the administration. As in the 1770 session, the marquis and his friends had gone into battle with everything on their side, yet once again they had failed to defeat the government in even a single division in the House of Commons. To the central core of the party, this was simply evidence that North had been able to use patronage to insulate himself from the will of the nation. After the Royal Marriage Act passed into law, the Rockinghams frequently lamented, both privately and in public, the growth of the "Immense & dangerous influence of the Crown."[83] "It has long Appeared," wrote Burke in June, "upon a Multitude of Trials and upon a variety of matters, that there is a determined, Systematical, and considerable majority in both houses in favour of the Court Scheme; an unremitted fight would only serve to exhibit a longer series of defeats."[84] By the summer of 1772, the Rockinghams were assuming the perspective as well as the leading basic premises of earlier country politicians, who like them had struggled from the outside against seemingly unassailable regimes.

CHAPTER EIGHT

The Rockinghams and the Influence of the Crown, 1772–1773

The effects of the Royal Marriage Act in the development of the Rockinghams' constitutional opinion were substantially magnified by a major crisis that began to divert the nation's attention just as the furore over royal matrimony was beginning to subside. The new crisis was a product of the near financial collapse of the East India Company. Eventually, it forced the Rockinghams, against formidable odds (and consequently to some extent with a sense of martyrdom), to defend with all their heart a traditional country-party position in Parliament and in the nation at large.

The East India Company was just beginning to gain public interest as the Rockinghams sought the sanctuary of their country estates at the close of the 1771–72 parliamentary session, and for some time the affair did not interrupt their private lives. Eventually, however, the company's problems had to be dealt with at the national level, and they drew the party into one of the most painful and emotive conflicts ever with the North ministry. A close examination of the Rockinghams' activities demonstrates that, in formulating their policy, they almost totally ignored the immediate political aspirations of their party. They gave up all chance of victory in Parliament, they combated both the administration and their major allies in opposition, and they found themselves at odds with a significant portion of the East India Company men too. They also did their reputation considerable harm, both within Parliament and outside it. Since the Falkland Islands crisis, the party leaders had shifted their focus from political expediency to credibility with the nation at large. Now they seemed to turn their back on both. The simple explanation is that, by 1772, neither of these concerns any longer competed in the Rockinghams' minds with the commitment they had made to oppose the undue influence of the crown. It is only by understanding this that the importance of the East India Company affair in redefining them as an antiministerial connection can be grasped.

The basic facts behind the East India Company issue are well documented.[1] By 1772, the company had been almost completely discredited in England. Its ignominy had resulted from two major factors. The first was a violent and bitter press campaign against the former governor, Robert Lord Clive,[2] which convinced the British public that the company's servants in India were generally a "crew of monsters."[3] The second was a set of grave financial problems, which became public knowledge just as the campaign against Clive reached its height. In 1773 Parliament was forced to subsidize the company heavily and, partly because of public criticism, to impose reforms that provided for regular government intervention in its affairs. An act of May 1773 gave the company tariff concessions on the export of its huge stocks of tea in England; the Loan Act, in June, approved a loan to the company of £1,400,000 at 4 per cent interest, placed severe restraints on its annual dividend, and established other financial reforms; and the Regulating Act, in the same month, brought about changes in the company's administration, both at home and in India, which made it more accountable to Parliament.

The majority of company stockholders were anything but happy with these measures. They believed that both the Loan Act and the Regulating Act were arbitrarily imposed and represented infringements of chartered rights. However, public opinion was completely against them, and the Rockinghams stood almost alone in helping them achieve more favourable terms and in resisting the principle of permanent government intervention in a chartered corporation. The Rockinghams' decision to take this approach was not arrived at without considerable anxiety. The leading members of the party had always considered propertied-class support crucial to their policies. "We have nothing but ourselves & public opinion to trust," the marquis once told Portland. "I think we have more of the Publick Opinion in our Favor (than any other Men have) & I am pleased with the Expectation that our Conduct will always be such, as to Increase the opinion formed and never to give Cause for its being Less."[4] Yet in this affair, he and his supporters felt compelled to make a stand that could only gain them public disapproval. It is clear, moreover, that they were not influenced by private pecuniary motives.

It has been argued that some of the important members of the party may have had substantial holdings in East India Company stocks and that they opposed the general principle of intervention because they feared from the beginning that the government would want to impose new limitations on the company's dividend – a measure that would likely have adverse effects on the value of their stocks.[5] A scrutiny of the East India Company stock ledgers,[6] however, demonstrates that the members of the party who usually participated in its decision-making process had little or nothing at stake financially.[7] Of much more importance in encouraging the leaders to side with the East India Company were their past commitments. In 1767, when the Chatham administration had made the original threat of government intervention, the Rockinghams had committed themselves to stand for the rights of chartered companies, and they had continued to do so between then and the autumn of 1772.[8] Even more to the point, the defence of the East India interest had, over the years, become inextricably entwined with the long-standing country principle of resistance to increases in crown patronage.

As early as 1768 the Rockinghams and others had used the principle of opposition to the undue influence of the crown in their attempts to prevent the government from meddling in the company's affairs. Opposition spokesmen had claimed that government intervention had to be resisted because it would give the ministers of the day, acting as the representatives of the crown, an opportunity to control and pressurize the directors, proprietors, and servants of this huge mercantile community, many of whom held seats in the House of Commons.[9] In only one respect did this diverge from the traditional country approach. It is well known that the country element in the House of Commons had been most vociferous throughout the eighteenth century in denouncing such great chartered corporations as the Bank of England, the South Sea Company, and the East India Company itself. However, the country spokesmen had been opposed to these corporations for the very same reason that the Rockinghams had chosen to protect them. They believed that the partnership which the companies had forged between the government of the day and specific commercial interests was likely to provide for a dangerous expansion of crown influence. They regularly pointed out that men who were employed by or had invested in these companies felt themselves to be unavoidably dependent on the good will of the ministry, because of their need to secure charters, monopolies, and other favours which the crown alone could provide. This was exactly the argument the Rockinghams used in the late sixties and early seventies. They defended a corporation which earlier country politicians had denounced, because they felt that government intervention would necessarily make the relationship between ministers and the company more profound and direct. If ultimately their principles induced them to make a response that would at one time have been unlike a country response, the principle itself was undeniably based on a widely recognized country tradition.

It is plain that before the opening of Parliament in November, the Rockinghams felt obliged above all to resist any measures that might augment the crown's influence. In October, Rockingham foresaw that the government would respond to the company's distress not only by imposing reforms but also by attempting to establish some permanent controls. He told Burke that he considered it "very probable that the subministers and the Lesser tools of ministry will highly arraign the conduct of E[ast] India affairs, which have drawn the Company's finances into this dilemma and may very plausibly urge that it is become very necessary that Government should have an immediate and intimate connexion with all the affairs of the Company."[10] Rockingham realized that this would bring his party's principle to the fore. He said, in the same letter, that he was "afraid the *public at large* will not be disinclined to the E[ast] India Company running into debt providing the ... money is paid to the Revenue, and for the same reasons, will be too apt to concur and to suffer Government to intermeddle in the very interior of the Company's affairs. All thinking men must already acknowledge that the influence of the Crown and the means of corruption are become very dangerous to the Constitution and yet the enormous addition of power, which Government are aiming at, by subjecting the E[ast] India Company to their control, does not strike and alarm so much as it ought." Dowdeswell[11] and the Duke of Portland[12] enunciated views very similar to these, and even Sir George Savile, who detested the East India Company and refused to join in its defence, expressed fears of the "*constitutional* consequences [of] giving up the management of the East Indies to Government."[13] As Professor Bowen has recently noted,[14] Burke at this point confessed that he knew little about Indian affairs. Characteristically, he agreed to take whatever line his colleagues felt was right.[15] This included supporting the "Province and Duty of Parliament to superintend the affairs of this Company."[16] Arguably, if Dowdeswell and the marquis had thought it appropriate, they could have persuaded Burke to produce a measure like the East India Bill that he eventually promoted in 1783.[17] However, it is equally clear that Burke, too, was extremely concerned about the possibility of the company's revenues and patronage falling "into the Hands of the Crown."[18]

The central figures in the party (presumably, including Burke) seem eventually to have realized that almost any sort of intervention by Parliament or the ministry in the affairs of the East India Company could result in the expansion of the crown's influence. This placed them in a rather serious dilemma. They understood that because of public prejudice against the East India Company, their popularity would suffer if they came to its defence. They also knew that they would have little chance of gaining support for their stand from other groups and interests in Parliament.[19] However, they could not escape their principles. The archetypal country-party country gentleman that Sir Lewis Namier described[20] came into Parliament above all to demonstrate his virtuous devotion to pristine values in face of the corruption and vulgarity of the court. The Rockinghams were much the same. When they saw that a principle to which they had voiced allegiance in the past was involved, they considered it impossible to turn their backs, no matter how uncomfortable it made them. This did not of course mean that they had to be very energetic. In late 1772, their initial response was to seek ways in which they could get their position on public record without going to great lengths to fight a potentially frustrating battle in Parliament. It was with this possibility in mind that Rockingham, expressing concern at the "awkward situation," began once again to contemplate the idea of a general party secession from Parliament[21] – an idea with which Dowdeswell, the Duke of Richmond, and Burke readily agreed.

When Dowdeswell, Richmond, and Burke discussed Rockingham's proposal among themselves, they decided that secession should be "enter'd into unanimously and with Spirit"[22] as a public demonstration of their views. This proved impossible, partly because of Rockingham's characteristic country-gentleman qualities. Burke and Dowdeswell wanted a meeting of all the party supporters at Harrowden or London in order to bring them into the plan.[23] But Rockingham "consider'd the matter over and over ... without decision"[24] and in the end did nothing. As late as 17 November he informed Dowdeswell, "I do not feel myself at all so established in Health, as to enable me to come" to a meeting.[25] Thereafter, the idea of secession was abandoned.

Partly as a consequence of Rockingham's indecision, the party was totally unprepared when Parliament reconvened. On the opening day, Burke, Portland, and Savile were the only leading members of the party who even appeared. Savile had no intention of taking a stand, and he soon returned to the country. Portland confessed, "What should be done, except keeping the affairs of the Company out of the power of the Crown I scarcely have any formed idea upon; how to effect that ... I am as much at a loss."[26] At this stage, Dowdeswell was content "staying quietly [at home] ... and leaving the conduct of business in Parliament to the King's Ministers."[27] He finally appeared about a week late.[28] Rockingham himself stayed at Wentworth enjoying bad health until well into the new year.[29] The

Duke of Richmond, the man who was soon to take up the opposition attack on behalf of the East India Company with more enthusiasm than anyone else in England, was hunting and entertaining guests at his Goodwood estates. He resisted Burke's efforts to coax him to London with the argument that any opposition to government on this issue was hopeless and would serve no purpose. "You laugh at me for staying a foxhunting" he wrote. "I would give that up or any Thing else to do real publick good, but to do none I am unwilling to break up a Party of My Friends and Neighbours."[30]

While the overall attendance of party members improved very little during the session, a small group of the leaders did, after a poor start, turn out quite regularly. In the Commons, Dowdeswell and Burke spoke in many of the debates, and they received fairly regular support from Lord John Cavendish. In the Lords, the Duke of Richmond became energetic enough, after his late arrival, to all but make up for the fact that he did not receive a great deal of help from the rest of his aristocratic friends. The stand they took was simply that defined by Dowdeswell – that "the Company had a right by charter to conduct its own affairs as to itself appeared most just and reasonable."[31] When they could not denounce a government measure for taking powers "out of those hands in wh[ich] the authority has vested them, and transfer[ring] them to the Crown,"[32] they labelled it unfair or an invasion of chartered rights.

The party spokesmen were able to find few allies in Parliament. Their relations with the Chathams continued to deteriorate. It was Chatham's administration that had made the initial intervention in the company's affairs in 1767, and therefore it was convenient for his followers to give up opposition on this issue. They supported most of the administration's measures in the Commons and concentrated on attacking the company for corruption.[33] The Rockinghams were alienated from some of their friends as well. Among these, four MPs who had risen to influence in the House of Commons – Lord George Germain, Charles Wolfran Cornwall,[34] and the two Thomas Townshends[35] – all separated permanently from the party while this issue was before Parliament. None of these men had been devoted Rockinghams, but they had supported the party from time to time. Undoubtedly, this issue made their decision to sever their connection with it a relatively easy one.

The party was unable to gain support even from many East India Company men in the Commons. Of the twelve members who in recent years had been company directors, only two were at all active on the opposition side.[36] Even Sir George Colebrooke and Robert Gregory, who normally followed the Rockinghams in Parliament, did little or nothing to help the party or cooperate with it. Similarly, only three or four out of eleven nabobs were at all helpful.[37] There was, in fact, a good reason why these men were reluctant to ally their efforts with those of the Rockinghams. Their company's troubles were taking up a great deal of Parliament's time and costing the British taxpayers and their own stockholders a substantial amount of money. Everybody, therefore, wanted to pin responsibility for the unhappy situation on someone. The company's present and former servants in India were being assailed in the press and scrutinized by a select committee in the House of Commons,[38] and there was considerable speculation against the directors.[39] Clearly, therefore, neither set had anything to gain by drawing the ire of the administration.

The alignment of forces in Parliament had one other rather ironic aspect. The representatives of radical opinion in metropolitan London supported the opposition.[40] Radical London opinion had traditionally shared country animosity towards government-sanctioned monopolies, and in the sixties it had been responsible, under Lord Mayor William Beckford's leadership, for a considerable amount of public criticism of the East India Company in particular.[41] However, like the Rockinghams, London radicalism had also been a staunch advocate of the doctrine of resistance to the undue influence of the crown. Therefore, London and the Rockinghams had something in common by 1772, and even city politicians such as John Sawbridge and James Townsend, who normally supported Chatham and Shelburne in the Commons, now joined forces with the Rockinghams in defence of chartered rights.

The London politicians were a very small group in the Lower House, and their help was of little immediate consequence. In fact, the total opposition was able to offer only slight resistance. During the passage of the Restraining Bill in December, the Rockinghams forced one division in the Lords and two in the Commons and lost them by votes of 26 to 6,[42] 114 to 45,[43] and 153 to 28,[44] respectively. These results were indicative of things to come. During the debates on the resolutions in the Commons that were to make up the Loan and Regulating Acts, they did not bother to attempt even one more division. The Duke of Richmond, when he at last managed to get to town, led a hard-fought and spirited campaign against the Regulating Act in the East India Company's General Court of Proprietors. For a short period he managed to draw the support of the majority, but in the end he achieved little of consequence except the abandonment of clauses that seemed directly to challenge the company's right to its territorial acquisitions and revenues.[45] Rockingham threw himself fully into the parliamentary battle against the bill in May and

June, and he wrote to many of his rank and file to persuade their attendance. The fact that the bill passed the Commons on 10 June by a vote of 131 to 21,[46] and the Lords on 19 June by 74 to 17,[47] demonstrates that his endeavours were largely in vain.

At the end of the session, the Rockinghams had little to be happy about. They had been humiliated by their lack of strength in Parliament, they had been totally alienated from the other major opposition party, they had lost some close friends, and they had found themselves in opposition to many of the men whose cause they thought they were championing. The only success they could claim was on a side issue, and this success was neither completely their own nor of much value to them. In the Commons in May, they had helped exonerate Clive from the allegations of the select committee.[48] Evidence suggests that here, too, the party was motivated chiefly by principle. The leaders had refused from the beginning to go along with the attack on company servants, because they saw it as part of a government conspiracy to take possession of the patronage of the company. As Rockingham argued:

The East India directors, & the Ministry join in proving the Misconduct, & Rapaciousness of the ... Company's Servants in India ... The Result will naturally be, that *Parliament* – ie the *Ministry* must take the Super direction of the E: I: Company's Affairs. The Lucrative offices, & Appointments relating to the E.I: Company's Affairs will virtually fall into the Patronage of the Crown, Such an Addition to the ways & means of Corruption which is at least equal to all the appointments of the Crown – In Army – Navy – & Revenue, Church & C must be felt, when already what the Crown possesses in Patronage has nearly overbalanced the Boasted Equipage of this Constitution ... The danger is Imminent I Fear unavoidable.[49]

In Burke's case, the defence of Clive is a direct contrast to the position he was to take many years later, when he not only spearheaded the impeachment of Governor General Warren Hastings[50] but assailed the company's employees at all levels for corruption in India.[51] It is clear, however, that the contrast is not indicative of any real change in Burke's attitude towards the nabobs. He was as convinced of their guilt in the earlier period as he was later.[52] In November 1772 he told Rockingham that the company's "present embarrassment is not from a defect of substance, but merely from a difficulty with regard to Cash: Into this difficulty they never could have fallen by the mismanagements of their servants abroad, though these have been, I make no Doubt, very considerable and very culpable."[53] Burke refrained for the most part from attacking the servants publicly only because, like the other leading members of his party, he feared that the government would use evidence of wrongdoing as an excuse to take over the company and expand the patronage of the crown.

After studying this affair, one might well feel justified in doubting whether the Rockinghams could be considered to have made a party stand at all, since their effort was seemingly so irresolute. The division lists in the House of Commons demonstrate that many members of the party attended irregularly or not at all. Even Burke, who worked more energetically than any of the others except perhaps Richmond, periodically retreated from the Commons and from his work with the proprietors.[54] There is no question, however, that all the important members of the party did believe it was their responsibility to support the principle to which they had committed themselves in the past. This responsibility was not neglected, despite the unattractive odds they faced within Parliament and the unsympathetic atmosphere outside it. If the Rockinghams were sometimes less than enthusiastic, mainly because they found it difficult to face up to the hopeless task of opposition, they made their position clear when suitable opportunities presented themselves. There can be little doubt, moreover, that many of the rank and file supported party policy and the central principle on which it was based. Thus, for instance, when Viscount Torrington[55] first heard that Parliament was being summoned, he told Portland, "I suppose East India Busyness is the cause ... We ought to take care, and be prepared, as I daresay, Government wishes to have ... their Emoluments, which however badly managed, they may be at present, doth not affect the constitution of this country, which It certainly could, if at the disposal of the Crown."[56]

Rockingham himself was not as energetic as he might have been.[57] However, he did not hesitate to make his position known,[58] primarily because he believed that a day would come when people would thank the party for attempting to protect the constitution. At the end of the session, he and his colleagues in the House of Lords submitted a protest that publicly clarified their position: "If the boundless fund of Corruption furnished by this Bill to the Servants of the Crown should efface every Idea of Honour, Publick Spirit, and Independence from every Rank of People; after struggling vainly against these Evils, we have nothing left but the Satisfaction of recording our Names to Posterity as those who resisted the Whole of this iniquitous system."[59] Considering the strength of public feeling and the force of political pressures, it is really quite extraordinary that the party took such steps.

One would have little choice but to speak in very laudatory terms of the Rockinghams' actions if one believed that the competition for power was important to them.[60] They unquestionably risked doing considerable long-term damage to their political future in order to stand up for their principles. What their performance could be used to demonstrate, however, is how little they really cared about the struggle for office. In all their correspondence before and during the session, none of them ever suggested that they should modify their stand against the influence of the crown in order to accommodate political circumstances. Very early in the fight, the Duke of Portland, for one, described the party's responsibilities in words that seem directly to indicate a country-party sense of priorities. The "formation of any plan will be attended with infinite difficulties," he warned. "That *immediate* popularity may be risked I can not deny, but at the same time I recur to the principles of our Union as a Party & upon that ground I think I see that the popularity of the day has never been courted by Us, that Difficulties have never been tamely submitted to. That we have been satisfied with the consciousness of having done what was right & that *That* was the only rule for our conduct."[61]

When it was all over, the party leaders – except perhaps Burke and Richmond, who continued gallantly but futilely to lead a rearguard action in the general court[62] – appear to have been a rather contented group of losers. To them, as to many country politicians, the fact that they had been able to seize an opportunity to demonstrate support for principle was far more important than the loss of political advantage. In July 1773, Dowdeswell was positively glowing with pride. Interestingly, he, like Burke, realized that the Rockinghams' relative freedom from the lure of place and pension gave them advantages over other followings when it came to standing up for principles. "Our indifference to the emoluments of office," he wrote, "except where they may be accompanied also by the honour of it, our steady & temperate adherence to our principles, whether in place or in opposition, do not suit Gentlemen who are anxious for the profits of office & indifferent to the means of obtaining it."[63] Dowdeswell, the one-time Tory, had been with the Rockinghams almost from the beginning. He had watched the ambitious politicians desert them in 1766. He had observed how different the marquis's priorities were from those of the old Duke of Newcastle. And he had seen politically motivated connections like those of the Duke of Bedford and George Grenville defect to the court. If he believed that the Rockinghams were significantly less concerned than other connections about the attractions of office, he had solid grounds for coming to that conclusion.

It would perhaps be going too far to argue that the marquis and his friends actually wanted to avoid political power. They did, after all,

form two administrations of their own. They knew that the Whigs
had originally established their influence in the nation at least partly
on the basis of "long possession of Government,"[64] and they were
certainly resentful of George III for presiding over the decline of the
Whigs.[65] It is evident, on the other hand, that Burke was not far off
the mark when he estimated that "honest disinterested intentions,
plentiful fortunes, assured rank, and quiet homes" had left all the
leading members of the party "but indifferently qualifyd for storming
a Citadel."[66] Two years before Rockingham's death, Charles James
Fox, the man who was to succeed him, complained, "You think you
can best serve the country by continuing in a fruitless opposition, I
think it is impossible to serve it at all but by coming into power."[67]
These two men could not have been less alike. Fox was a politician
who desperately needed high office. Rockingham was the leading figure in a connection of country aristocrats and gentlemen who had little difficulty living without it.

The marquis and his friends cannot be described simply as a country connection by 1773. Nor should they be used as evidence to substantiate the existence of a genuine country party in eighteenth-
century politics. They remained committed, as will be seen, to a court
Whig constitutional ideology. Moreover, they were far too loyal to
their party. Country-party politicians are supposed to have been independent in every sense of the term. We have learned to believe that
they were free to decide all issues without concern not only about the
pursuit of place and pension but about political allegiances. No one
could claim that the Rockinghams fulfilled the latter require-
ment.[68] Yet it is also clear that in their day-to-day political activities
the Rockinghams displayed most of the characteristics of a country
party, and that through their large following they did a great deal to
keep the essential country traditions alive and well in British politics.
Modern scholarship has recently made public two essays on party
written in the early 1760s by the Tory country gentleman Sir Roger
Newdigate. In one of these essays, Newdigate wrote the following
description of Whigs in reply to a writer's claim that the majority in
British society were of that party:

"If by Whigs he means the friends of liberty of the constitution rather than of
the person or family of any King whatsoever he is right. They are and always
will be the majority of the nation, being composed of the moderates of both
parties who successively opposed the attempts of both Whig and Tory administrations to advance prerogative upon the ruin of liberty from the reign
of the first Charles to this day ... Virtue unblemished ... acting according to
the spirit of liberty and the constitution ... disdaining corruption because its

[*sic*] needs it not and seeking no interests but the interests of the whole people of Great Britain, will always be supported by the majority of this kingdom."[69]

This explanation implies that there was a considerable body of men in eighteenth-century politics who went into Parliament not for place and pension, but mainly to demonstrate their devotion to principle and their concern for the constitution. Whether a large number of them ever remained uncommitted to party or connection or to an alliance of one form or another is a matter of conjecture. What seems evident, however, is that a substantial proportion of them were country-party types who felt varying degrees of commitment either to Whigs or to Tories. In normal circumstances, these men were likely to vote roughly on the basis of party affiliation. Thus, many of the Whigs among them tended to support the oligarchy under the first two Hanoverians and then to oppose the governments of both North and Pitt. The Tories tended to oppose the Whig oligarchy and to support both North and Pitt. However, because of their disinterested approach, no government could afford to take any of them for granted. This Walpole discovered during the excise crisis, and North discovered it when the American war was lost. At such times (and also on occasions when opposition spokesmen called for a reduction of government corruption and spending), both Whigs and Tories of the country variety had a tendency to vote the same way. The marquis and his friends were country politicians with a strong Whig bias, just as Newdigate and his friends were country politicians with a Tory bias. The Rockinghams, however, suffered from a rather severe identity crisis because their party allegiance was to a connection which in the not very distant past had been considered a creature of the court.

The East India Company issue did more than anything the Rockinghams had ever experienced to confirm and strengthen the country side of their character. At the beginning of their long term in opposition, their feeling of kinship with the court Whigs had forced them to consider themselves as future ministers.[70] This perspective had weakened significantly with the party's decline and defeat in the House of Commons between 1770 and 1772. The East India Company issue in a sense put the finishing touches to it. The Rockinghams did not altogether lose their sense of identification with the court Whigs in 1773. Indeed, their value system would always be deeply affected by some important ideals they derived from their predecessors.[71] But in the formulation of party political activities and in their day-to-day reaction to events, their country-party mentality was to predominate for the remainder of their time in the political wilderness. The marquis and his friends had lost parliamentary battles against the North government on a regular basis since 1770, but never quite as decisively over a prolonged period as in this particular affair. In the previous session, crucial divisions in the Commons had produced government majorities by as few as eighteen votes.[72] Now, however, government support was so great and the opposition so badly discredited and split that the Rockinghams realized there was no way they could defeat North in the House of Commons in normal circumstances. This lifted from their shoulders as never before the responsibility of carrying on the quest for power, and it allowed them to relax in a role to which by nature and temperament they were better suited.

The East India issue was a milestone in the Rockinghams' development of country-party qualities, because it profoundly reinforced their distrust of the central government. Historians observing the Whig party in later years under Fox and Earl Grey have described the "neurotic fear of the court – and deep ... suspicion of executive power"[73] that were fundamental to the development of the parliamentary reform program. The Rockinghams' support for the policy of opposition to the undue influence of the crown in the early 1770s shows that this fear and suspicion had a long tradition within the Whig party. The East India affair was certainly not the only factor that prompted the Rockinghams to take up this principle. They had been doing so increasingly in their political activities before 1772. But it is evident that this issue represents the culmination of an important stage in their development in that, from then on, the principle became the central pillar in their political platform.

During the early years of the American Revolution, the marquis was to attend the House of Lords only sporadically, and his speeches were infrequent and for the most part brief. However, the one subject that could still rouse his interest and emotion was government waste and corruption. In 1777, for instance, when Parliament was asked to pay the arrears in the civil list, he responded with a long and emotional speech, urging that "a further increase of the present overgrown influence of the Crown, would ... enable the Ministers to carry on the delusive system which has been fatally adopted and which ... must tend to the ruin ... of this once great empire."[74] The concern evident in his correspondence in these years demonstrates something of an obsession. Over and over again, he warned his friends that his "Majestys Advisers" feared "the Influence of the Crown getting out of their Hands."[75] Similarly, he warned: "Causes of the increase of the power and influence of the Crown (which I take to be the grand disorder of the State) are by no means latent, but are easily traced to have arisen from various new Circumstances."[76] When British reversals in the American Revolutionary War brought back hope of victory against the North regime, this part of the Rockinghams' platform was to emerge more clearly than any other. Ultimately, it would temper their court Whig defensiveness towards the system just enough to allow them to take the historic step of committing the party to moderate measures of amendment. Consequently, in 1780 they gave their staunch support to John Dunning's[77] famous motion in the House of Commons, which declared "that the influence of the Crown has increased, is increasing and ought to be diminished,"[78] and they also promulgated their program of "economical reform." The East India Company issue completed the process of weaving this traditional country-party antiministerial principle into the fibre of their political ideology. As such, it played an important role in the transition through which the conservative court Whigs of their past became the reformist Whigs of their future.

The Rockingham Whigs in 1773

The most prolonged, aggressive, and determined political battle ever waged by Rockingham began just a few weeks after his party's humiliating defeat in Parliament over the East India Company affair. To anyone concerned about analyses of the marquis's character, one of the most interesting facets of his energetic performance in this battle is that it originated almost entirely in personal economic considerations. Through it, as Rockingham well knew, there was little chance of altering the course of his party's decline in the House of Commons or of redeeming his party with the nation at large. The virtually complete success he attained, however, demonstrates that when really animated, he had the ability to become a much more powerful force in the general realm of politics than he had been during the past few years.

On 4 September the marquis received a letter from one of his close friends, Lord Bessborough,[1] warning him of a proposal in the Irish Parliament to tax the estates of absentee landlords. According to the information, North and his cabinet had recently promised that if such a tax was to receive the approval of the Irish Parliament in its next sitting, the Privy Council would advise the king to assent to it.[2] Since the annual rent from Rockingham's extensive holdings in Ireland was about £10,000,[3] the effects of such a tax on his income would be significant if not critical. At first, however, he was inclined to take Bessborough's warning lightly:

I confess I do not feel much alarm'd: I think an old Friend & acquaintance of your Lordships and mine [Lord Mansfield], whose weight in Council is great, would never suffer such an Invasion of Justice, Equity & Policy ... I own the more I consider this matter the less likely it appears to Me that an English Privy Council could dare to advise the Kings Assent – I cannot help thinking that there is a little degree of Trick in its having been so strongly stated to

Your Lordship; for undoubtedly the Ministry here will wish that if it is proposed in Ireland, it May be objected to, by Your Lordships Friends there; & it will sufficiently answer the good purpose of Ministers here, if they can create confusion among all Parties in Ireland.[4]

At the same time, he made it clear that if "this measure should be taken in Ireland," he would "lose no time in coming to London" to fight it. When Bessborough wrote back and told him that there was "not the least doubt"[5] that the measure was in the offing, Rockingham kept his promise.

Immediately, he gave up the country life and set out for the capital. In a matter of days he met with Burke,[6] and the two began an intensive campaign to influence as many people and interests as possible against the proposed tax. The first thing they did was discuss the matter with four other English aristocrats who had a large vested interest in the affair, including the Earl of Upper Ossory[7] who was normally a government supporter (and who appears to have been Bessborough's original source). They then sent a communal letter to North, requesting "Authentick Information Concerning a Matter in which we are so nearly Concerned" and stating the intention to "pursue every legal method of Opposition to a project in every light so unjust and Impolitick."[8] They and one or two employees also compiled lists of those in England who held estates both at home and in Ireland,[9] and when North's reply arrived with confirmation of Bessborough's intelligence,[10] they began to approach these people. Between late October and early December, they sent out no less than five circular letters[11] to nearly a hundred individuals, apprising them of the proposed tax and suggesting the need for concerted action, and then keeping them up to date on events. One of those contacted was Welbore Ellis, the joint vice-treasurer of Ireland, who later informed the marquis, "I have fully executed ... my promise ... of enforcing my sentiments of this Tax on both Sides of the water where I thought they might be urged with any propriety or effect."[12]

Rockingham and Burke also did their utmost to arouse the City of London.[13] In this undertaking they had two things going for them. First, John Wilkes was now supreme in the city. In the previous mayoralty election, his friend and political supporter, Frederick Bull,[14] had triumphed over the candidates of the rival radical faction as well as over those of the administration. Although Wilkes's supporters and the Rockinghams had not been on good terms since 1770, Wilkes himself had displayed no desire to alienate the leaders of the party and was to some extent obliged to them because they were still paying him the small annual stipend. Secondly, and probably more to the point, the city was likely to be classified as an absentee landlord because it owned a substantial amount of land in Ulster which had been granted to it as part of the plantations of 1609. In early November, Wilkes and Bull promised to do "any thing that can be desired,"[15] and the latter agreed to call a meeting of the Common Council to consider strategies.

During November, a tax of two shillings in the pound on the estates of landlords who were absent for six months of the year or more was considered in the Irish House of Commons, and after some long debates it was defeated by a small majority. Consequently, it proved unnecessary for Rockingham to exert the full force of his potential opposition against the British government. Even so, the effects of his efforts made a very strong impression in England, and it is extremely doubtful that North could have kept his promise to support the tax if it had succeeded. As early as 29 October, North had written to Lord Harcourt,[16] the lord lieutenant of Ireland: "I always apprehended that it would cause much uneasiness ... but the uneasiness which it does cause has exceeded my apprehension. The cry is universal against it. Friend and foe, those who have and those who have not estates in Ireland, join in condemning and abusing it."[17]

A major reason for the defeat of the measure in Ireland was that the government there, under pressure from North, withdrew its support.[18] However, some direct intervention by Rockingham and Burke also played a significant part. Before the tax was debated, the marquis wrote to a number of his friends and encouraged them to do all they could to sway public opinion. On 7 November one of them advised him, "Rely upon it the Tide of popularity is decisively turnd against every Idea of the Tax, Your Intention of being heard by Counsel against the Measure alarms the most sanguine for it. I am at this present Moment making Ground for you in certain Counties and Cities to back you by Petition against the act of their Representatives in Case the Bill should pass the House."[19] While his leader's influence was thus brought to bear outside Parliament, Burke wrote to Sir Charles Bingham,[20] an opposition MP in Ireland, and, in his characteristically imaginative fashion, supplied arguments against the tax based on a comprehensive theory of empire. Interestingly, at the time when disturbances such as the Boston Tea Party were about to push Britain to the brink of war in America,[21] the central underlying principle in Burke's imperial policy was the supremacy of the mother country. Among other things he said:

An authority sufficient to preserve ... unity, and ... consolidate the various parts that compose ... [the British Empire] must reside somewhere; that ...

can only be in England ... But if any of the parts which ... are placed in a sub-ordinate situation will assume to themselves the power of hindering or checking the resort of their municipal subjects to the centre or even to any other part of the empire, they arrogate to themselves the imperial rights, which do not, which cannot, belong to them, and ... destroy the happy arrangement of the entire empire ...

What is taxing the resort to and residence in any place but declaring that your connexion with that place is a grievance? Is not such an Irish tax as is now proposed a virtual declaration that England is a foreign country, and a renunciation ... of the principle of *common naturalization* which runs through this whole empire? ...

If in Ireland we lay it down as a maxim that residence in Great Britain is a political evil, and to be discouraged by penal taxes, you must necessarily reject all the privileges and benefits which are connected with such a residence.[22]

This is Burke fulfilling his role as a party man to the best of his ability in these early years of opposition. Here we see him using all his creative juices and eloquence to achieve an objective clearly mapped out for him by one of his leaders. He should not, however, be considered disingenuous. He was not promulgating principles that he was not prepared to live with. Later in his career, even when he was being most outspoken in the cause of American liberties (indeed, even when he was reaching the point of conceding the need for American independence), he also, in some measure at least, actively endeavoured to protect whatever he felt in his heart he could protect of England's central overriding authority in the empire.[23] Bingham apparently used Burke's arguments with effect. When the bill was defeated, he told Burke, "I got great applause thanks to your Friendly assistance, for the support I gave against the Tax, and I had the Pleasure to hear from many Gentlemen, that my arguments had the greatest weight with them, as they came undecided into the House ... No one knows that I heard from you or that your Powers contributed so much to the throwing out of this infamous attempt of Administration."[24]

Historians have tended to stress the importance of Burke's role in defeating the tax, obviously not without justification.[25] However, they have at the same time failed to give due credit to the marquis. While supervising the opposition attack, Rockingham made no less than three trips to London in October and November[26] and personally took a hand in writing up many important documents. The initial letter to Lord North appears to have been his, and not Burke's as has been assumed. The principles and ideas in it – that "all of us ... have the Right of free Subjects of Choosing our Habitation in whatever part of His Majesty's Dominions we shall esteem most Convenient"; that such a tax amounts "in Effect" to a "Fine for our Abode in this Country"; that its "manifest Tendency is to lessen the value of all Landed property" in Ireland; and that it "leads directly to a separation of these Kingdoms in Interest and Affection" – were a direct rephrasing of sentiments Rockingham had expressed in his letter to Bessborough on 20 September. He also wrote at least the first two (and most important) circular letters himself,[27] and besides corresponding privately with numerous individuals both at home and in Ireland, he spent a good deal of time visiting prominent people with whom he felt it would be worthwhile to converse directly.[28] Rockingham's new-found vigour drew praise even from Burke, who later commented that it was "amazing with what spirit and activity ... [Rockingham] exerted himself on the occasion."[29]

This demonstrates how capable Rockingham could be in playing the game of politics when he was sufficiently interested, but it also supports the contention that for the most part during his career he was relatively uninterested. Between 1768 and 1773, Rockingham showed concern about a number of matters in Parliament, including the Nullum Tempus Bill, the Middlesex election, the Jury Bill, and the Royal Marriage Bill. Between 1768 and 1770, he also promoted the union movement with enthusiasm. Yet his attention even to these issues was erratic and was continually either interrupted or delayed by periods of almost total inactivity. Nothing in all Rockingham's years as a politician had ever evoked in him anything like the determination, aggressiveness, and energy which the proposed Irish absentee tax did. He had never before composed one single document for the purposes of political propaganda, yet between September and December 1773, he set about the task as though it came to him naturally. The difference was that now some of his personal wealth and property were at stake, and this type of thing was much more important to him than making a mark in national politics.

Linda Colley has pointed to numerous similarities between the Rockinghams in general and the Tories who defied the Whig oligarchies in the period 1714–60.[30] Both, she notes, faced powerful government regimes and thus turned to certain extraparliamentary expedients to overcome their political weakness. They formed alliances outside Parliament, exploited the press, and became involved in various campaigns in an effort to draw public sympathy. At one time or another, they also turned to programs of reform to modify the system from which they naturally became estranged. Professor Colley is to be commended for this. It might be argued, however, that she would have been more precise if she had drawn her comparison between the Rockinghams and the country-party element within the Tory party. She might then also have stressed a common disinclination towards place, pension, and power on the national level. This, as much as anything else, kept both groups out of office for so long and helped produce the sense of victimization that encouraged them to behave the way they did. Arguably, it was also crucial in pulling both together against the court and ensuring that each emerged, for a time at least, "an easily recognised, self-conscious, and durable political group."[31]

In some respects, the marquis and his friends changed between 1768 and 1773. Rockingham overcame his inability to speak out in the House of Lords, and learned to take a leading part against the government, as when opposing the Royal Marriage Bill in 1772. Although he seldom won any compliments for his oratory, he appears at least to have discovered how to relax in front of an audience and how to give a passable and even competent performance. The House of Lords thus seems to have been less intimidating to him than before. However, the general environment of national politics appears to have grown only slightly more attractive. He continued to find it distasteful "to come to London & to Enter into the Hurry of Intricate & difficult Business which must instantly ensue."[32] After early 1771, his inclination to stay in the country does not seem quite so exceptional considering that from then on there never seemed to be much probability of major victories against North.

Even so, historians who see Rockingham as a power-hungry politician should compare his conduct in the second half of 1773 with that in earlier periods when success had seemed imminent. In the summer of 1769, he and his friends abandoned the capital when the extremely important petitioning movement was gathering force, and imprudently left business in the hands of a small group of men whose lack of restraint they knew to be dangerous. Later in the same year, when the campaign of protest was nearing completion, Rockingham resisted leaving the security of Wentworth for so long that when Parliament reassembled, the opposition was unable to press its advantage effectively. At the same time, after coaxing Burke to get the *Thoughts* finished because of certain political advantages he hoped to garner, Rockingham caused a considerable delay in publication because of his tardiness in merely offering criticism.

Ironically, the Rockinghams had difficulty pursuing even secession in a sustained and convincing manner. They talked about withdrawing en masse from Parliament in 1771 and 1772 but never really carried through. Later, in 1777, when they used secession to protest

North's large majorities over the American war, they did so in a very feeble and unenthusiastic way and for only a short time.[33] Their behaviour was very different from that of their much more politically ambitious successor, Charles James Fox, in the 1790s. When Fox found the battle against William Pitt the Younger[34] hopeless, he seceded seriously. He retreated from parliamentary affairs for four long years.[35] The difference is that he was far more devastated than the Rockinghams by insignificance in Parliament. They often felt uncomfortable about leaving the country for the capital when things were going their way, but when the fight went against them, they were unlikely to be so disheartened as to want to give up politics entirely. Fox, on the other hand, like Lord Temple in 1770, was so dejected that he seriously considered announcing his retirement.

As has been seen, when Rockingham, Portland, Dowdeswell, and Richmond witnessed the destruction of the union movement and began to recognize the futility of the fight against North, they evinced few signs of genuine regret. Instead of becoming frustrated with one another or quarrelsome, they drew more closely together with expressions of mutual admiration and love of the party. While Burke was the one man in the central core of the party who showed the kind of interest in affairs at the centre which might be held as a thirst for place and power, his total veneration for the marquis and others, and his consequent willingness to "assimilate to their Character" (to put it in his own words),[36] enabled him to restrain this ambition indefinitely. If the Rockinghams' relative indifference to office and other attributes gave them much in common with the country gentlemen who had consistently opposed their court Whig ancestors, we must not forget that throughout their career they also managed to retain a number of important court Whig preconceptions. Before expanding on this and examining the characteristics that made the party something of an oddity (if not a contradiction of terms) in the eighteenth century, it should perhaps be pointed out that in a number of important respects the marquis and his friends were very much a product of the age and society in which they lived. For the most part, the principles and policies they espoused in the late 1760s and early 1770s directly reflected propertied-class opinion. For that reason, a study such as this provides some extremely useful insights into the ideals and prejudices that operated within the government process as a whole. Some of these were to have far-reaching effects on the course of British history.

Of the repercussions of this period, the war with the American colonies, which followed on the heels of the Boston Tea Party of December 1773, was undoubtedly the most important. It must be admitted that in general the Rockinghams' attitude towards the Americans was less intransigent than that of most politicians of their time. In repealing the Stamp Act in 1766, they had come forth as the proponents of moderation and conciliation, and a few years later, the need to justify their earlier actions demanded that in some measure they should continue to do so. Thus, during the crisis that followed the passage of the Townshend duties, while repeatedly enunciating the maxim that Parliament was supreme and had a right to pass whatever laws and regulations were thought necessary for the maintenance of imperial policies, they attacked the government for having imposed the new duties. They also supported (albeit rather unobtrusively) the small minority of people who wanted the duty on tea repealed. However, the salient point is that their call for conciliation after 1767 was noticeably less bold than it had been earlier. While this was partly a result of their desire to find common ground with the Grenvilles and to work towards the construction of the new broad and comprehensive Whig ministry, it was also indicative of the fact that opinion in Britain had hardened a good deal since they had been in power. Even in 1768, before the movement for a united opposition had begun, Dowdeswell and Rockingham himself – as evinced by his admonition of the Bostonians for their misbehaviour – shared the predominant belief of the general public that colonial resistance had gone too far.

One of the more intelligent comments on this subject in 1768 came from Savile. He realized that a conflict of interest was inevitable when a mother country attempted to control and restrain a distant, growing, and increasingly competitive protectorate whose aspirations in some major areas contrasted with her own. "I am afraid these same Colonists are above our heads," he observed, "and I am almost ready to think that G[eorge] G[renville]'s act [the Stamp Act] only brought on a crisis 20 or possibly 50 years sooner than was necessary. This indeed is regarding Colonies almost all the ill that can be done, for in my opinion ... it is in the nature of things that some time or other Colonies so situated must assume to themselves the *rights* of nature & resist those of Law; which is Rebellion. By *rights* of nature I mean advantages of situation or their natural powers."[37] It is interesting that although Savile could grasp the depth and dimensions of the problem, he, like most of his contemporaries, was fundamentally unprepared to allow nature to take its course.

Some historians attempting to explain why the British were unsuccessful in dealing with the American problem during the crucial years preceding the revolution have focused on certain political exigencies.[38] They have pointed to the inadequate representation of American interests in the House of Commons, the weak and disjointed state of the opposition parties that had espoused conciliatory views, and the general lack of ability among the members of the North cabinet whose responsibility it was to deal with colonial affairs. No doubt these things were relevant, but they should not be emphasized at the expense of a much more important factor – public opinion. The American Revolution broke out because the British and the colonists had been on a collision course for years over the fundamental question of what the imperial Parliament could or could not do. British opinion was that Parliament could "make laws and statutes of sufficient force and validity to bind the colonies and peoples of America *in all cases whatsoever.*" This the Americans never accepted. Many of them claimed during the agitation over the Stamp Act that they could not be taxed without their consent, especially not for revenue purposes, and after 1767 they were adamant on this point. The repeal of the Stamp Act and the Townshend duties did nothing towards finding a long-term solution to this central overriding issue.

One can only speculate what effect a large and vociferous American cell in the House of Commons would have had on Anglo-American relations, but it seems unlikely that it would have made a great deal of difference. In fact, one could argue that it would have made the polarization even more pronounced. Since 1765, the American colonists' determination to oppose imperial legislation on the grounds of right had done a great deal to turn opinion in England against them. The Rockinghams, as Dowdeswell's letter to the marquis in July 1768 demonstrates, were determined that they would never support the colonists on this basis. Animosities would surely have been heightened if the members of the House of Commons had been informed of opinions such as those of the Committee of Correspondence of Massachusetts Bay. The committee reprimanded its colonial agent in 1769 for his part in a proposed petition to Parliament, "because the Right of the Inhabitants of the colonies to be Taxed only by their own Representatives is not therein exp[ressly] asserted."[39] Nor would the situation have been improved if attitudes like that of the colonial agent for New York had been voiced more plainly. The fear among the English propertied classes for the supremacy of Parliament was not only based on the fact that many Americans were asserting maxims that were ill suited to the principles of mercantilism; it was also because the colonists were clearly anxious to escape a host of restrictions and controls besides those encompassed in the Revenue Act of 1767. In early 1770, when the New York agent first heard that the London merchants had agreed to petition against the Townshend duties, he told a friend on the other side of the Atlantic, "Ye

No[rth] American merch[an]ts have joined in a petition to Parliament for the Repeal of one Revenue Act only." This, he asserted, "will by no means answer your end," since the "whole system of oppressive laws [must] be repealed."[40] The fact is that what the Americans wanted most, the British were diametrically opposed to granting. Consequently, it is doubtful that if the Americans had had a better opportunity to state their claims, the British would have been any more willing to listen.

The individuals who composed the North cabinet may not by nature have been well equipped to handle a problem as delicate and complex as this in the early seventies. It is clear, however, that neither the Rockinghams nor the Chathams, nor apparently anyone else, had any profound insight into the problem or any constructive plans for solving it. Moreover, it is difficult to see what the ministers could have done had they tried. They unquestionably realized that to grant the colonists more concessions after repealing the bulk of the Townshend duties would be extremely unpopular both within Parliament and outside it. They retained the duty on tea in 1770 and protected it three years later for the same major reason that the Rockinghams were so timid about advocating repeal – public concern for the supremacy of Parliament. Late in 1774, when they brought forth their four Coercive Acts in response to the Boston Tea Party and thereby pushed the crisis to the brink of war, the strength of feeling in the House of Commons convinced them that they were taking precisely the correct line. While the members were debating the first of these acts, Burke wrote to the Committee of Correspondence of the General Assembly of New York. He described the situation fairly accurately when he said:

The popular current, both within doors and without, at present sets strongly against America. There were not indeed wanting some few persons in the House of Commons, who disaproved of the Bill, and who expressed their disapprobation in the strongest and most explicit Terms. But their arguments upon this point made so little impression that it was not thought advisable to divide the House. Those who spoke in opposition, did it, more for the acquittal of their own honour, and discharge of their own consciences ... than from any sort of hope ... of bringing any considerable Number to their opinion; or even of keeping in that opinion several of those who had formerly concurred in the same general Line of Policy with regard to the Colonies.[41]

During the session, the Rockinghams were as timid as ever. When news first reached England of the Boston Tea Party, they were totally disinclined to take up the cause of colonial liberties. In February, Burke informed the marquis with tacit approval:

It was the D. of Richmonds, Mr. Dowdeswells and Lord FitzWilliam's as well as Lrd J. Cavendishes Sentiment that your Lordships friends in the House of Peers ought to absent themselves, and not to countenance the interested Petulance of those Paltry discontented People, who without embracing your principles, or giving you any sort of support, think to make use of your Weight to give consequence to every occasional spurt of opposition they think proper to make in order to put the Ministry in mind, that they are to be bought by private contract, as unconnected individuals. When you mean opposition, you are able to take it up on your own Grounds, and at your own time.[42]

It is true that some members of the party – notably Burke and to a lesser degree Dowdeswell – did speak out against North's coercive measures from the beginning. However, they also took pains to demonstrate that they supported the legislative authority of Britain over America and disapproved of the colonists' acts of resistance. A great many of their followers refused to oppose the government at all, and one of the Cavendishes actually voiced approbation of the Boston Port Bill.[43]

The Chatham-Shelburne politicians were similarly equivocal. Barré, like Cavendish, supported the first of the acts, and the party in general did not begin to take a stand directly against the government until the third act was proposed and the danger of a full-scale military conflict began to seem very real. It is extremely doubtful that better relations between the two opposition groups would have made any significant impression on the course of events. The opposition politicians were reluctant to take up the Americans' cause not because they were disunited but, as in the past, because they were concerned for the supremacy of Parliament and because they knew that almost everyone in Great Britain was at least as concerned as they were. Moreover, even if they had come together, discussed the issue thoroughly, and decided to oppose the government with resolution, the independent country gentlemen would still have backed (and indeed demanded) an authoritarian approach, and North's majorities would still have been very large. In retrospect, it is far from certain that if the Rockinghams had remained in office after 1766, they would have been any more successful in avoiding the conflict than North was.

One glaring example of the same lack of real understanding of this problem that can be seen from their actions in the period 1767–70 came to light during the events leading to the passage of the Tea Act in 1773. This act of course caused a great deal of resentment in America and was thus an important factor in the development of the revolution. The reason for the colonists' anger was that it removed the duty which the East India Company had previously been required to pay when exporting tea from England, but it did nothing about the threepence-per-pound import duty that had been imposed on the Americans by the Revenue Act of 1767.[44] Because this enabled the East India Company to export tea more cheaply and thereby undersell its competitors in America, the colonists viewed it as an attempt to force them to buy goods on which they were being unconstitutionally taxed. One would think that anyone who was extremely concerned about American rights would realize this. But the Rockinghams, like almost everyone else in the mother country, overlooked the danger. The only member of the party who criticized the Tea Act was Dowdeswell, and his concern was not based on the possibility that the Americans would feel offended; his fear was that because the export duty alone was being repealed, the colonists would not buy the tea and therefore the legislation would do nothing to help the East India Company. On 26 April he observed that "no proposition with regard to the duty laid upon tea imported into America" had been made. He argued that if North intended "to leave that duty as it is," he would not be serving the East India Company at all. "It is not the bargain that prevents the export, but that there was a duty laid there upon the import," he stated. "I tell the n[oble] L[ord] now if he dont take off the duty, they wont take the tea."[45] Dowdeswell is perhaps to be applauded for at least realizing what few others in Britain did. However, it is apparent that over the previous few months, the party as a whole had largely ignored an opportunity to press this issue at a time when it might have done so with some influence.

The Tea Act of 1773 was originally formulated because the proprietors of the East India Company sitting in a meeting of the General Court on 7 January had recommended that the directors apply to the government for relief. The directors were instructed to obtain the right "to export to Foreign Dominions," duty free, "a part of their Surplus Quantity of Tea" and to request the removal of "the three pence per pound Duty in America."[46] Over the next few weeks, the directors took this proposition to North as a part of the basis for the petition to Parliament for the much-needed loan. On 9 February,[47] they reported back that the first lord of the Treasury "did not give hopes that the three pence Per Pound Duty on Tea in America could be taken off but that he was disposed to promote the Export of Teas" duty free. The proprietors decided to apply on this basis.

Unquestionably, the Rockinghams were well aware of all this. At this stage, not only Richmond but also the marquis and Dowdeswell were working in conjunction with Dempster and their friend Daniel Wier[48] in an effort to pressure the directors.[49] As Rockingham's papers at Sheffield demonstrate, he was kept up to date on all the negotiations between the directors and the government in January and February, and was acquainted with each of the various propositions discussed.[50] Yet his sole concern was to prevent the directors from agreeing to measures that might give the government a right to take control of the company. He showed little if any concern about the Americans. Moreover, the propositions which the Duke of Richmond tried to get the proprietors to adopt in February called not only for the "repeal of the 3 pence duty on tea imported into America" but for "*either*" that "*or*" the repeal of the export duty.[51] Thus, the party leaders in general were so out of touch with American opinion that it had not yet occurred to them that many colonists would be unlikely to change their attitude about tea duties just because the East India Company could supply tea at a lower price.

The Rockinghams' policy in American affairs since 1765 had, in essence, not been greatly dissimilar from that of Lord North. They had repealed the Stamp Act for the sake of British trade, and a few years later he had repealed most of the Townshend duties for the same reason. They sponsored the Declaratory Act in order to maintain Parliament's authority, and he retained the duty on tea to demonstrate that the principles expressed in that act had some meaning. They were just as anxious to support the Declaratory Act as North was to support the tax on tea. Had the legislation of 1767 never been passed, the conflict presumably would not have broken out so quickly; but in view of the fact that the Americans were voicing dissatisfaction with a host of existing restrictions, limitations, and controls even before that legislation was contemplated,[52] it is very likely that, over the years, resentment would have pushed them on to strong measures of resistance anyway. If the Rockinghams had been in office, faced with an angry British public and limited by their concern for "the proper subordination of America, as a fundamental, incontrovertible Maxim, in the Government of this Empire,"[53] they would have found it very difficult to give in to their friends across the ocean. At some point, therefore, they might well have found themselves in the position of the North ministry in 1774.

What seems patently clear about the Rockinghams' response to the American problem during the prewar years is that it represented the orthodox eighteenth-century approach. The same could be said of the other more general policies the marquis and his friends adopted while playing the game of politics between 1768 and 1773. Initially, as they clung to an image of a court Whig past and worked to establish a new united ministry, their most prominent platform was that of opposition to Bute, the cabal, and secret influence. The stand against secret influence had, to a greater or lesser extent, been championed by every connection that had at one time or other practised opposition between 1761 and 1770. After 1770 the cry of favouritism was not entirely abandoned. Throughout the following decade, the Rockinghams and their allies continued to see evidence of its existence, and they blamed such people as Charles Jenkinson, Rockingham's old friend Lord Mansfield, and even Bute himself for having undue weight in the Closet. In January 1775, Burke told his leader that it "would conduce greatly to our acting with some regularity if we knew who the Ministry were." He added, "I have great reason to suspect that Jenkinson governs every thing ... A trusty person set at his door to follow him in his motions, would give great lights ... To follow Jenkinson, will be to discover my Lord Bute, and my Lord Mansfield, and another person [the king] as considerable as either of them."[54] However, for the most part, this approach no longer suited political exigencies, and the secret influence theory fell into the background of opposition mythology as the crown's influence began to seem the greater and more immediate problem.

Despite their inability to win the approval of most independent MPs over specific issues (such as the Jury Bill or the East India Company) in which they took a stand against the influence of the crown, the Rockinghams were not really far out of step with the feelings of the "sober part of the people"[55] or the "men of weight and character,"[56] whom they most wanted to represent. As is well known, concern about the advantages that crown patronage gave to the executive had been prevalent among independent elements in the House of Commons since the seventeenth century, and evidence suggests that it still was. George Grenville's Controverted Elections Act, for instance, succeeded in 1770 and was made permanent in 1774 (each time despite government resistance) because of the general desire to have a legislature that was less subservient to the crown and the executive. At times, a considerable proportion of the independents were willing to back measures which even the Rockinghams balked at in order to work towards that end. One such measure was John Sawbridges's annual bill for shortening the duration of Parliament. When Sawbridge first proposed this bill on 25 April 1771, he made it clear that his purpose was the same as that which had induced men to call for short Parliaments since 1716: "In the course of seven years representatives forget their constituents and long parliaments naturally become independent of the people. What is the consequence? They become dependent on the crown whose influencing power is by the vast increase of places become almost irresistible."[57] On that day, only fifty-four members voted in the minority, partly because it was very late in the session and many had already returned to their homes for the summer recess. However, when Sawbridge submitted his bill again in March 1772, eighty-three people supported him. Among them was Sir Roger Newdigate and, apparently, numerous other independents, for the Chathams and city radicals could have mustered no more that thirty votes and the vast majority of the Rockinghams either voted with the court or abstained.[58]

The reason for the decline of the Rockingham party (and for that matter, of the opposition generally) was not so much that people stopped worrying about overpowerful executives; it was more that they had come to see them as the lesser of two evils – the other evil being the excesses of the government's many antagonists between 1768 and 1773. During this period, the independent members of the House of Commons were horrified at the misbehaviour of the London mobs, the radicals, the press, the East India Company servants, and the colonists. This increasingly tended to draw them closer to Lord North. One of the best indications of the reaction that set in is the degree to which North and his associates learned to play on it during the debates. In the jury controversy, for instance, they were quick to point out that unless Mansfield and the King's Bench judges were upheld, "Your Wilkes's, your Junius's, and your Bill of Rights men, urged like spiteful toads, by malice and hunger, would spit their impotent venom in our faces."[59] And in meeting the attacks of the opposition over the state of the navy during the Falkland Islands issue, they argued: "Our patriots make every thing an occasion for a commonplace declamation against wicked and foolish ministers, and patch together scraps which one of them retails in the newspapers, and others carefully glean up; one half of them being constantly dupes to the artifices of the other."[60]

Even the Rockinghams displayed numerous signs of reaction towards the apparent excesses of the time. They, too, were alarmed by the riots both at home and in America in 1768 and 1769, by the rashness of the radicals during the petitioning movement and in the London remonstrance of March 1770, by the impetuosity of the printers and London magistrates in early 1771, and to some extent by the alleged rapaciousness of the East India Company servants in 1772–73. Like most people from the propertied classes, they identified two major types of evil in the nation; but they regarded the executive evil as the greater, and therefore they always ended up in opposition. Any government not formed by the court Whigs of old or the Rockingham Whigs of new was by nature incapable of proceeding in a good or just manner and had to be resisted. In their determination to strike a blow against the administration, they often contributed to or appeared to support excesses which, in different circumstances, they might have been as anxious as anyone to repress. They seemed constantly linked with all the violence and abuses of the time, and for this reason they lost a great deal of credit with the independents.

If their principle of opposition to the influence of the crown was not incompatible with the values of independent gentlemen, obviously it was also not incompatible with the values of other parties that remained in opposition during this period. Both the Chathams and the city radicals had taken it up in fighting the government over the Middlesex election, the rights of juries, the Royal Marriage Act, and so on. In 1772 and 1773, London had even joined the marquis and his friends in defence of one of its traditional enemies, the East India Company, in order to affirm support for it. The growth of reaction to the influence of the crown among antiministerial forces between 1768 and 1773 was to have a pervading effect on the policies of all opposition parties for a further decade. Towards the end of the American Revolution, this concern was expressed directly, not only in Dunnings's famous motion of 1780 and in the Rockingham's program of "economical reform," but in more radical causes such as Christopher Wyvill's[61] celebrated association movement.[62]

Part of the reason why the Rockinghams, Chathams, and radicals were not able to work together over a prolonged period, despite their common determination to resist the undue influence of the crown, is that in the realm of constitutional thought this was all they were able to agree on. In 1769 and 1770, the city politicians adopted a program of reform which, over the following years, was expanded and promoted with growing determination. The Rockinghams' refusal to accept any part of this program did much to alienate them from the radicals and ensured that the two groups were never able to overcome their differences, despite the fact that they found themselves perpetually on the same side in the House of Commons. Moreover, since Chatham was willing to go along with the radicals' ideas to some extent, it contributed to the breakdown of relations between the Rockinghams and his party. The inability of these three groups to find a mutually acceptable constitutional platform has never really been understood. In order to explain it properly, one needs to compare the ideals of the two parties whose disagreement was most pronounced – the Rockinghams and the radicals.

Like the marquis and his friends, the London politicians who advocated reform in the 1760s and 1770s had much in common with the
country-party politicians of the early eighteenth century. The problem was, however, that in some basic respects they were country in a
way that the Rockinghams, primarily because of enduring court
Whig preconceptions, could never be. Since 1688, when the vast majority of the members of the propertied classes had grown almost to
worship the revolution settlement and the system of government established through it, the proponents of country doctrine had always
been distinguishable by their belief that the constitution, however
good, was imperfect. They were the men who in such well-known
publications as *Cato's Letters*, the *Craftsman*, and the *Monitor* continually warned of imperfections: "The Design of the *Revolution* was not
accomplish'd, the Benefit of it was not secured to us, the just Expectations of the Nation could not be answer'd unless the *Freedom of Elections* and the *Frequency, Integrity, and Independency of Parliaments* were
sufficiently provided for. These are the essentials of *British Liberty*. Defects in other Parts of the *Constitution* can never be fatal, if These are
preserved intire."[63] Their discontent centred, of course, mainly on the
fact that Parliament – and, above all, the House of Commons – was
subservient to the executive because of the strength of crown and
ministerial influence. It was this that led them to call for reform measures such as place and pension bills, oaths against bribery in elections, and shorter Parliaments. While such expedients (aimed entirely
at restoring the principles on which the revolution settlement was
thought to have been based) were conservative, country spokesmen
displayed a tendency towards radicalism in the emphasis they constantly placed on the importance of the "people." Often the difference
between them and the majority of the members of the propertied
classes was only one of degree: everyone agreed that it was essential
that the will of the public should be reflected in the actions of the representatives in Parliament and of the administration; but the country
politicians stressed this over and over again, and they were prepared
to give the people a greater say in the normal operations of government and a much more direct control over their representatives than
most men of substance were inclined to think appropriate. In statements such as the following they sound distinctly democratic and
egalitarian even in the twentieth century:

In Truth, every private Subject has a Right to watch over the Steps of those
who would betray their Country, nor is he to take their Word about the Motives of their Designs, but to judge of their Designs by the Event ... Some will
tell us, that this is setting up the *Mob* for Statesmen, and the Censurers of

States ... [but it] is certain, that the whole People, who are the Publick, are the best Judges whether Things go ill or well with the Publick ... In short the People often judge better than their Superiors, and have not so many Byasses to judge wrong, and Politicians often rail at the People, chiefly because they have given the People occasion to rail.[64]

This concern for the people helped make some country politicians – those described by H.T. Dickinson as "radical country Whigs" – not only receptive to ideas for making specific alterations in the constitution but anxious to eliminate its theocratic base.[65] They disliked the union between church and state because it fostered a central man-made religious authority over individual conscience and individual interpretation of the Scriptures. As has been seen, Savile seems to have backed the call for ending subscription in 1772 for precisely this reason.[66]

In the 1760s, the London politicians for the most part gave vent to their dissatisfaction with the existing constitution merely by reiterating the ideals of earlier country parties. In promoting amendment, they contented themselves with adopting all the traditional schemes for limiting royal and ministerial influence. However, in the early 1770s, they became radicals in a genuine sense as an increasingly strong conviction that the current system of government was not adequately equipped to reflect the views of the public prompted them to push the country concern for the people to some of its logical conclusions. A good deal has been written about the antiministerialism that developed in London during the first ten years of the reign as a result of a number of circumstances, including the economic discontent that accompanied the postwar depression, the resignation of the city's idol William Pitt in 1761, the Wilkes and general warrants business, and the Middlesex election issue.[67] In the seventies, this antiministerialism was increased and in a sense became more an antiestablishmentism as a result of further economic discontent, the refusal of the king and Parliament to heed the petitions of 1769, the extremely emotive jury and printers' affairs, and the government's policy of naval conscription during the Falkland Islands crisis. All of these seemed to make it all too apparent that the king, the ministry, and the Houses of Parliament were no longer concerned for the interests of the public. City leaders began to lash out, not only at crown and ministerial influence but also at the classes monopolizing the power structure and therefore at the existing system of representation, which they believed was "insufficient, partial, and unjust," and kept Parliament subject to "the root of corruption and treasury influence, as well as aristocratic tyranny."[68] While desiring to change the system of representation, they also wanted to extend the franchise in more areas to a greater number of people, since "government is only a trust from the people for their good, and in several instances, so far from possessing an absolute power, we ought to acknowledge, that ... [Parliament has] no power at all ... Many things are so closely woven in with the constitution, like the trial by jury, that they cannot be separated, unless the body of people expressly declare otherwise, after free and full consideration."[69]

Despite the fact that in these years the Rockinghams became something closely resembling a typical eighteenth-century country party, they never totally lost sight of their court Whig roots. Despite all the evidence to the contrary, they continued earnestly to believe that they were Whigs of the type that had monopolized successive administrations for more than half a century before George III's reign. Consequently, they could not countenance a number of country-party premises. In particular, they found it very difficult to accept the most basic assumption that initially led both the country and radical politicians to programs of reform – the assumption that the constitution was in any genuine sense imperfect. Throughout previous reigns, it had been the court Whigs who had venerated the constitution the most and had constantly attempted to defend it against reform.[70] The marquis and his friends, who felt it was in every way their duty to "restore the principles and policy of the Whigs,"[71] carried on this tradition. They consistently worked to protect the constitution and all the conventions in church and state on which their predecessors had stood. Near the end of his life, and after witnessing the horrors of the French Revolution, Burke was to take immense pride in this fact:

I was connected with men of high place in the community. They loved Liberty ... Perhaps their politicks, as usual, took a tincture from their character, and they cultivated what they loved. The Liberty they pursued was a Liberty inseparable from order, from virtue, from morals, and from religion, and was neither hypocritically nor fanatically followed. They did not wish, that Liberty, in itself one of the first of blessings, should in it's perversion become the greatest curse which could fall upon mankind. To preserve the Constitution entire, and practically equal to all the great ends of it's formation, not in one single part, but in all it's parts, was to them the first object. Popularity and power they regarded alike. These were with them only different means of obtaining that object; and had no preference over each other in their minds, but as one or the other might afford a surer or a less certain prospect of arriving at that end. It is some consolation to me, in the chearless gloom which darkens the evening of my life, that with them I commenced my political career, and never for a moment, in reality, nor in appearance, for any length of time, was separated from their good wishes and good opinion.[72]

How far the marquis himself was prepared to go in the early years to defend the existing constitution is seen in a letter he wrote in 1772 to a supporter who had previously displayed an inclination to accept the idea of shorter parliaments.

I seriously think the genuine Constitution of this country is in great danger & not merely from bad Men being ministers but from the prevalency of Self interest in Individuals in Parl[iament]: & from the little attention which the publick at large at present shew on all political Matters, even tho' the principles of the Constitution are invaded ... I own I do not absolutely agree with you in regard to your opinion of short Parliaments being a remedy for the corruption of the House of Commons ... If the body of Constituents were in fact more incorrupt than the body of Representatives, it Might have some effect, but I fear the whole is at present in a general state of Corruption, & one immediate consequence would follow that every Representative who could not early reward his Constitutients by procuring Government Favours for them would be rejected at the first Election.[73]

This letter demonstrates the rather delicate position in which the Rockinghams had placed themselves in recent years by championing the principle of opposition to the undue influence of the crown. Just as country parties had done before them, they had been claiming that this influence gave administrations an unfair advantage in the House of Commons, but they could not admit that this was indicative of any fundamental weakness in the constitution. Therefore, the marquis was arguing that it was not the influence of the crown in itself that was the problem; it was the susceptibility to it not only of the representatives but of the people themselves. The solution, he was saying, did not lie in constitutional change (for governments would always be able to procure favours) but in a revival of the country's moral standards. "The Publick at large," he continued, "are languid at present & afford but little encouragement to ... Men, either to give themselves Much trouble or much expence: In time there May & I hope will arrise a more general patriotick spirit & that both the Men of Rank & Fortune & the Actual Constituents will cooperate together. The Race Now is whether the Men of Rank &c or the Constituents are the *Most* Corrupt. The Race Must be which shall be the *least* corrupt."

The Rockinghams' Whiggishness, then, made it difficult for them to go along with those who believed that the constitution was in need of serious alteration. It also helped make their attitude towards society incompatible with the country and radical attitudes. This caused them to be particularly antipathetic towards schemes for giving the people a stronger and broader voice in affairs of government. It should be said, however, that they did believe that the will of the people was extremely important, and over the years they continued to cultivate public opinion whenever it was possible to do so without impinging on some of their more salient principles. One finds in their letters, with almost monotonous regularity, such phrases as "I am fully convinced that the publick in general are glad of peace,"[74] "the general disposition of the publick,"[75] "I can not but think that the publick in general will be more inclined to join in an attack upon ministers,"[76] and "Lord Chatham ... can not assent to *our friends* getting the credit with the publick which on this and all occasions they have deserved."[77] The Rockinghams also thought that the House of Commons should act in such a way as to bring the will of the people to bear on the actions of government. Thus, in the *Thoughts*, they could assail the members of the House for their actions during the Middlesex election issue because the "virtue, spirit, and essence of a House of Commons consists in its being the express image of the feelings of the nation. It was not instituted to be a controul *upon* the people, as of late it has been taught, by a doctrine of the most pernicious tendency. It was designed as a controul *for* the people."[78]

It is evident, however, that their conception of the relationship between the people and their representatives was very different from that of the country and radical politicians. The latter saw MPs as the servants of the public almost in the modern sense of the term. The members were commissioned by the people directly (or ought to be), and were continually accountable to them for all their public actions both in and out of Parliament and on a long-term and day-to-day basis. To ensure that MPs conducted themselves for the public good, the people had a right, and indeed a duty, to be constantly vigilant and to be prepared to intervene directly and frequently – through petitions, instructions, and so on. The Rockinghams, on the other hand, considered that the representative, though responsible to the people, was for the most part free to interpret the people's will in his own way and to act on their behalf as he saw fit. He was almost something of an enlightened despot, providing his constituents with leadership while concerning himself with their welfare. It was this attitude, for instance, that led Lord John Cavendish to write during the petitioning movement: "I have no doubt the Gentlemen of the county will be ready to do anything; but we have been a great many years teaching them to acquiesce & to be contented with what their members do for them; if we encourage them to take everything into consideration they may choose to interpose much oftener than I am likely to think convenient."[79] It also prompted Burke to assert a few years later, in his oft-quoted speech to the electors at Bristol:

It ought to be the happiness and glory of a Representative, to live in the strictest union, the closest correspondence, and the most unreserved communication with his constituents. Their wishes ought to have great weight with him ... But, his unbiassed opinion, his mature judgement, his enlightened conscience, he ought not to sacrifice to you; to any man, or to any sett of men living. These he does not derive from your pleasure; no, nor from the Law and the Constitution. They are a trust from Providence, for the abuse of which he is deeply answerable. Your Representative owes you, not his industry only, but his judgement; and he betrays, instead of serving you, if he sacrifices it to your opinion.[80]

The Rockingham's decision to back the merchants' protest against the Stamp Act in 1765–66 and to go along with the campaign of 1769 demonstrates that they felt that the people had a right to intervene in exceptional circumstances. But they were not anxious to see this right exercised a great deal – or, in normal circumstances, at all. In the *Thoughts* they claimed that the "*interposition of the body of the people itself*" is only justified when "it shall appear, by some flagrant and notorious act, by some capital innovation, that these Representatives are going to over-leap the fences of the law, and to introduce an arbitrary power. This interposition is a most unpleasant remedy ... to be used ... only, when it is evident that nothing else can hold the constitution to its true principles."[81]

Clearly, the Rockinghams did not share the country respect for the intelligence of their constituents or for their capacity to act in a reasonable manner. While they held that only the people could put the constitution back on its just principles, they did not wish to see them do it by taking matters into their own hands. What they hoped was that one day the constituents might learn to "repose a perfect confidence"[82] in those of their "natural" leaders who were motivated solely by concern for the good of the nation (that is, of course, in the Rockinghams themselves) and who would act under their instruction. "All direction of publick humour and opinion must originate in a few,"[83] Burke argued, and the "people are not answerable for their supine acquiescence ... God and nature never made them to think or to Act without Guidance and direction."[84]

Any party with views such as these was naturally not going to have much sympathy for measures aimed at enhancing the power of the people. The Rockinghams' attitude was obviously very heavily affected by their "aristocratic conception of politics."[85] If the people were to start taking more initiative and responsibility in public affairs, the Rockinghams and others like them were likely to see their influence suffer. In Yorkshire, Rockingham was constantly aware of threats to his position as things stood. He often found it necessary, for instance, to speak out against those who wanted to "bar the operation of the landed weight in Peers Possession"[86] during elections, and in later years he feared the powerful association movement as much for its proponents' determination to act irrespective of aristocratic authority as for their extremism.[87] However, Rockingham's attitude and that of his friends was not just a result of concern for the privileges of the aristocracy. There can be little doubt that their feelings of kinship with the court Whigs of the past did much to impress on their minds how important this concern was (or perhaps to make it seem more important than it should have seemed). They believed that their forefathers had predominated over the nation not so much because they had been commissioned directly by the people but because they had achieved a natural importance through qualities such as rank, position, and property: "Persons in your Station of Life ought [to] have long Views," Burke once told one of the peers in the party in a well-known and much-quoted letter:

You people of great families and hereditary Trusts and fortunes ... if you are what you ought to be are the great Oaks that shade a Country and perpetuate your benefits from Generation to Generation ... The immediate power of [a person such as yourself] or a Marquis of R[ockingha]m is not so much of moment but if their conduct and example hands down their principles to their successors; then their houses become the publick repositories and offices of Record for the constitution ... It has been remarked that there were two eminent families at Rome that for several ages were distinguished uniformly, by opposite Characters and principles. The Claudian and Valerian. The former were high and haughty but publick spirited, firm, and active and attached to the aristocracy ... Any one who looks attentively to their History will see that the ballance of that famous constitution was kept up for some ages by the personal Characters, dispositions, and traditionary politicks of certain families as by any thing in the Laws and order of the State.[88]

Even more telling is the passage in the *Thoughts* in which the party compared William Pitt the Elder (the future Earl of Chatham) with Newcastle and his colleagues in the old Whig oligarchy:

It was more strongly and evidently the interest of the new Court Faction, to get rid of the great Whig connexions, than to destroy Mr. Pitt. The power of that gentleman was vast indeed and merited; but it was in a great degree personal, and therefore transient. Theirs was rooted in the country. For, with a good deal less of popularity, they possessed a far more natural and fixed influence. Long possession of Government; vast property; obligations of favours given and received; connexion of office; ties of blood, of alliance, of friendship ... the name of Whig, dear to the majority of the people; the zeal early begun and steadily continued to the Royal Family.[89]

While the Rockinghams were quite prepared not to live up to the example the old Whigs had set for them, in so far as the attainment of office and power was concerned, they unquestionably wanted the Whig party to remain a force in the nation. They felt that it had originally established itself on more tangible foundations than the power of the people, and they were determined that those would not be pulled from beneath them by a new quasi-egalitarianism.

The Rockinghams, then, rejected the idea of substantial change because, unlike the radicals, they did not share the country politician's belief that the constitution was flawed in any significant way. In the late seventies and early eighties, their country-party fear of the influence of the crown would allow them to overcome their court Whig defensiveness toward the constitution just enough to develop their economical reform program. In this program, however, they proposed only moderate measures and the kind they felt would not substantially meddle with what they considered the basic structures of their predecessors' system. The proposals they offered were not inconsequential. They called for the abolition of some fifty places in the royal household and the government. Burke estimated that this would result in a savings of some £200,000 annually.[90] However, not only was this a less radical solution than that offered by any major group either inside or outside the ministry in the seventies and eighties, but it was also meant to defend and preserve the system as much as to change it. When the Rockinghams designed their program, they were alarmed at the progress being made by Christopher Wyvill in Yorkshire, and they believed that the call for reform in Britain was so strong that unless the governing classes could demonstrate that the constitution was flexible enough to accept moderate change, the purveyors of radical and really threatening ideas would have their way. "Little more time remains for us," Burke told the Duke of Portland in January 1780. "It will not be borne by the people, who are hungering & thirsting after substantial reformation, that we should balk their appetite."[91] At that point, the party's most dynamic new recruit, Charles James Fox, was courting the reform movement directly.[92] The other leaders believed it was suddenly necessary for them to protect the Whig constitution through mild alterations. This rationale Burke explained most succinctly when introducing his civil establishment legislation on 11 February 1780.[93] He reiterated the same message when reflecting on his public life a decade and a half after this legislation had been passed into law. In 1796 he felt compelled to acknowledge that it had been "not my love, but my hatred to innovation, that produced my Plan of Reform":

Without troubling myself with the exactness of the logical diagram, I considered them as things substantially opposite. It was to prevent that evil, that I proposed the measures ... I had ... a State to preserve, as well as a State to reform. I had a People to gratify, but not to inflame, or to mislead. I do not claim half the credit for what I did, as for what I prevented from being done. In that situation of the publick mind, I did not undertake, as was then proposed, to new model the House of Commons or the House of Lords; or to change the authority under which any officer of the Crown acted, who was suffered at all to exist. Crown, Lords, Commons, judicial system, system of administration, existed as they had existed before; and in the mode and manner in which they had always existed. My measures were, what I then truly stated them to the House to be, in their intent, healing and mediatorial ... I have ever abhorred, since the first dawn of my understanding to this it's obscure twilight, all the operations of opinion, fancy, inclination, and will, in the affairs of Government, where only a sovereign reason, paramount to all forms of legislation and administration, should dictate. Government is made for the very purpose of opposing that reason to will and to caprice, in the reformers or in the reformed, in the governors or in the governed, in Kings, in Senates, or in People.[94]

The Rockinghams' moderation was, in a real sense, connected with their attitude towards party (in itself anathema to country values). They loved their own connection, they believed it to be the one that had done so much to establish and sustain the existing conventions of government, and therefore they defended those conventions just as they constantly defended their past policies. Their immense party feeling was unquestionably one of their most noteworthy characteristics. Besides helping to shape their attitude towards the constitution, it did much to enable the marquis and his friends to survive many unrewarding years in opposition; above all, it gave them, through Burke's famous work of 1770, a substantial influence in their country's political development long after their own career had ended.

Earlier in the century, Lord Bolingbroke, in his widely read *Dissertation*,[95] had attempted to construct a party to end all parties, but Burke in the *Thoughts* called for the establishment of a party to end all parties except one – that one being the Rockingham Whigs. Initially, the difference does not perhaps seem great, particularly since both men were ultimately promoting the same type of grand alliance against the government of the day. It seems more significant, however, when one considers that merely to suggest that a party of any sort should become a permanent facility in the government process was to take a stand directly against the mainstream of eighteenth-century ideals. Bolingbroke had not been able to foresee a role for his own party past the time when it would overthrow the existing government, because he, like most men of his day, still viewed detachment and independence in politics as one of the great virtues. Party was a threat to that virtue and, as such, was unacceptable. Thus, he could not even give it a fixed leadership and was reduced, in later works, to calling on his "Patriot King" to provide for its development.

Burke's party, on the other hand, had existed and been clearly definable under the court Whig oligarchy for many decades before George III's ascendancy. The challenge for him was not to construct but simply to recreate this one following by drawing the other groups and connections into the marquis's fold. It was not only desirable but was "essentially necessary for" its members' "full performance of their public duty"[96] that the party should in all circumstances continue to function in the future. In his efforts to justify the Rockinghams, Burke inadvertently provided an excellent defence not just for the one party but for the perpetual struggle among parties in general, in a constant competition for office:

It is the business of the speculative philosopher to mark the proper ends of government. It is the business of the politician, who is the philosopher in action, to find out proper means towards those ends, and to employ them with effect. Therefore every honourable connexion will avow it as their first purpose, to pursue every just method to put the men who hold their opinions into such a condition as may enable them to carry their common plans into execution, with all the power and authority of the State. As this power is attached to certain situations, it is their duty to contend for those situations. Without a proscription of others, they are bound to give to their own party the preference in all things; and by no means, for private considerations, to accept any offers of power in which the whole body is not included.[97]

This was the message that politicians and theorists of the nineteenth century were to draw on so heavily in their efforts to rationalize party government. To point out that in his determination to exalt, expand, and develop the one connection, Burke failed to grasp the implications of his own reasoning is not to deny his accomplishment.[98] In defending party, he enunciated ideas that no author of a major work had previously put forward, and he did so in a manner that later generations would find extremely compelling. When viewing British politics in the years during which the *Thoughts* was written, however, the historian is impressed as much with the spirit displayed by all the leading members of the connection as with the abilities of the work's noted author. From the beginning, Burke was prepared not only to love the Rockingham Whigs but to embrace all their social, political, and constitutional values. By applauding party and illustrating its benefits, he was directly venting their genuine concern for the advancement and perpetuation of their own group and the need to justify their loyalty to something that most people found distasteful. It was, of course, the growth of the same type of loyalty among politicians in general that in later years evolved into the disciplined and cohesive party system. If the majority of the important Rockinghams had not possessed this loyalty, Burke could not have written as he did.

Any discussion of the Rockinghams' constitutional philosophy must of necessity concentrate almost exclusively on a few of the leaders. Their views were probably fairly representative of those of the vast majority of the more committed party members. In concluding the discussion, however, it is essential to point out that they were not representative of the ideas of many of the least committed members, among whom authentic country attitudes tended to be even more influential. Despite their rather dramatic decline in the House of Commons from 1770 onwards, the Rockinghams did not lose their semi-independent following. Such people as Charles Turner and Sir George Savile refused to support the party in awkward issues such as that concerning the East India Company, but for the most part they remained on good terms with the marquis and they continued to follow his lead when their scruples permitted. That is why, for instance, when Dowdeswell submitted his Jury Bill in 1771 he was able to muster seventy-one votes in a thin House, even though the administration, the Chathams, and the vast majority of the independent MPs outside his own following were against him. Because such men as Turner and Savile prided themselves on their independence, they could not share the party spirit displayed by the marquis and many of his closer friends, and they did not have the same feeling of kinship with the court Whigs of the past. Consequently, they were less devoted to the constitution, and in their deep-seated distrust of government and their indifference to place and pension, they were somewhat more strictly controlled by country doctrines. They sincerely considered it the duty of MPs to follow the opinions of those they represented, rather than take the lead. "I hold a leasehold under my constituents,"[99] Savile once said, and in later years he and Turner supported the association movement because they felt that the constitution was no longer able to reflect the voice of the nation adequately.[100] Savile's general willingness to go along with the more extensive reform campaign during the next few years imposed the first real strains on his relationship with Rockingham.

Even though the Rockinghams reflected the values of their time and place in British society, they were in some respects almost unique. They were countrylike politicians who believed they were court Whigs of a bygone era; they approached the constitution with a conservatism that reflected a pervading desire to protect the past, but they clung together out of mutual admiration and love of their party in a way that foreshadowed political conventions of the future; and despite their party feeling, they managed to attract a number of men who prided themselves on their independence. Moreover, after following the course of their career over a number of years, the historian is obliged to concede that they were faithful to their principles to a degree that was extraordinary in their day. This does not, of course, mean that they were gifted with any exceptional abilities when it came to formulating policies or deciding what was best for Britain and the empire. Indeed, their platform between 1768 and 1773 was extremely limited and almost totally negative: it could be summed up as opposition to secret influence, opposition to the undue influence of the crown, opposition to the government, and defence of existing conventions both at home and in America. It cannot be denied, however, that they placed more emphasis on principle in general than most politicians of their time and that once they had established their principles they seldom if ever deserted them. Their most pervading principle was indeed that of consistency, and one finds it very difficult to substantiate a charge of inconsistency against them.

It is true that their stand on the American problem was rather equivocal, but the most fortunate thing about the issue was that their original policy enabled them to take virtually any line they felt desirable. The marquis was almost justified when he told Joseph Harrison[101] in the spring of 1769, "I imagine some late appearance of G[eorge] G[renville] acting in a Sort of Concert with our Friends, must be to a degree a Matter of Surprise & must Occasion Various Speculation. – It may be to be proper to remark – that he adopts many of our Points – not us his & it may also be to be remarked, that his Language & C, of late has softened upon the Subject of ... America."[102] Rockingham might have added that his own language also had softened somewhat, partly though by no means entirely for the sake of accommodation with Grenville. However, the point is that as both the founder of the Declaratory Act and an exponent of conciliation, he had a perfect right to change his language; Grenville did not. Before the union movement, Grenville had emerged as the nation's champion of firm measures and had again and again denounced the Rockinghams and everyone else who considered the policy of appeasement. Moreover, he had made his stand on some clearly enunciated principles. He had told Pownall in July 1768:

I have done my Duty by endeavouring to assert the Sovereignty of the King & Parlt of Great Britain over all the Dominions belonging to the Crown & to make all the Subjects of the Kingdom contribute to the public Burthens for their own Defence according to their abilities & situation. I thought that we had the clearest Right imaginable & that we were bound by every Tye of Justice & of wisdom to do this, & I am convinced it would have been accomplish'd without any considerable Difficulty if America had not received such Encouragem't to oppose it from *hence* as no other People would have resisted.[103]

Grenville's conduct over the next three years at times seemed almost a direct contradiction of these maxims.

The Rockinghams' attempts to draw both the Grenvilles and the Chathams into their following between 1768 and 1770 might on the surface seem somewhat irregular, since both these parties had previously been anathema to them. Three points may be offered in their defence. First, they did not change any of their principles for the sake of union. Not only with respect to America but in the other major issue that confronted them – the Wilkes and Middlesex election affair – it was Grenville and not they who did the about-face. Secondly, as Dowdeswell's manifesto of 1767 demonstrates, union was to the Rockinghams a most important principle in itself. Only through it, they believed, could they ever fulfil their obligation to recreate the "broad and comprehensive" court Whig oligarchy and destroy secret influence. Moreover, whereas Chatham displayed a strong inclination to abandon the union movement for office in late 1770 and the Grenvilles did do so in early 1771, the Rockinghams were faithful to it until their allies had made their priorities clear. Thirdly, in their general approach to their allies they evinced no fundamental lack of uniformity. While Chatham and Temple went out of their way to create the false impression that they were willing to give the marquis and his friends the lead, the Rockinghams did everything possible to make their intentions known from the beginning. Among other things, in the *Thoughts* they not only proposed an arrangement, but they attempted to make it clear that one could only be achieved if the other parties were willing to rally to their banner and give them a predominance both in opposition and in any future administration.

In dealing with the proposed Irish absentee tax, both Rockingham and Burke tended to exploit constitutional ideals and theories of empire for the sake of the marquis's financial well-being. However, they believed in the premises they were propagating. The most basic point they put forward was that the tax would contribute to a breakdown of the unity of the British Empire because it would divide the kingdom in "Interest and Affection" and work towards the destruction of authority at the centre. This was perfectly consistent with every view they had ever expressed with respect to the relationship between England and her overseas dominions. They had always maintained, and would continue to maintain, that it was essential that policies be designed to preserve the "authority of Great Britain"[104] while at the same time creating an atmosphere of *"mutual confidence and affection, upon which the glory and safety of the British empire depend."*[105] Because their reasoning was naturally biased, they exaggerated the effect which the tax was likely to have and they did not give due consideration to its possible benefits, but they cannot be said to have disregarded their principles. Having taken this stand, Burke, for one, continued to adhere to it, even after his leader's death had erased all personal economic considerations. In 1797, when a similar tax was considered in the Irish House of Commons, he attacked a number of his friends for supporting it; he said they were "running the full length of Jacobinism – and meaning something little short of the disunion of the two Kingdoms."[106]

If all this sounds like an apologia for the Rockinghams, even their severest critics must concede that in at least two controversies during this period they proved remarkably willing to stand up for their principles in very awkward circumstances. The most obvious of the two was, of course, the East India Company affair. Admittedly, they hesitated at first and attempted to avoid it, but when they were forced to decide between their principle of opposition to the undue influence of the crown and political expediency, they unanimously came down in favour of the former. They gave up all chance of victory in Parliament, combatting the administration, the Chatham-Shelburnes, the independents, as well as a significant portion of the East India Company men, and they did their reputation both within and outside Parliament considerable harm. The other issue was the Middlesex election. As has been seen, in order to prove their consistency, the Rockinghams insisted on agitating this matter long after it was politically realistic to do so and after even Chatham had come to the conclusion that it would be wiser to drop it.

Arguably, the Rockinghams' loyalty to principle was a critical factor in maintaining good relations with their independent echelon. People such as Savile looked on the political forum as a place to prove their allegiance to ideals, and they appreciated the fact that the leading members of the party were determined to adhere to their own at virtually any cost. During the East India Company affair Savile, though unable to follow the party line himself, realized that his friends were sincere, and instead of attempting to dissuade them from their policy, he advised them not to waste this "opportunity of foretelling with a gravity arising from the subject the fatal consequences, (constitutional ones) we dread from it."[107] Moreover, he found that they were as appreciative of his position at such times as he was of theirs. Because Rockingham believed that principles were extremely important, he had a great deal of respect for Savile's, and he never showed the slightest sign of irritation when Savile refused to acquiesce in party measures. One of the best indications of the understanding that existed between them emerged during the Irish absentee tax business. Although the marquis had much at stake in this affair and took such a strong line with respect to it, Savile, in his objective and independent manner, decided he could not oppose the tax. He knew, however, that he was expected to give his unbiased views on all occasions and therefore had no qualms not only about making his position clear to Rockingham but also about presenting the other side of the argument. He told the marquis, "We are two nations not one in many matters absolutely, in some matters hostile, for we have a separate purse. If you was to be taxed in Northamptonshire for not living there, it would be absurd; but if Northamptonshire had a separate purse, and all her landlords were in rich neighbour countries, I don't know exactly how far I should think I might go if I were a Northamptonshireman."[108] Rockingham took this as well-meant advice from a friend and later merely commented that Savile's "doubt seems to be, Whether the *Measure* is really a bad one for *Ireland*. He has no doubt it is bad and even unjust towards *us* and *England*."[109]

Thus, while the leading members of the party deserve full credit for their consistency and their concern and respect for principles, it is unrealistic to accept, as some modern scholars seem to, the glowing descriptions of nineteenth-century Whig historians.[110] This study has shown that the Rockinghams tended to be very spasmodic in focusing on the problems that faced England and the empire in these years, and they showed no exceptional understanding of the major public issues they confronted. Moreover, it now seems abundantly clear that in order to conduct themselves in such an honourable way with respect to their principles, they did not have to forgo anything they really valued. Others, including Chatham and Grenville, had been professional politicians all their lives, and they not only wanted but desperately needed high office. Their stature both among their followings and in their own eyes had always depended substantially on proximity to the seat of power. One can sympathize with Grenville, who became interested in union in late 1768 not out of principle but because it offered him a last desperate chance to force himself on the king and thereby sustain the loyalty of the few men who had not immediately deserted him when they suspected that he was no longer a realistic contender.

The Marquis had to face no similar problems. It is true that he lost some friends over the years – the Yorkes, Dartmouth, Germain, and Meredith – but, of these, only Meredith had ever been very close to the party. The vast majority of Rockingham's supporters remained with him, and no matter how low his political fortunes sank, he could still boast that although the "Publick & opposition seem at present asleep ... I dont find the least Variation among any of those we call *our Friends.*"[111] Rockingham, Dowdeswell, Portland, and the rest could defy political expediency for the sake of higher purposes because, compared with their allies, they really did not care a great deal about it. Much has been said of this already, but it is perhaps appropriate to conclude by quoting Burke, who in a letter to William Baker on 12 October 1777 left a fairly accurate picture of what it was like to operate in conjunction with the landed aristocrats and gentlemen at the highest level of the connection:

Ill success, ill health, minds too delicate for the rough and toilsome Business of our time, a want of the stimulus of ambition, a degeneracy of the Nation, which they are not lofty enough to despise, nor skillful enough to cure, have, all together, I am afraid contributed very much to weaken the Spring of Characters, whose fault it never was to be too elastick and too firmly braced ... My chief employment for many years has been that woful one, of a *flapper.* I begin to think it time to leave it off ... I am persuaded that the men who will not move, when you want to teize them out of their inactivity, will begin to reproach yours, when you let them alone.[112]

The Rockinghams did ardently want recompense for their efforts, and their policies were as carefully calculated to achieve it as those of other connections were to achieve power and office. In a sense, it was public approval they sought, but more than just immediate approval.

Indeed, they repudiated that on entering the fight over the East India Company. The "formation of any plan will be attended with infinite difficulties I ... forsee," Portland told his leader in November 1772, "& that *immediate* popularity may be risked I can not deny, but at the same time I recur to the principles of our Union as a Party & upon that ground I think I see that the popularity of the day has never been courted by Us, that Difficulties have never been tamely submitted to. That we have been satisfied with the consciousness of having done what was right & that *That* was the only rule for our conduct."[113] Richmond once said of Rockingham that "because he acts honestly and fairly as he certainly does," he thinks "it will produce a like return."[114]

This would seem to be one of the keys to understanding the party as a whole. Rockingham, Dowdeswell, Portland, Lord John Cavendish, and even Burke believed that by making a stand to ward off the present dangers to the constitution and by taking pains at all times to maintain their consistency, they would at some future period win lasting and universal commendation. "The Publick at large sometimes makes a sudden Wheel," Rockingham said in December 1772, "& become violent against those who lead them into Errors, notwithstanding they themselves had early adopted & even been favourable in the outset to those very Errors."[115] He does not appear to have felt at all sure that this would occur soon or even in his lifetime, but he was determined that posterity would look back and see that in an era of widespread corruption, the party he loved so much had stood out from all others in its purity, its integrity, and its persistence in the cause of constitutional government and the public good. In his letters he often made references to history, which demonstrate that although he saw himself as an eighteenth-century Whig, he also – while warning the public of the dangers of the influence of the crown in the early 1770s – had begun to identify with the men of the previous century who had risked life and liberty in the fight against the tyranny of the Stuarts. At one point, he told Turner:

Charles the 1st & his Ministers had not the advantage of a Diffusive Patronage to Create *Influence*, & therefore strove to Create a high undefined Prerogative in the Crown which might operate in Terrorem, & bend Men's Minds to Obedience, whose Affections they had not the Ways, & Means of Influencing. Thomas Earl of Strafforde[116] in the early part of his Life Opposed & felt the lash of the Tyranny, unfortunately for him a Gracious Monarch afterwards soothed him into the loss of his Head – High undefined Prerogative in its very Nature was Odious & all Men dreaded it. I pay due Honour, & Credit to the Men, who made the Noble struggle, & who warded that Mischief from this Country. The Lash at present is a much Severer Trial on Mens Virtue. There is something so Mild, & Alluring in coming under the Benign Influence of the Crown. It not only, ratifies the Individual but also affords him the opportunity of exerting one of the Best Principles of the Human Heart – His Social love – in behalf of his Friends – Relations &c. So that one ought not to wonder that many Men either wont see the danger, or are not of such rigid Stuff as can Withstand the Temptation.[117]

What Rockingham really wanted was for future historians to believe that he and his devoted friends had been "of such rigid stuff."

The party that Rockingham, Dowdeswell, and Burke had forged by 1773 remained largely unaltered in its membership, its court Whig ideology, and its country Whig values until Rockingham's death in 1782. Anyone attempting to account for the apparent change in the Whigs that occurred at that point would be wise to focus closely on the personalities of Rockingham and Fox. When the marquis was gone, there was no one left with the authority to restrain his energetic, ambitious, and virtually irrepressible new successor. By then, Dowdeswell too had died, and although Burke was influential with Fox, in the long run he was unable to direct him firmly. The Duke of Portland and Lord John Cavendish lacked both the energy and the personal magnitude to exert any real control, and Richmond had left the fold to take up the cause of radical reform. In this situation, Fox was able to fashion the deep suspicion of crown and executive, which the party had learned in the early seventies, into a substantial program of parliamentary amendment.[118]

In the final analysis, an understanding of the Rockinghams' particular blend of qualities can help the historian elucidate political alliances in the late eighteenth century. Unfortunately, it does not simplify the picture. The Rockinghams championed too many country objectives to be viewed as part of a Whig-versus-Tory struggle, and their court Whig biases remained too strong to fit them conveniently into a country-against-court explanation. Moreover, they cannot be written off merely as a faction vying for power in a Namierite assessment that divides politicians into three clear-cut groups: a court party of office holders, independents, and factions.[119] A reasonable approach, however, would be to build on Namier's analysis by adding four more categories. This would identify: (1) a court party of office holders; (2) independents; (3) factions such as those of Chatham, Grenville, and the Duke of Bedford when out of power and trying to get in; (4) the city radicals, whose chief interests were the rights of the City of London and reform, but certainly not high ministerial office; (5) country Tories such as Newdigate and Bagot; (6) court/country

Whigs, meaning Rockingham and his most committed regular associates, who were men of country values but whose self-concept and
social, political, and constitutional ideology had been heavily influenced by the need to defend the Whig establishment in the previous
reign;[120] and (7) country Whigs, including the twenty or twenty-five
men at the periphery of the Rockingham connection (in terms, that is,
of commitment) who were country first, Whig second, and court not
at all. Sir George Savile, Charles Turner, and others could not be devoted to the party or its court Whig past, but they were nonetheless
an important and generally supportive sub-group whose opinions
mattered deeply.

All this points to the complicated nature of political alignments in
the first two or more decades of George III's reign. When attempting
to generalize about them, it is difficult to find anything more precise
than "a complex admixture of small alliances and connections."[121]
During the early years of North's regime, country-party and other
standards were often raised by Whigs against a court composed as,
P.D.G. Thomas has observed, of both Whigs and Tories.[122] In the early
years of the American conflict, Tory country gentlemen and independent country gentlemen often sided with the court against an opposition that consisted of court-country and country Whigs, the
Grenvilles prior to 1770, the Chatham-Shelburnes, the city radicals,
and, presumably, some independent country gentlemen. In the late
1770s and early 1780s, when all the country groups, tired of high taxation and humiliation at war,[123] tended to turn against North, court-
country and country Whigs found themselves regularly voting with
country Tories and independent country gentlemen, as well as with
the Shelburnes and city radicals, over issues such as the Rockinghams' country-party program of economical reform. Clearly, to speak
of any sort of lasting dichotomy in national politics – until, perhaps,
the polarization in British society resulting from the French Revolution – is superficial and bound to cause distortions.[124]

The Rockinghams in Both Houses of Parliament, 1768–1773

THE HOUSE OF COMMONS

Those who were MPs for less than the entire period are indicated by the dates following their constituency.

Abdy, Sir Anthony Thomas (?1720–75), MP Knaresborough
A'Court, William (c. 1708–81), MP Heytesbury
Adams, George (1731–89), MP Lichfield, 1770–
Anson, Thomas (1695–1773), MP Lichfield, 1768–70
Aufrere, George René (1715–1801), MP Stamford
Baker, William (1743–1824), MP Plympton Erle
Barrow, Charles (1707–89), MP Gloucester
Beauclerk, Aubrey (1740–1802), MP Aldborough
Bentinck, Lord Charles Edward (1774–1819), MP Carlisle*
Bethell, Hugh (1727–72), MP Beverley, 1768–72
Bridges, Sir Brook (1733–91), MP Kent
Bullock, John (1731–1809), MP Maldon*
Bullock, Joseph (1731–1808), MP Wendover, 1770–
Burke, Edmund (1729–97), MP Wendover
Burke, William (1729–98), MP Great Bedwyn
Byng, George (?1735–89), MP Wigan*
Cavendish, Lord Frederick (1729–1803), MP Derby
Cavendish, Lord George Augustus (?1727–94), MP Derbyshire
Cavendish, Henry (1732–1804), MP Lostwithiel
Cavendish, Lord John (1732–96), MP York
Cholmley, Nathaniel (1721–91), MP Boroughbridge

---

* Contested election. There were twenty-four in 1768.

Clayton, Robert (?1740–99), MP Bletchingley
Codrington, Sir William (1719–92), MP Tewkesbury
Coke, Wenman (c. 1717–76), MP Derby, 1772–
Colebrooke, Sir George (1729–1809), MP Arundel
Conolly, Thomas (?1737–1803), MP Chichester
Cornish, Samuel (c. 1715–70), MP New Shoreham
Coxe, Richard Hippisley (1742–86), MP Somerset
Curwen, Henry (1728–78), MP Cumberland*
Damer, Hon. John (1744–76), MP Gatton
Damer, John (1720–83), MP Dorchester*
Dawnay, Hon. John (1728–80), MP Malton
Dempster, George (1732–1818), MP Perth Burghs*
Dowdeswell, William (1721–75), MP Worcestershire
Fenwick, Thomas (?1729–1794), MP Westmorland*
Fetherstonhaugh, Sir Matthew (1714–74), MP Portsmouth
Finch, Savile (c. 1736–88), MP Malton
Fletcher, Henry (c. 1727–1807), MP Cumberland*
Foley, Edward (1747–1803), MP Droitwich
Foley, Thomas (1716–77), MP Herefordshire
Foley, Thomas (1742–43), MP Herefordshire
Frankland, Thomas (1718–84), MP Thirsk
Frankland, William (1720–1805), MP Thirsk
Garth Turnour, Edward Turnour 1st Baron Winterton [I] (1734–88),
    MP Bramber 1768 – 14 Feb. 1769*
Gregory, Robert (?1729–1810), MP Maidstone*
Grey, Hon. Booth (1740–1802), MP Leicester*
Hanbury, John (1744–84), MP Monmouthshire
Harbord, Harbord (1734–1810), MP Norwich*
Hewett, John (c. 1721–87), MP Nottinghamshire
Hotham, Beaumont (1737–1814), MP Wigan*
Keppel, Hon. Augustus (1725–86), MP New Windsor
Lascelles, Daniel (1714–84), MP Northallerton
Lascelles, Edward (1740–1820), MP Northallerton
Lascelles, Edwin (1713–95), MP Yorkshire
Lennox, Lord George Henry (1737–1805), MP Sussex
Lowdes, Charles (?1699–1783), MP Bramber 1768 – 14 Feb. 1769*
Ludlow, Peter, 1st Earl Ludlow [I] (1730–1803), MP Huntingdonshire*
Luther, John (?1739–86), MP Essex*
Mauger, Joshua (1725–88), MP Poole*
Meredith, Sir William (?1725–90), MP Liverpool[1]
Milles, Richard (c. 1735–1820), MP Canterbury*
Montagu, Frederick (1733–1800), MP Higham Ferrers

Murray, James (1727–99), MP Kirkcudbright

Musgrave, George (?1740–1824), MP Carlisle*

Norris, John (b. 1740), MP Rye

Offley, John (?1717–84), MP East Retford

Osbaldeston, Fontayne Wentworth (1696–1770), MP Scarborough 1768–1770*

Pennyman, Sir James (1736–1808), MP Scarborough 1770–*

Plumer, William (1736–1822), MP Herefordshire

Plumptre, John (1711–91), MP Nottingham

Radcliffe, John (1738–83), MP St Albans

Salt, Samuel (c. 1723–92), MP Liskeard

Saunders, Sir Charles (c. 1713–75), MP Hedon

Savile, Sir George (1726–84), MP Yorkshire

Scawen, James (1734–1801), MP Mitchell*

Scudamore, John (1727–96), MP Hereford

Skipwith, Thomas George (?1735–90), MP Warwickshire, 1769–

Standert, Frederick (c. 1705–85), MP Bletchingley, 1769–

Thompson, Beilby (1742–99), MP Hedon

Tollemache, Hon. Wilbraham (1739–1821), MP Northamptonshire, 1771–

Trecothick, Barlow (?1718–75), MP London*

Verney, Ralph, 2nd Earl Verney [I], (1714–91), MP Buckinghamshire

Walsingham (formerly Boyle), Hon. Robert (1736–80), MP Knaresborough

Weddell, William (1736–92), MP Kingston-upon-Hull*

West, James (1703–72), MP Boroughbridge, 1768–1772

Whitmore, William (1714–71), MP Bridgnorth, 1768–1771

In the *Rise of Party in England: The Rockingham Whigs, 1760–82*,[2] Dr O'Gorman estimates the party membership to have been considerably smaller than this. Among those listed above whom he does not consider Rockingham men are the two, Damers who voted regularly in opposition and who were the son and brother of Lord Milton, who was a consistent Rockingham supporter in the House of Lords; Mauger, who stood at Poole with the backing of Rockingham, Newcastle, and James West; and Luther, Radcliffe, and the three Foleys, who respectively were the friends of Abdy, Lord Torrington, and Dowdeswell. The links between such men and the leading members of the party appear to have been strong enough to warrant categorizing them as Rockinghams. However, in many cases the discrepancy between the two estimates appears to be simply a reflection of dissimilar definitions of the independent Rockinghams. Because a more liberal defintion was used here, such men as Henry Cavendish, the two Franklands, Hanbury, the three Lascelles, Milles, Salt, Aufrere, Bethel and John Bullock are considered part of the following. These men all seem to have adhered to the party line in the divisions in the House of Commons, and a number of them are described as friends in the correspondence of Newcastle,

Rockingham, Portland, or Burke. It is to be admitted, however, that the line separating many independent Rockinghams from many genuine independents is a very thin one and virtually impossible to draw without error.

THE HOUSE OF LORDS

Abergavenny, George Neville, 17th Baron (1727–85)
Albemarle, George Keppel, 3rd Earl of (1724–72)
Archer, Andrew Archer, 2nd Baron (1736–78)
Bessborough, William Ponsonby, 2nd Earl of [I] (1704–93)
Boyle, Edmund Boyle, 2nd Baron (1742–98)
Devonshire, William Cavendish, 5th Duke of (1748–1811)
Dorset, John Frederick Sackville, 3rd Duke of (1745–99, inherited title 1769)
Effingham, Thomas Howard, 3rd Earl of (1746/7–91)
Fitzwilliam, William Fitzwilliam, later Wentworth, 2nd Earl (1748–1833)
Manchester, George Montagu, 4th Duke of (1737–88)
Milton, Joseph Damer, 1st Baron (1718–98)
Monson, John Monson, 2nd Baron (1727–74)
Portland, William Henry Cavendish Bentinck, 3rd Duke of (1738–1809)
Richmond, Charles Lennox, 3rd Duke of (1734/5–1806)
Rockingham, Charles Watson-Wentworth, 2nd Marquis of (1730–82)
Scarborough, Richard Lumley-Saunderson, 4th Earl of (1725–82)
Sondes, Lewis Monson, 1st Baron (1728–95)
Stamford, Harry Grey, 4th Earl of (1737–1819)
Torrington, George Byng, 4th Viscount (1740–1812)
Winchilsea, Daniel Finch, 8th Earl of (1689–1769; on his death the title passed
    to George Finch, 1752–1826)

All the above consistently signed the many protests which the party submitted over the years in the House of Lords.[3] Moreover, they all either corresponded with the leading members of the party or were, at one point or another, described by those members as friends. The only doubtful man among them is Manchester, who at times seemed to take the Chatham line. In this particular period, however, Manchester appears to have considered himself a Rockingham.[4]

Notes

ABBREVIATIONS

BL British Library
BM British Museum
HMC Historical Manuscripts Commission
NUL Nottingham University Library
PRO Public Record Office
SCL Sheffield City Library
WCL William L. Clements Library
WWM Wentworth Woodhouse Muniments

INTRODUCTION

1 Charles Watson-Wentworth, 2nd Marquis of Rockingham (1730–82).
2 (1729–97), MP 1765–94.
3 Burke, *Correspondence*, 7: 52–3, Burke to William Weddell, 31 January 1792.
4 William Henry Cavendish Bentinck, 3rd Duke of Portland (1738–1809).
5 (1721–75), MP 1747–54, 1761–75.
6 (1723–96), MP 1754–84, 1794–96.
7 8th Baronet (1726–84), MP 1759–83.
8 Namier, *Structure of Politics*, 5–6.
9 The marquis and his friends are described as a power-hungry faction in Namier and Brooke, *History of Parliament*, 1:190.
10 This is a central theme in Langford's, *First Rockingham Administration*; see, in particular, 283–7.
11 For the most recent discussions of country-party attributes, see Hayton, "The 'Country' Interest and the Party System, 1689–c.1720," and Dickinson, *Liberty and Property,* 91–118, 163–92. For an overview of contemporary literature and argument, see Gunn, *Factions No More*, 97–112.

12 (1676–1745), 1st Earl of Orford.

13 (1695?–1754).

14 Clark, *Revolution and Rebellion*, 142.

15 For a fuller discussion of membership in the Rockingham fold, see below, 23, and the appendix.

16 Thomas, "Party Politics in Eighteenth-Century Britain."

17 5th Baronet (1719–1806), MP 1742–47, 1751–80.

18 (1728–98), MP 1754–80.

19 6th Baronet (?1697–1778), MP 1754–74.

20 Among the Tories who turned against North during the course of the war and supported economical reform were Richard Hill (1733–1808), MP 1780–1806; Thomas Lister (1752–1806), MP 1773–90; John Parker (?1754–97), MP 1780–82; John Parker (?1735–88), MP 1761–84; Lucy Knightley (1742–91), MP 1763–68, 1773–84; William Drake (1723–96), MP 1746–96; Clement Tudway (1734–1815), MP 1761–1815; Sir John Rous, 6th Baronet (1750–1827), MP 1780–96; Henry Dawkins (1728–1814), MP 1760–68, 1769–74, 1776–84; Sir Watkin Williams Wynn, 4th Baronet (1748–89), MP 1772–89. By 1780, Newdigate was also voting against government on a least one motion relative to the influence of the crown. However, he and Bagot did not contest the 1780 election. Mordaunt retired from Parliament in 1774.

21 Thomas, "Party Politics in Eighteenth-Century Britain," 207.

22 Thomas Pelham-Holles, 1st Duke of Newcastle (1693–1768).

23 William Keppel, 2nd Earl of Albemarle (1702–54).

24 William Cavendish, 4th Duke of Devonshire (1720–64).

25 This point is made by Langford, *First Rockingham Administration*, 288.

26 See Browning, *Political and Constitutional Ideas of the Court Whigs*, and Dickinson, *Liberty and Property*, 57–162.

27 (1749–1806), MP 1768–1806.

28 (1736–1839), MP 1788–1802, later (1802) 6th Duke of Bedford.

29 Charles Grey, 2nd Earl Grey (1764–1855).

30 For a discussion of the more radical approach before the French Revolution, see Dickinson, *Liberty and Property*, 195–231.

31 Burke, *Writings and Speeches*, 2: 243–7.

32 Ibid., 264.

33 Ibid., 266–7.

34 See, Langford, *First Rockingham Administration*.

35 This is also the central argument of the party's other well-known political publication in this period, *Observations on a Late State of the Nation*; see, Burke, *Writings and Speeches*, 2:102–219. For discussions of these works, see below, 58–9, 88–95.

36 O'Gorman, *Rise of Party*, 409–59.

37 The bill proposed by John Crewe (1742–1829), MP 1765–1802.

38 The bill proposed by Philip Jennings Clerke (1722–88), MP 1768–88.

201 Notes to pages 8–12

39 See, Elofson, "Rockingham Whigs and the Country Tradition."
40 William Pitt, 1st Earl of Chatham (1708–78), MP 1735–66.
41 See Namier and Brooke, *History of Parliament*, 1:186.
42 Ibid., 190.
43 A recent work that could do this is O'Brien, *Great Melody*; see, in particular, xxxii–lix.
44 (1838–1928).
45 (1800–59).
46 Including John Brewer, see below, 62.
47 See below, 58. In his survey of the Rockinghams' career (*Rise of Party*), Professor O'Gorman acknowledges that the party leaders were concerned about ideals. However, he does not stress how much stronger that concern was than other objectives, including public office. Nor does he offer an extensive elaboration of Rockingham constitutional thought. The one realistic study that recognizes the depth of the party's concern for principles is Langford's, *First Rockingham Administration*. It concentrates on the party in the fledgling stage before it had been able to work out any sort of extensive constitutional ideology.

CHAPTER ONE

1 O'Gorman, *Voters, Patrons and Parties*, especially 317–83; Bradley, *Religion, Revolution and English Radicalism*. Evidence of the growth of party politics is also found in Phillips, *Electoral Behavior in Unreformed England*. The polarity in the four boroughs studied, however, is described as "anti-ministerial" or "opposition" against "ministerial," rather than Whig versus Tory (114–23). The reader is also directed to Money, *Experience and Identity*, especially 189–95.
2 See, for instance, Burke, *Correspondence*, 3:76, 78, 97.
3 Ibid., 3: 382–3, Burke to Fox, 8 October 1777.
4 See Namier and Brooke, *History of Parliament*, 1:442.
5 See Hill, *Parliamentary Parties, 1742–1832*.
6 Clark, "The Decline of Party," 517–19; Namier, *England in the Age of the American Revolution*, 192–5.
7 Brooke, *King George III*, 159.
8 Professor Frank O'Gorman argues that the nineteenth-century two-party dichotomy began some fifty years before 1832 (*British Two-Party System*, 14). Recent research, however, has warned against assuming that even in the 1780s men who saw themselves as Whigs could be considered of the same following even when cooperating closely together on a regular basis (Christie, "Anatomy of the Opposition").
9 Professor Christie makes this argument in "Parliamentary Politics," 102, 112. Paul Langford notes that "at the local level, particularly in the larger

constituencies, and where great landed interests could trace back a contin-
uous tradition of loyalty to one of the great parties, the old slogans continued to be used at election time, though without much reference to the
actual control at Westminster of those elected" ("Old Whigs, Old Tories,
and the American Revolution," 106). James Bradley remarks on the distinction between local versions of the Whig party and the Rockinghams
(*Religion, Revolution and English Radicalism*, 412–17). However, he seems to
have drawn the conclusion that the Rockinghams were the only connection to which members of the local groups could be expected to have re-
sorted on the national level.

10 The party surrounding George Grenville (1712–70), MP 1741–70.
11 The party surrounding John Russell, 4th Duke of Bedford (1710–71).
12 Augustus Henry Fitzroy, 3rd Duke of Grafton (1735–1811).
13 The party surrounding Frederick styled Lord North (1732–92), later (1790)
   2nd Earl of Guilford, MP 1754–90.
14 (1709–70), MP 1747–70, Lord Mayor of London 1762–63, 1769–70.
15 (1737–87), MP 1767–74, 1782–87.
16 Professor Christie has recently convincingly put forth this thesis with respect to parties throughout the 1770s and 1780s ("Party in Politics"; "The
   Anatomy of the Opposition").
17 See below, 23.
18 Christie, "Party in Politics," 55.
19 See, Brewer, *The Sinews of Power*, especially 64–87.
20 Rubini, *Court and Country*, 37–8, 68–92, 171–7; Dickinson, *Liberty and Property*, 163–92; Langford, *Polite and Commercial People*, 22–33, 53–7, 185–9,
   230–1; Colley, *Defiance of Oligarchy*, 85–101, 204–62.
21 Including William Hussey (1725–1813), MP 1765–1813; Francis Page
   (?1726–1803), MP 1768–1801; Sir John Palmer (1735–1817), MP 1765–80; Sir
   Thomas Clavering (1719–94), MP 1753–60, 1768–90.
22 Others were Sir James Dashwood (1715–79), MP 1761–68; Sir William Dol-
   ben (1727–1814), MP 1768–77; Sir Edward Blackett (1719–1804), MP 1768–
   74; Edward Southwell (1738–77), MP 1761–76.
23 Including Charles Marsham (1744–1811), MP 1768–90; Sir Mathew Ridley
   (1745–1813), MP 1768–1812.
24 Including William Drake (1723–96), MP 1746–96; Thomas More
   Molyneaux (?1724–76), MP 1759–76. See Lawson, *George Grenville*, 264–6,
   276–7.
25 Including Sir John Glynne (1712–77), MP 1753–77; Richard Lowdes
   (?1707–75), MP 1741–74; Sir Henry Hoghton (1728–95), MP 1768–95.
26 See below, 158, 182–3.
27 Walpole, *Memoirs*, 3:109–13.
28 See below, 182.
29 (1732–95), MP 1768–95.

30 See below, 128.
31 Besides Brooke's work cited above, 9, see Brewer, *Party Ideology and Popular Politics*, 257, and O'Gorman, *Rise of Party*, 474.
32 For the Rockingham following in both Houses of Parliament, see the appendix.
33 Often, Rockingham did not meet with his leading supporters at all on political matters when Parliament was not in session, or he only contacted them when he could do so without disrupting his social life and his attention to the racing circuit. See below, 39, 132. See also Brooke, *King George III*, 122.
34 Langford, *First Rockingham Administration*, especially 271–89. Professor Langford confirmed the earlier work of Collyer ("Rockingham Connection and Country Opinion").
35 For a solid account of the activities of some of the "old Whigs," see Browning, *Duke of Newcastle*.
36 For a view of Newcastle's sense of his own inefficacy, see, for instance, Bateson, *Narrative of the Changes in the Ministry*, 115–16.
37 (1703–32), MP 1741–72.
38 Formerly John Thornhagh (c.1721–87), MP 1747–74.
39 (?1717–84), MP 1747–74.
40 George Keppel, 3rd Earl of Albemarle (1724–72).
41 Daniel Finch, 2nd Earl of Nottingham and 7th Earl of Winchilsea (1689–1769).
42 William Ponsonby, 2nd Earl of Bessborough [I] and 1st Baron Ponsonby (1704–93), MP 1742–58.
43 Sheffield City Library (SCL), Wentworth Woodhouse Muniments (WWM), R1–1356, Dowdeswell to Rockingham, 8 February 1771.
44 SCL, WWM, R1–1425, Portland to Rockingham, 9 January 1773.
45 SCL, WWM, R1–1413, Portland to Rockingham, 21 November 1772.
46 Richmond, "Duke of Richmond's Memorandum," 479.
47 For Rockingham's early life, see Guttridge, "Early Career of Lord Rockingham."
48 Young, *Six Months Tour through the North of England*, 1:271.
49 Namier and Brooke, *History of Parliament*, 1:427–31.
50 See below, 64–5.
51 1726–1811.
52 Coke, *Letters and Journals*, 2:357.
53 Langford, *First Rockingham Administration*, 278.
54 Charles Barrow (1707–89), MP 1751–89, and Sir William Codrington, 2nd Baronet (1719–92), MP 1761–92.
55 Thomas, "Check List of MPs," 220–6.
56 SCL, WWM, R1–1413, Portland to Rockingham, 21 November 1772.
57 William L. Clements Library (WCL), Dowdeswell Papers, Dowdeswell to Burke, 18 October 1772.

58 Burke, *Correspondence*, 1:302, Burke to O'Hara, 28 March [1767].
59 (1759–1806), MP 1781–1806.
60 Burke, *Correspondence*, 1:266, Burke to Rockingham, 21 August 1766.
61 Ibid., 1:290, Burke to Charles O'Hara, 15 January [1767].
62 For Burke's position in the party between Dowdeswell and Fox, see Burke, *Writings and Speeches*, 3:1–9.
63 See O'Brien, *Great Melody*, especially xxxviii-xli, xlvi, 99–105, 135. O'Brien supports the views expressed by Morley in *Burke*, Guttridge in *English Whiggism*, and Cone in *Burke and the Nature of Politics*.
64 O'Brien, *Great Melody*, xliv-lix.
65 See Burke, *Writings and Speeches*, 3:45.
66 Ibid., 3:325.
67 Burke, *Correspondence*, 2:377, Burke to Richmond [post 15 November 1772].
68 Ibid., 2:5.
69 See below, 72, 75–6, 79.
70 O'Brien, *Great Melody*, 129–35.
71 For the *Thoughts*, see below, 89–95, and Burke, *Writings and Speeches*, 2:243–7.
72 See below, 148.
73 Burke, *Writings and Speeches*, 3:1–47; see also, O'Gorman, *Rise of Party*, 259–62.
74 O'Brien, *Great Melody*, 99–105; Burke, *Writings and Speeches*, 3:26–7.
75 From 1761 until 1780 the other was filled by Rockingham's friend Edwin Lascelles (1713–95), MP 1744–90.
76 Nottingham University Library (NUL), Portland Papers (PWF) 5302, B. Hotham to Portland, 28 November 1769.
77 For instance, in the East India Company issue of 1772–73, when many of his colleagues supported the company against government interference, he temporarily separated from them. See Cobbett, *Parliamentary History*, 17:464.
78 Lord Charles Edward Bentinck (1744–1819), MP 1766–74, 1775–1802; Henry Curwen (1728–78), MP 1768–74; Thomas Fenwick (?1729–94), MP 1768–74; Henry Fletcher (c.1727–1807), MP 1768–1806; Beaumont Hotham (1737–1814), MP 1768–75; George Musgrave (?1740–1824), MP 1768–74.
79 William Cavendish (1720–64).
80 (1729–1803), MP 1751–80.
81 (?1727–94), MP 1751–80, 1781–94.
82 (1732–1804), MP 1768–74.
83 Sir Anthony Abdy, 5th Baronet (?1720–75), MP 1763–75; William A'Court (c.1708–81), MP 1751–81; Aubrey Beauclerk (1740–1802), MP 1761–74.
84 Walpole, *Memoirs*, 2:17.

85 Burke, *Correspondence*, 1:326, William Burke to Edmund Burke [post 4 September 1767].
86 Charles Lennox, 3rd Duke of Richmond (1735–1806).
87 (1746–1830), MP 1766–84.
88 That led by William Pitt, 1st Earl of Chatham (1708–78), MP 1735–66.
89 Coke, *Letters and Journals*, 2:180.
90 Burke, *Correspondence*, 1:321, Burke to Rockingham, 18 August 1767.
91 Ibid.
92 Brooke, *Chatham Administration*, 162–217.
93 See below, 151–2, 154, and Elofson, "The Rockingham Whigs in Transition."
94 Burke, *Correspondence*, 2:371, Richmond to Burke, 15 November 1772.
95 (1725–86), MP 1755–82.
96 (c. 1713–65), MP 1750–75.
97 See appendix.
98 William Cavendish, 5th Duke of Devonshire (1748–1811).
99 Leinster, *Correspondence*, 517, Kildare to Leinster, 4 May [1768].
100 William Fitzwilliam, 4th Earl Fitzwilliam (1748–1833).
101 Andrew Archer, 2nd Lord Archer (1736–78), MP 1761–68.
102 George Harry Grey, 4th Earl of Stamford (1737–1819).
103 George Neville, 17th Baron and 1st Earl of Abergavenny (1727–85).
104 Richard Lumley-Saunderson, 4th Earl of Scarborough (1725–82).
105 See appendix.
106 O'Gorman, *Rise of Party*, 320. Professor O'Gorman's estimate is accepted by others (Christie, "Parliamentary Politics," 116).
107 (1744–84), MP 1766–84.
108 (?1727–83), MP 1768–83.
109 See below, 81.
110 (1720–1805), MP 1768–74; (1718–84), MP 1747–80, 1784.
111 (1715–1801), MP 1765–74.
112 Professor Christie speaks of some nineteen Tories who in the 1770s "were adopting a very independent stance, some of them being hardly distinguishable from Rockinghamites" ("Party in Politics," 56). There were a number of Whigs about whom the same could be said; it is very difficult to decide exactly how many but probably at least twenty-five. For a full list of the Rockinghams in both Houses, see the appendix.
113 (formerly Boyle) (1736–80), MP 1758–80.
114 (1732–1818), MP 1761–90.
115 (?1729–1810), MP 1768–84.
116 (1736–92), MP 1766–92.
117 (1742–99), MP 1768–84, 1790–96.
118 (1721–91), MP 1756–94.
119 (1696–1770), MP 1766–70.

120 Christie, "Party in Politics," 55–6.
121 (?1720–75), MP 1763–75.
122 (?1739–86), MP 1763–84.
123 2nd Baronet (1719–92), MP 1761–92.
124 (1707–89), MP 1751–89.
125 This could be the case, for instance, in Colley, *In Defiance of Oligarchy*, and Hill, *Parliamentary Parties, 1742–1832*, 3–89.
126 Colley, "Eighteenth-Century English Radicalism," 4–21.
127 See below, 185–6.
128 Dickinson, *Liberty and Property*, 167.
129 See Christie, *Myth and Reality*, 261–83; Black, *The Association*, 1–82.
130 Wyvill, *Political Papers*, 1:32.
131 Burke, *Writings and Speeches*, 2:210.
132 Burke, *Correspondence*, 2:101, Burke to Rockingham, 29 October 1769.
133 For the court Whig view, see Browning, *Political and Constitutional Ideas*.
134 *Grenville Papers*, 4:392, Thomas Whatley to George Grenville, 28 October 1768.
135 Burke, *Writings and Speeches*, 2:215.
136 Burke, *Correspondence*, 2:92, Rockingham to Burke, 15 October 1769.
137 John Stuart, 3rd Earl of Bute (1713–92).
138 See Brewer, "Misfortunes of Lord Bute," 3–43.
139 Paul Langford has designated this period "Cumberland's Administration"(*First Rockingham Administration*, 70–108).
140 William Augustus (1721–65).
141 See, Langford, *First Rockingham Administration*, 109–98, for the Rockinghams' handling of America, and 236–63 for the demise of the administration.
142 For the negotiations of July 1767, see Brooke, *Chatham Administration*, 162–217, and *King George III*, 141–2; O'Gorman, *Rise of Party*, 206–8; Lawson, *George Grenville*, 241–5; and Rea, *English Press in Politics*, 135–8.
143 Bedford, *Correspondence*, 3:373, Bedford to Rockingham, 16 July 1767.
144 Ibid.
145 Bateson, *Narrative of the Changes in the Ministry.*
146 Almon, *Political Register*, 1:4.
147 Augusta of Saxe Gotha (1719–72).
148 (1725–97), MP 1757–64, 1768–69, 1774–90.
149 (1731–64).
150 See Rudé, *Wilkes and Liberty*, 17–35.
151 For this administration, see Lawson, *George Grenville*.
152 Almon, *Political Register*, 1:3.
153 See Langford, *First Rockingham Administration*.
154 NUL, PWF, 8984, Rockingham to Portland, 28 August 1766.
155 See Brewer, "Party and the Double Cabinet," 3–21.

156 Burke, *Writings and Speeches*, 2:56.
157 *Grenville Papers*, 4:7, Temple to Grenville, 18 March 1767.
158 The negotiations of 1767 are a case in point. See also below, 32–4.
159 See below, 90–2.
160 See below, 35, 58–9.
161 *Monitor*, 22 May 1762.
162 Almon, *Political Register*, 1:8.
163 Almon, *Biographical, Literary and Political Anecdotes*, 3:32.
164 Almon, *Political Register*, 1:3.
165 Ibid.
166 Walpole, *Memoirs*, 2:196.
167 Burke, *Writings and Speeches*, 2:270.
168 Walpole, *Memoirs*, 2:196.
169 See, for instance, Brooke, *King George III*, 159–61; Langford, *Polite and Commercial People*, 521–4; Pares, *George III and the Politicians*, 93–118.
170 Augustus Henry Fitzroy, 3rd Duke of Grafton (1725–1811).
171 (1733–1805), MP 1761–80.
172 *Grenville Papers*, 4:120–1, Whately to Grenville, 29 July 1767.
173 (c.1728–72), MP 1761–72.
174 *Grenville Papers*, 4:125, Grenville to Whately, 30 July 1767.
175 Ibid., 145, Whately to Grenville, 1 August 1767.
176 SCL, WWM, R1–842. Dowdeswell entitled his piece "Thoughts on the present state of publick affairs and the propriety of accepting or declining administration, Written the 23d & 24 of July 1767."
177 According to the *Thoughts*, this was the central accomplishment of the party's first administration; see below, 35.
178 Burke, *Writings and Speeches*, 2:275.

CHAPTER TWO

1 Frederick North, styled Lord North (1732–92), MP 1754–90.
2 See below, 186–9.
3 See below, 109; Christie, "The Marquis of Rockingham and Lord North's Offer of a Coalition," 109–32; O'Gorman, *Rise of Party*, 422–3.
4 Ibid., 446–53.
5 That centred on William Petty, formerly Fitzmaurice, 2nd Earl of Shelburne (1737–1805), later (1784) 1st Marquis of Lansdowne.
6 See Hill, *Parliamentary Parties, 1742–1832*, 110–27; O'Gorman, *British Two-Party System*, 14.
7 Christie, "Anatomy of the Opposition," 77. See also his "Party in Politics," 47–68.
8 Brooke, *Chatham Administration*, 139.
9 Franklin, *Writings*, 5:464, Franklin to Joseph Galoway, 2 July 1768.

10 For instance, on 20 July Sir William Meredith informed the Duke of Portland, "It seems as if things were verging towards Mr. Grenville. As the
Bedfords are provoking Ld. Chatham's people to resign, they must have
somebody in view & who can that be, but Mr. Grenville?" See Nottingham University Library (NUL), Portland Papers (PWF) 6727.

11 British Museum (BM), Hardwicke Papers, British Library (BL), Add. Ms.
35568:289, Sir Joseph Yorke to Hardwicke, 20 July 1768; Burke, *Correspondence*, 2:3, Burke to Rockingham, 18 July 1768.

12 See also Phillimore, *Memoirs and Correspondence of Lord Lyttleton*,
749–50, Temple to Lyttleton, 14 August 1768.

13 See Burke, *Correspondence*, 2:4, Burke to Rockingham, 18 July 1768.

14 BM, Newcastle Papers, BL, Add. Ms. 32991:94, Newcastle to Rockingham, 12 September 1768; ibid., 206, 8 October 1768; ibid., 230, 11 October
1768.

15 Ibid., 236, Newcastle to Portland, 11 October 1768.

16 Ibid., 264, Newcastle to Richmond, 17 October 1768.

17 Ibid., 228, Frederick Cavendish to Newcastle [October 1768].

18 Chatham, *Correspondence*, 3:338, Chatham to Grafton, 12 October 1768.

19 BM, Newcastle Papers, BL, Add. Ms. 32991:331, Albemarle to Newcastle,
8 October 1768.

20 Lawson, *George Grenville*, 269.

21 Namier and Brooke, *History of Parliament*, 2:543–4.

22 See George III, *Letters to Lord Bute*, 240.

23 Lawson, *George Grenville*, 277–93.

24 BM, Grenville Papers, BL, Add. Ms. 42086:36, Whately to Grenville, 9 May
1768.

25 Ibid., 62, Whately to Grenville, 13 July 1768.

26 5 Geo. III, c. 12.

27 See Thomas's *British Politics and the Stamp Act Crisis, Townshend Duties Crisis*, and *Tea Party to Independence*.

28 Besides Thomas, *British Politics*, see Langford, *First Rockingham Administration*, 109–98.

29 5 Geo. III, c. 33. It called on the colonists to make provisions for British
troops stationed among them.

30 (1725–1767), MP 1747–67.

31 7 Geo. III, c. 46. It taxed enumerated commodities and also explicitly af-
firmed the mother country's right to tax for revenue purposes with the
following statement in the preamble: "Whereas it is expedient that a Revenue should be raised, in Your Majesty's Dominions in *America*, the Administration of Justice, and the Support of Civil Government, in such
Provinces where it shall be found necessary; and towards further defray-
ing the Expences of defending, protecting, and securing the said Dominions."

32 Sainsbury, *Disaffected Patriots*.
33 Bradley, *Religion, Revolution and English Radicalism*.
34 See, in particular, Thomas, *Townshend Duties Crisis*, 1–17, 94–120, and *Tea Party to Independence*, 48–87.
35 Rogers, *Whigs and Cities*, 1–220.
36 As Professor Bradley notes it was not necessary for the laws to be enforced (*Religion, Revolution and English Radicalism*, 84–90).
37 Johnson, "Letters of William Samuel Johnson," 424–5, Johnson to Pitkin, 6 March 1770.
38 See below, 51–2.
39 See below, 57–8.
40 "Correspondence between William Strahan and David Hall," 330, Strahan to Hall, 3 February 1768; see also *Public Advertiser*, 6 August 1768.
41 (1732–1810).
42 See *Grenville Papers* beginning at 4:319; Grenville's letterbook at the Huntington Library, California; and Great Britain, HMC, *Various Collections*, 6:95ff.
43 BM, Grenville Papers, Add. Ms. 42086:70, Knox to Grenville, 23 July 1768.
44 For a more generous view of Grenville's approach to the American problem, see Lawson, "George Grenville and America," 561–76.
45 (?1718–75), MP 1768–74.
46 Johnson, "Letters of William Samuel Johnson," 267, Johnson to Pitkin, 12 March 1768. On 19 January 1768, James West wrote to Newcastle, "I am sorry to tell [you] … that the opposition to Ald Trecothick gains great strength, from his actions as a friend to the Colonies, in opposition to the Trade of Great Britain" (BM, Newcastle Papers, BL, Add. Ms. 32988:48).
47 Langford, "Rockingham Whigs and America," 145. For a discussion of Burke's views on America, which mirrored those of the party leadership in general, see Burke, *Writings and Speeches*, 3:42–7.
48 Sheffield City Library (SCL), Wentworth Woodhouse Muniments (WWM), R13–10, Thomas Cushing, in the name of the House of Representatives of Massachusetts Bay, to Rockingham, 22 June 1768.
49 William L. Clements Library (WCL), Dowdeswell Papers, Dowdeswell to Rockingham, 10 August 1768.
50 SCL, WWM, R1–1077, Savile to Rockingham, 31 July 1768.
51 See O'Brien, *Great Melody*, 126–7.
52 See below, 52, 88.
53 See Burke's "Speech on American Taxation," (*Writings and Speeches*, 2:406–63).
54 Burke, *Writings and Speeches*, 3:59.
55 BM, Newcastle Papers, BL, Add. Ms. 32991:95, Newcastle to Rockingham, 12 September 1768.

56 Ibid., 224, Newcastle to Frederick Cavendish, 10 October 1768.
57 By 1768 Britons generally were coming to the conclusion that the Rockingham administration's repeal of the Stamp Act had been a mistake. It
   appeared to have encouraged the Americans to believe that by causing a
   great stir at any one time, they could obtain whatever concessions they
   wanted. See, for instance, Chatham, *Correspondence*, 4:253–4, Shelburne
   to Chatham [26 May 1767].
58 BM, Newcastle Papers, BL, Add. Ms. 32990:75, Newcastle to Bessborough, 16 May 1768.
59 For the latest word on this, see Christie, "Parliamentary Politics," 115
   and n55.
60 Ibid.
61 *Grenville Papers*, 4:392, Whately to Grenville, 28 October 1768.
62 BM, Newcastle Papers, BL, Add. Ms. 32991:403, Albemarle to Newcastle
   [7 November 1768].
63 5th Baronet (1736–1802), MP 1757–84.
64 See Anderson, "Pascal Paoli," 180; Carrington, "The Corsican Constitution," 481–503; and Throsler, *Pasquale Paoli*.
65 James Boswell, who spent considerable time in Corsica and admired both
   the island and its people, started a subscription for funds for Corsica at
   this time, and he received support from Barlow Trecothick and other politicians. For Boswell's views on Corsica, see his *Account of Corsica*.
66 See, for instance, the comments in the *Public Advertiser*, 21 June and
   15 July 1768.
67 For comments on the insignificance of the island, see the *Public Advertiser*, 6 July 1768. On 20 July, Sir Joseph Yorke informed his brother, "Corsica will not bring on a war I think, for the City don't take it up warmly,
   but there seems an inclination to give poor Paoli some assistance" (BM,
   Hardwicke Papers, BL, Add. Ms. 35368:289.
68 BM, Newcastle Papers, BL, Add. Ms. 32991:403, Albemarle to Newcastle
   [7 November 1768].
69 When the matter was debated in the Commons, no one suggested that
   Britain should send military assistance. See nn 70 and 72 below.
70 BM, BL, Eg. Ms. 215:105.
71 (1729–1807), MP 1763–80.
72 BM, BL, Eg. Ms. 215:161–95.
73 (1726–1802), MP 1761–90.
74 (1709–70), MP 1747–70.
75 Langford, *First Rockingham Administration*, 136–9, 269–70.
76 See below, 75–6.
77 Langford, *First Rockingham Administration*, 109–98.
78 No doubt it was to avoid making enemies among the London radicals
   that they had bothered to continue paying a small annual stipend to John

Wilkes since his animated dispute with the Grenville ministry some years earlier (see below, 55). For the city's opposition press in the 1760s and 1770s, see Rea, *English Press in Politics*.

79 For this conflict, see Bonsall, *Sir James Lowther*, 81–140; Hughes, *North Country Life*, vol. 2; and Turbeville, *History of Welbeck Abbey*, 2:101–36.

80 (1736–1802), MP 1757–84. Husband of Lady Mary Stuart (1740–1824).

81 SCL, WWM, R1–931, 9 July 1767. The property had been in the Portland family's possession since 1705.

82 SCL, WWM, R1–932, R. Herbert (surveyor general) to the lords of the Treasury.

83 SCL, WWM, R1–933, Portland to Grafton, 2 September 1767.

84 SCL, WWM, R1–944, Portland to Grafton, 1 January 1768.

85 SCL, WWM, R1–942, Sir Grey Cooper to Portland, 22 December 1767.

86 (c.1727–1807), MP 1768–1806.

87 (1728–78), MP 1761–74.

88 (?1731–1814), MP 1786–96.

89 Rockingham even took the precaution of instructing Portland to get his friends to town and to tell them to be prepared "to stay the evening, or all night" if necessary (NUL, PWF 9003, 13 February 1768).

90 BM, Hardwicke Papers, BL, Add. Ms. 35430:269, Abdy to Charles Yorke, 15 September 1768.

91 Ibid., 126, Rockingham to Charles Yorke, 31 October 1768; BM, Newcastle Papers, BL, Add. Ms. 32991A:373, Rockingham to Newcastle, 2 November 1768; BM, Hardwicke Papers, BL, Add. Ms. 35430:130, Rockingham to Yorke, 12 November 1768; NUL, PWF 2841, Robert Clayton to Portland, 15 November 1768; BM, Papers, BL, Add. Ms. 35039:291, Lord John Cavendish to Yorke [January 1769].

92 BM, Newcastle Papers, BL, Add. Ms. 32991:425, Rockingham to Newcastle, 12 November 1768.

93 *Journals of the House of Commons* (hereafter, *Commons Journals*), 32:289.

94 *Journals of the House of Lords* (hereafter *Lords Journals*), 32:299.

95 SCL, WWM, R1–1038, Portland to Rockingham [23 April 1768]; BM, Newcastle Papers, BL, Add. Ms. 32989:371, Portland to Newcastle, 23 April 1768.

96 BM, BL, Eg. Ms. 215:18.

97 Ibid., 219:94, 9 March 1769. On 5 April, Lord John Cavendish moved that counsel "be admitted to be heard" on the charges against Lawson (*Commons Journals*, 32:359).

98 Ibid., 32:361.

99 BM, BL, Eg. Ms. 219:159, 6 April 1769.

100 Ibid. 219:309, 24 April 1769. This motion was proposed by Henry Seymour, a Grenville, but it is very likely that the Rockinghams were the principal instigators. Burke and Savile supported the motion in debate.

101 BM, Newcastle Papers, BL, Add. Ms. 32989:381, 2 April 1768.
102 Burke, *Correspondence*, 2:197, Burke to Rockingham, 16 February 1771.
103 Ibid., 197 and n.
104 Dickinson, *Liberty and Property*, 121–62.
105 SCL, WWM, R1–1078, Newcastle to Rockingham, 1 August 1768.
106 Barré spoke for the measure.
107 (?1708–77), MP 1756–77.
108 (1727–59).
109 (1724–73), MP 1763–73.
110 (?1721–87), MP 1762–84.
111 (1722–1805), MP 1767–80.
112 BM, BL, Eg. Ms. 215:105–25, 8 November 1768.
113 On 7 December (*Commons Journals*, 32:92; BM, BL, Eg. Ms. 215:270).
114 On 25 January 1769 (Cobbett, *Parl. Hist.*, 16:480–4; BM, BL, Eg. Ms. 215:94–102).
115 On 14 March (Cobbett, *Parl. Hist.*, 603).
116 BM, BL, Eg. Ms. 215:105–28.
117 Ibid., 215:105, 128. Grenville supported the principle of an inquiry on these grounds and said he would second it at a later date, but he voted against the motion for the time being. By attacking the order sent out by the secretary of state, Grenville was able to speak for American rights without going against the authority of Parliament – which he had constantly championed in connection with the American problem.
118 Lawson, "George Grenville and America," 576.
119 Cobbett, *Parl. Hist.*, 16:476–9.
120 Ibid., 476–7 and n.
121 The petition was presented on 26 January (ibid., 484–5).
122 (c. 1710–76).
123 On 8 February (Cobbett, *Parl. Hist.*, 16:494–510).
124 Ibid., 488.
125 De Berdt, "Letters," 355, De Berdt to Cushing, 1 February 1767.
126 Burke, *Writings and Speeches*, 2:232.
127 6 Geo. III, c. 12.
128 For a thorough discussion of this act, see Langford, *First Rockingham Administration*, 151–3, 190–1.
129 Burke, *Writings and Speeches*, 2:406–63, and 3:102–68, 183–220.
130 SCL, WWM, R1–1186, Rockingham to Joseph Harrison, 19 May 1769.
131 (1709–87), the collector of customs in Boston.
132 SCL, WWM, R1–1186, Joseph Harrison to Rockingham, 13 February 1769.
133 The best source for this is still Rudé, *Wilkes and Liberty.*
134 His conviction for republishing the *North Briton* no. 45 and for printing and publishing "Essay on Women" was confirmed on 15 June (*Gentleman's Magazine* 38[1768]:299). He was sentenced on 18 June (ibid., 300).

135 (1730–98), MP 1761–90.

136 William Murray, Earl of Mansfield (1705–93), MP 1742–56.

137 Thomas Thynne, 3rd Viscount (1734–96), later (1789) Marquis of Bath.

138 Rudé presents evidence that, as early as April 1768, the cabinet and the king had decided to expel Wilkes (*Wilkes and Liberty*, 66). However, it appears that at some stage a change of policy occurred, for on 14 November Lord North (who was then the chancellor of the exchequer) informed his father that "the Administration were well inclined to do nothing upon the subject of Mr. Wilkes, but he has resolved to force his cause upon them and upon the house ... I do not see how ... [this] can end without his expulsion" Bodleian Library, North Papers, d, 24:52.

139 *Lords Journals*, 32:213.

140 *Commons Journals*, 32:175–6; Cobbett, *Parl. Hist.*, 16:544.

141 *Commons Journals*, 32:545–67.

142 Albemarle, *Memoirs of Marquis of Rockingham*, 2:235–6, Chas. Price to Rockingham, 16 November [1773].

143 See, for instance, Walpole's comments, in his *Correspondence*, 23:19–22, Walpole to Mann, 12 May 1768.

144 The proclivity for rioting, particularly in London in this difficult period, is also demonstrated in that associated with a feud between one James Stephens and the government over imprisonment for debt (Innes, "The King's Bench Prison," 250–98).

145 Rea, *English Press in Politics*, 156–73.

146 BM, BL, Eg. Ms. 217:133.

147 (?1737–1821), MP 1768–84, 1790–94, 1817–21.

148 The vote was 1143 for Wilkes and 296 for Luttrell.

149 Burke, *Writings and Speeches*, 2:229.

150 (1737–87), MP 1767–74, 1782–87.

151 (1722–79), MP 1768–79; see SCL, WWM, BK-109, Glynn to Burke, 7 March 1769; SCL, WWM, R1–1184, James Adair to Rockingham, 17 May 1769; BM, Wilkes Papers, BL, Add. Ms. 30868:95, Adair to Wilkes [April/May 1769].

152 See, for instance, Hume, *Letters*, 2:197, Hume to Rev. Blair, 28 March 1769.

153 Rea, *English Press in Politcs*, 160.

154 Cobbett, *Parl. Hist.*, 16:598–601.

155 BM, Hardwicke Papers, BL, Add. Ms. 35430:153, Rockingham to Charles Yorke, 28 February 1769.

156 Ibid., 153.

157 Cobbett, *Parl. Hist.*, 16: 600. In fact, reasonably extensive accounts were to be submitted for the scrutiny of the House in January and February 1770 (*Commons Journals*, 32: 626–70, 729–30). For an interesting discussion of what these accounts demonstrate and George III's financial problems, see Reitan, "The Civil List in Eighteenth Century British Politics," 318–37.

158 Cobbett, *Parl. Hist.*, 16:600.
159 Ibid.
160 See below, 83–4.
161 Paul Langford believes that Dowdeswell had a hand, in particular, in "some of the earlier portions, relating to questions of taxation and finance" (Burke, *Writings and Speeches*, 2:105–6).
162 Ibid., 210.
163 Ibid., 214.
164 Great Britain, HMC, *Charlemont Mss.*, 1:294, Mountmorres to Charlemont, 11 May 1769.
165 Ibid.

CHAPTER THREE

1 See Langford, "Old Whigs, Old Tories," 106–30; Christie, "Parliamentary Politics," 101–22, and "Party in Politics," 47–68.
2 *The Sentiments of an English Freeholder.*
3 It was published on 16 June (*Public Advertiser*) and was entitled *The Question Stated, Whether the Freeholders of Middlesex Lost Their Right by Voting for Mr. Wilkes at the Last Election.*
4 William L. Clements Library (WCL), Dowdeswell Papers, Dowdeswell to Rockingham, 5 September 1769; Burke, *Correspondence*, 2:25, Rockingham to Burke, 15 May 1769; Nottingham University Library (NUL), (PWF) 6731, Meredith to Portland, 9 June 1769.
5 Meredith, *The Question Stated*, 18.
6 Ibid., 20.
7 Ibid., 19.
8 Rudé, *Wilkes and Liberty*, 105–34.
9 Ibid., 113–21. Professor Rudé leaves the impression that the Rockinghams were very active. He speaks of "vigorous campaigning" by party members (113) while providing evidence of their involvement in various counties.
10 Brewer, *Party Ideology and Popular Politics*, 179.
11 Ibid.
12 Rudé, *Wilkes and Liberty*, 105–48.
13 Ibid., 135–48.
14 Burke, *Correspondence*, 2:26, Burke to Charles O'Hara, 31 May 1769.
15 *Annual Register* 12(1769):102–3. It was presented to the king at St James's Palace by John Glynn, John Sawbridge, James Townsend, and George Bellas – all known Wilkites.
16 The petition is quoted in ibid., 197–200; Almon, *Political Register*, 4:347–9.
17 It was presented on 5 July (*Annual Register* 12[1769]:113).
18 On 18 July the petition was approved by a meeting of the "free and independent citizens" of the city (ibid., 116). There is a copy of it in Almon,

Political Register, 4:115–16; *General Evening Post*, 6 January 1770; *London Chronicle*, 25 November 1769.

19 Burke, *Correspondence*, 2:96, Burke to Charles O'Hara, 24 October [1769].

20 John Hobart, 2nd Earl of Buckinghamshire (1723–93).

21 British Museum (BM), Grenville Papers, British Library (BL), Add. Ms. 42087:69, 21 September 1769.

22 Albemarle, *Memoirs of Marquis of Rockingham*, 2:133, Savile to Rockingham, 24 September 1769.

23 Sheffield City Library (SCL), Wentworth Woodhouse Muniments (WWM), R10–5–1, Abdy to Rockingham, 10 September 1769. Both Abdy and Savile did eventually support the petitioning campaign after they witnessed the strong support for it in their respective counties. In the letters quoted here, they were giving vent to initial reactions.

24 Burke, *Correspondence*, 2:61, Rockingham to Burke, 1 September 1769.

25 Ibid., 2:37, Rockingham to Burke, 29 June 1769.

26 SCL, WWM, R1–1209, Rockingham to Stephen Crofts, 11 July 1769.

27 (1713–95), MP 1744–90.

28 *Public Advertiser*; Wyvill, *Political Papers*, 1:xi.

29 Burke, *Correspondence*, 2:61–2, Rockingham to Burke, 1, 3 September 1769.

30 Ibid., 2:62–3.

31 (1721–91), MP 1756–74.

32 (1742–99), MP 1768–84, 1790–96.

33 Burke, *Correspondence*, 2:61–2, Rockingham to Burke, 1,3 September 1769.

34 SCL, WWM, R10–3, Dring to Rockingham, 1 October 1769.

35 Albemarle, *Memoirs of Marquis of Rockingham*, 2:104–5, Rockingham to Dowdeswell, 19 September 1769.

36 WCL, Dowdeswell Papers, Dowdeswell to Rockingham, 5 September 1769.

37 Burke, *Writings and Speeches*, 2:269.

38 Rudé, *Wilkes and Liberty*, 105–34.

39 Burke, *Correspondence*, 2:41, Burke to Rockingham, 2 July 1769.

40 SCL, WWM, R1–1224.

41 Albemarle, *Memoirs of Marquis of Rockingham*, 2:106, Rockingham to Dowdeswell, 19 September 1769; NUL, PWF 2662, Cavendish to Portland [28 September 1769].

42 WCL, Dowdeswell Papers, Dowdeswell to Rockingham [late September 1769].

43 *Annual Register* 12(1769):205.

44 NUL, PWF 2662, J. Cavendish to Portland [28 September 1769].

45 3rd Baronet (1734–83), MP 1761–68.

46 *Annual Register* 12(1769):205.

47 SCL, WWM, R10–15A, Rockingham to Dowdeswell [19 September 1769].

48 SCL, WWM, R10–8, Dring to Rockingham, 3 October 1769.

49 The correspondence concerning the distribution and signing of the petition is among Rockingham's papers at Sheffield, (SCL, WWM, R10–8 to R10–15).

50 Rudé, *Wilkes and Liberty*, 135.

51 SCL, WWM, R10–13–1, Dring to Rockingham, 29 November 1769.

52 SCL, WWM, R1–1247, Savile to Rockingham, 7 November 1769.

53 The petition was not presented until 8 January 1770 (*Public Advertiser*).

54 Rudé, *Wilkes and Liberty*, 143–5.

55 *Public Advertiser*, 9 December 1769.

56 SCL, WWM, R1–1251, 9 December 1769.

57 SCL, WWM, R1–1254.

58 *Daily Advertiser*, 2 October 1769.

59 (1727–1802), MP 1764–1802.

60 BM, Liverpool Papers, BL, Add. Ms. 38206:150, Robinson to Charles Jenkinson, 3 November 1769.

61 SCL, WWM, R1–1173, Mawbey to Rockingham, 19 March 1769; Ibid., Cavendish to Rockingham, 1 July 1769.

62 (1729–1809), MP 1754–74.

63 (?1740–99), MP 1768–84, 1787–99.

64 *Public Advertiser*, 17, 27, 28 June 1769.

65 SCL, WWM, R1–1200, 21 June 1769, and R1–1205, J. Cavendish to Rockingham, 1 July 1769.

66 SCL, WWM, BK1–143, Abdy to Burke, 4 November 1769.

67 SCL, WWM, R1–1205, J. Cavendish to Rockingham, 1 July 1769.

68 Ibid.

69 *Annual Register* 12(1769):90.

70 (1733–1800), MP 1759–90; Monatagu was also a Rockingham supporter.

71 Great Britain, HMC, *Foljambe Mss.*, 146–7, Savile to Hewett, 2 September 1769; NUL, PWF 6884, Montagu to Portland, 3 October [1769].

72 Ibid.

73 Ibid.

74 Burke, *Correspondence*, 2:53, Dowdeswell to Burke, 10 August 1769.

75 [d. 1793].

76 BM, Hardwicke Papers, BL, Add. Ms. 35609:43, Chas. Cocks to Hardwicke, 17 September 1769.

77 WCL, Dowdeswell Papers, 5 September 1769.

78 Burke, *Correspondence*, 2:67, Richmond to Burke, 2 September 1769.

79 SCL, WWM, R1–1237, Meredith to Rockingham, 18 October 1769.

80 Burke, *Correspondence*, 2:71–4, Burke to Rockingham [6 September 1769]. For his speech at the Aylesbury meeting, see *Public Advertiser*, 15 September 1770.

81 Ibid.
82 (c.1715–76).
83 Burke, *Correspondence*, 2:86, Burke to O'Hara, 27 September 1769.
84 Walpole, *Correspondence*, 23:163, Walpole to Mann, 31 December 1769.
85 There are lists of the minority for divisions on the Middlesex election issue for 9 and 25 January 1770. See Namier and Brooke, *History of Parliament*, 1:528–9. My own analysis places some fifty-eight members of the minority in the independent category. This does not include those men I would categorize as independent Rockinghams. There were twenty-one of these men in the minority.
86 Burke, *Correspondence*, 2:76, Burke to Rockingham, 9 September 1769.
87 Some twenty politicians in the House of Commons.
88 Burke, *Correspondence*, 2:43, Burke to Rockingham, 9 July 1769.
89 Public Record Office (PRO), Chatham Papers, 23:5, Hood to Chatham, 16 April 1769; *Grenville Papers*, 4: 418, Whately to Grenville, 25 March 1769.
90 Thus, for instance, in the autumn Horace Walpole told a friend during a holiday in France: "I have no doubt of [the French minister, the Duc de Choiseul's] … having already tampered with Wilkes; but as he dreads the predominant star of Lord Chatham, I dropped, as by accident to a confident of the Ducs that if the latter did not wish a war, nothing could be so imprudent as to encourage Wilkes, whose faction would bring back Lord Chatham" (Walpole, *Correspondence*, 23:147, Walpole to Mann, 8 October 1769).
91 Grafton, *Autobiography and Correspondence*, 237.
92 *Grenville Papers*, 4: 403, diary for 23 November 1768; ibid., 398, Grenville to Suffolk, 25 November 1768. See also their letters in PRO, Chatham Papers, 62.
93 Great Britain, HMC, *Lothian Mss.*, 287, Grenville to Buckinghamshire, 16 August 1769.
94 Burke, *Correspondence*, 2:90, Rockingham to Burke, 15 October 1769; ibid., 91.
95 Ibid., 88, Burke to Rockingham, 9 October 1769.
96 Ibid., 91, Rockingham to Burke, 15 October 1769.
97 Ibid., 112–13, Burke to Rockingham, [24] November 1769; Albemarle, *Memoirs of Marquis of Rockingham*, 2:141 [November 1769]; NUL, PWF 5302, Hotham to Portland, 28 November 1769.
98 Ibid.
99 Burke, *Correspondence*, 2:113, Burke to Rockingham, [24] November 1769.
100 Ibid., 43, Burke to Rockingham, 9 July 1769.
101 Ibid., 92–3, Rockingham to Burke, 15 October 1769.
102 Ibid.
103 Ibid. This had at least been the case since they had left office in 1766.

CHAPTER FOUR

1 Burke, *Correspondence*, 2:121–2, Burke to Rockingham, 18 December 1769; William L. Clements Library (WCL), Dowdeswell Papers, Dowdeswell to Rockingham, 16 December 1769.
2 Public Record Office (PRO), Chatham Papers, 62:176, Temple to Lady Chatham, 5 December 1769.
3 Chatham, *Correspondence*, 2:388–9, Chatham to Calcraft [8 January 1770].
4 See above, 10, 30.
5 Cobbett, *Parl. Hist.*, 16:644–727.
6 Charles Pratt, 1st Baron Camden (1714–94).
7 John Manners, styled Marquis of Granby (1721–70).
8 (1731–83), later (1782) Baron Ashburton, MP 1768–82.
9 Cobbett, *Parl. Hist.*, 16:800.
10 *Annual Register* 13(1770):67; *Gentleman's Magazine* 40(1770):44; Chatham, *Correspondence*, 3:394–5, Temple to Lady Chatham, 16 January 1770; ibid. 395–400, Calcraft to Chatham, 20 January 1770.
11 (1715–83), MP 1742–70, joint vice-treasurer [I].
12 George Montagu, 4th Duke of Manchester (1737–88); George William Coventry, 6th Earl Coventry (1722–1809); John Peyto Verney, 14th Baron Willoughby de Broke (1738–1816).
13 Henry Fitzroy, 5th Duke of Beaufort (1744–1803).
14 Francis Hastings, 10th Earl of Huntingdon (1728–89).
15 (?1715–70), MP 1755–70.
16 (1733–1812), MP 1754–61, 1763–96, 1799–1801.
17 (c. 1710–81), MP 1754–74.
18 Cobbett, *Parl. Hist.*, 16:800.
19 Only General Charles Cornwallis, 2nd Earl Cornwallis (1738–1805), later (1792) 1st Marquis Cornwallis, the other vice-treasurer of Ireland, and Admiral Richard Howe, 4th Viscount Howe (1726–99), MP 1757–82, the treasurer of the navy, resigned with him. See Walpole, *Memoirs*, 4:58.
20 Cobbett, *Parl. Hist.*, 16:800–7.
21 Ibid., 811–13.
22 Philip Yorke, 2nd Earl of Hardwicke (1720–90).
23 (1722–70), MP 1747–70.
24 (1728–1801), MP 1753–84.
25 Another brother, Joseph (1724–92), also held a seat in the Commons (1751–80), but he was British ambassador at The Hague between 1761 and 1780 and he did not attend Parliament.
26 Philip Yorke, 1st Earl of Hardwicke (1690–1764).
27 British Museum (BM), Hardwicke Papers, British Library (BL), Add. Ms. 35362:261, Yorke to Hardwicke, 8 October 1769.

28 In the Hardwicke Papers there is a memorandum labelled "Private Memorial December the 30th 1770," in which Hardwicke recorded his recollections of the circumstances of the offers made to Charles and of the various pressures that came to bear on him at that time (BM, BL, Add. Ms. 35428:116–21). There is another memorandum, labelled "Memoirs begun 20th October 1772," in which Charles's wife did the same (ibid., 132–40).

29 Ibid., 118.

30 Ibid.

31 Ibid., 134.

32 Ibid., 133.

33 See below, 101, 130–1.

34 The most comprehensive biography of the king is still Brooke, *King George III*.

35 Hume, *Letters*, 2:213, Hume to Strachan, 25 January 1770.

36 Brooke, *King George III*, 159

37 Professor Brooke demonstrates the king's determination during the events of early 1770 (156–9). He also provides conclusive evidence that George III was thereafter the backbone of the North ministry's authoritarian policy with respect to America (163–216).

38 Hume, *Letters*, 2:214–15, Hume to Adam Smith, 6 February 1770.

39 BM, Hardwicke Papers, BL, Add. Ms. 35375:19–20, Yorke to Hardwicke, 5 January 1770.

40 Chatham, *Correspondence*, 3:394–5, Temple to Chatham, 16 January 1770.

41 Cobbett, *Parl. Hist.*, 16:755.

42 See, for instance, Phillimore, *Memoirs and Correspondence of Lord Lyttleton*, 753–4, Rockingham to Lyttleton, 20 January 1770; PRO, Chatham Papers, 62:188, Temple to Lady Chatham, 17 February 1770.

43 Before 9 January 1770, Rockingham had spoken only once since going into opposition in 1766. That was during the previous session (on 2 March 1769). For comment, see Walpole, *Memoirs*, 3:228.

44 Burke, *Correspondence*, 2:139, Burke to O'Hara, 21 May 1770.

45 Cobbett, *Parl. Hist.*, 16:742.

46 Walpole, *Memoirs*, 4:62–3.

47 Cobbett, *Parl. Hist.*, 16: 845. Two weeks later, Rockingham and Chatham submitted the same motion in the Lords (ibid., 849).

48 Walpole, *Memoirs*, 4:66.

49 John Stuart, Lord Mountstuart (1744–1814), MP 1766–76.

50 Walpole, *Memoirs*, 4:66.

51 Ibid., 66–7.

52 *Public Advertiser*, 15 March 1770.

53 Ibid.

54 7th Baronet (1719–94), MP 1754–60, 1768–90.

55 Cobbett, *Parl. Hist.*, 16:874–7; BM, BL, Eg. Ms. 212, 125; *Journals of the House of Commons (Commons Journals)*, 32:798–9.
56 Walpole, *Correspondence*, 23:198, Walpole to Mann, 15 March 1770.
57 Cobbett, *Parl. Hist.*, 16:895–9.
58 Ibid., 899–900.
59 See Rea, *English Press in Politics*, 174–87.
60 Walpole, *Correspondence*, 23:195–8, Walpole to Mann, 15 March 1770.
61 Malmesbury, *Letters*, 197–9, Harris to his son, 20 March 1770; Gibbon, *Letters*, 1:113, Gibbon to [his stepmother], 20 March 1770.
62 As distinguished from those John Brewer describes as men of "movable property" ("English Radicalism," 323). In the City many of the latter sort appear to have supported the radicals in this period and would have been less horrified.
63 On 9 January; see *Annual Register* 13(1770):71.
64 Malmesbury, *Letters*, 199, Harris to son, 20 March 1770.
65 Cobbett, *Parl. Hist.*, 16:925.
66 Walpole, *Correspondence*, 18:199–201, Walpole to Mann, 23 March 1770.
67 Walpole, *Memoirs*, 4:69.
68 On the eighteenth; (see Almon, *Memoirs of a Late Eminent Bookseller*, 58).
69 It was agreed to and presented on 28 March. See *Annual Register* 13(1770):85.
70 Chatham, *Correspondence*, 3:436, Calcraft to Chatham, 29 March 1770; ibid. 436–7, Chatham to Beckford, 10 March 1770.
71 *Gentleman's Magazine* 40(1770):188.
72 Chatham, *Correspondence*, 436–7, Calcraft to Chatham, 30 March 1770.
73 (1732–95), MP 1768–95.
74 Chatham, *Correspondence*, 436–7, Calcraft to Chatham, 30 March 1770.
75 Cobbett, *Parl. Hist.*, 16:954–5, 966.
76 Ibid., 978–9.
77 PRO, Chatham Papers, 66:104, Shelburne to Chatham [mid-May 1770]; ibid., 108, Shelburne to Chatham [mid-May 1770]. There is a copy of this remonstrance in the *Gentleman's Magazine* 40(1770):267.
78 Chatham, *Correspondence*, 3:447, Rockingham to Chatham, 27 April 1770; SCL, WWM, R87–2, Rockingham to [Chatham, 27 April 1770]; SCL, WWM, R87–3, Rockingham to [Chatham, 27 April 1770].
79 Chatham, *Correspondence*, 3:448, Chatham to Shelburne, 28 April 1770.
80 Cobbett, *Parl. Hist.*, 16:954–66.
81 PRO, Chatham Papers, 62:182, Shelburne to Chatham [12 May 1770]; Albemarle, *Memoirs of the Marquis of Rockingham*, 2:180–5, letters between Rockingham and Chatham, 10–14 May 1770.
82 Walpole, *Correspondence*, 23:215–16, Walpole to Mann, 24 May 1770.

83 Albemarle, *Memoirs of Marquis of Rockingham*, 2:185, Chatham to Rockingham, 14 May 1770.
84 See, for example, Chatham, *Correspondence*, 3:455, Rockingham to Chatham, 11 May 1770; PRO, Chatham Papers, 54:207, Rockingham to Chatham, 15 May 1770.
85 Cobbett, *Parl. Hist.*, 16:52–74; BM, BL, Eg. Ms. 221:3–53.
86 See, for example, Wedderburn's speech on 5 March (BM, BL, Eg. Ms. 221:43–4) and Burke's speech on 26 April (ibid., 222:20–3).
87 Burke submitted the resolutions on 9 May (Cobbett, *Parl. Hist.*, 16:1001–7) and Richmond on 18 May (ibid., 16:1010–28). For Burke's speech introducing the resolutions, the resolutions themselves, and a discussion of Burke's performance, see his *Writings and Speeches*, 2:323–4.
88 Walpole, *Memoirs*, 4:99.
89 Burke, *Correspondence*, 2:139, Burke to O'Hara, 21 May 1770.
90 For the *Thoughts* and a thorough discussion of the circumstances that produced it, see Burke, *Writings and Speeches*, 2:241–323.
91 Burke, *Correspondence*, 2:92, Rockingham to Burke, 15 October 1769.
92 Ibid., 101, Burke to Rockingham, 29 October 1769.
93 Ibid.
94 Burke, *Writings and Speeches*, 2:244–5.
95 Ibid., 246–7.
96 Albemarle, *Memoirs of Marquis of Rockingham*, 2:145–6, Portland to Rockingham, 3 December 1769.
97 Chatham, *Correspondence*, 3:491, Rockingham to Chatham, 20 November 1770.
98 Burke, *Writings and Speeches*, 2:276.
99 Ibid., 253.
100 Ibid., 274.
101 Ibid., 260–1.
102 Ibid., 261.
103 Ibid., 263.
104 Ibid., 264.
105 Ibid., 266.
106 Ibid., 269.
107 Ibid., 270.
108 Ibid.
109 Although O'Brien confuses secret influence, which Burke was principally concerned about in 1770, with the influence of the crown, which he was to be more concerned about in the seventies and early eighties (*Great Melody*, Chicago, 1992, li–lii; below, 172).
110 Burke, *Writings and Speeches*, 2:275.
111 Ibid., 276.
112 Burke, *Correspondence*, 2:176, Burke to Rockingham, 29 December 1770.

113 SCL, WWM, R1–842, "Thoughts on the present state of publick affairs and the propriety of accepting or declining administration, written 23d & 24 July 1767."

114 Burke, *Writings and Speeches*, 2:311.

115 Ibid., 312.

116 Ibid., 320–1.

117 This is basically the argument of O'Gorman (*Edmund Burke*, 23–44). Professor O'Gorman points out that Burke wanted to bring cohesion to his party through the *Thoughts*. However, while he estimates that Burke was trying to avoid provoking the other groups in opposition, he does not recognize how ardently the party was trying to draw other followings into the Rockingham fold. At this time, cohesion was something that the work promoted not just in the one group but in the opposition as a whole. This could only help to form one great party under the Rockinghams' direction.

118 See, for example, Morley, *Burke*, 75–8; Mansfield, *Statesmanship and Party Government*, 30; Burke, *Selected Letters*, 31; O'Brien, *Great Melody*, lxii–lxiii.

119 Burke, *Writings and Speeches*, 2:318.

120 Ibid., 315.

121 For further discussion, see below, 183–5.

122 Henry St John, 1st Viscount Bolingbroke (1678–1751), *Dissertation upon Parties*.

123 SCL, WWM, R1–1558, Richmond to Rockingham, 12 Februay 1771.

124 Burke, *Writings and Speeches*, 2:315.

125 *Principles of the Late Changes*, 34.

126 Cobbett, *Parl. Hist.*, 16:834.

127 Ibid., 753.

128 (1741–1811), MP 1768–80.

129 SCL, WWM, R1–1276, Dowdeswell to Rockingham, 1 February 1770.

130 See Sir George Savile's speech at the general meeting of the County of York, 25 September 1770, recorded in Wyvill, *Political Papers*, 1:xxvi–vii.

131 (1728–98), Edmund's cousin.

132 Burke, *Correspondence*, 2:126, William Burke to William Dennis, [3, 6,] April [1770].

133 (1728–98), MP 1754–80.

134 Burke, *Correspondence*, 2:126–7.

135 (1731–1814), MP 1754–74.

136 Walpole, *Memoirs*, 4:98.

137 Ibid.

138 William Murray, 1st Baron Mansfield (1705–96), later (1776) 1st Earl of Mansfield.

139 For an analysis of the effects that this bill would have had, see Kemp, "Crewe's Act 1782," 258–63.

140 BM, Grenville Papers, BL, Add. Ms. 42087:128, [Whately] to Grenville [7 February 1770].
141 Walpole, *Memoirs*, 4:100.
142 For the reform movement in London at this time, see Royle and Walvin, *English Radicals and Reformers*, 13–31; Brewer, "English Radicalism," 323–67, and *Party Ideology and Popular Politics*, 240–64; Dickinson, *Liberty and Property*, 195–231; and Sutherland "The City of London and the Opposition," 1–29.
143 See below, 177–83.
144 Walpole, *Memoirs*, 3:109–13; BM, Newcastle Papers, BL, Add. Ms. 32988:355, West to Newcastle, 17 February 1768.
145 Burke, *Writings and Speeches*, 2:269.
146 Ibid.
147 Ibid., 310.

CHAPTER FIVE

1 Burke, *Correspondence*, 2:137–8, Burke to O'Hara, 21 May 1770.
2 Burke, *Writings and Speeches*, 2:321.
3 Public Record Office (PRO), Chatham Papers, 61:151, Temple to Chatham [May 1770].
4 Ibid., 25:53.
5 Sheffield City Library (SCL), Wentworth Woodhouse Muniments (WWM), R1–1315, Manchester to Rockingham, 8 October 1770.
6 Lord George Sackville Germain (1716–85), MP 1741–82.
7 Great Britain, HMC, *Stopford-Sackville Mss.*, 1:133, Germain to Irwin, 30 October 1770.
8 (1705–70), MP 1747–68; not to be confused with his father whose name was also William and who represented this constituency until 1768 as a Newcastle-Rockingham supporter.
9 (1726–76), MP 1768–76.
10 SCL, WWM, R1–1304, Rockingham to Dowdeswell, 15 June 1770.
11 Ibid, Rockingham to Dowdeswell, 15 June 1770.
12 On 25 June; see *Annual Register* 13(1770):120.
13 Wilkes, *Correspondence*, 4:59–60, Wilkes to his daughter, 26 June 1770.
14 *Annual Register* 13(1770):119.
15 SCL, WWM, R1–1303, J. Cavendish to Rockingham [10 June 1770]; ibid., R1–1304, Rockingham to Dowdeswell, 15 June 1770.
16 Wilkes, *Correspondence*, 4:64, Wilkes to his daughter, 29 June 1770.
17 Almon, *Political Register*, 4:345.
18 (1731–91).
19 Macaulay, *Observations on a Pamphlet, Entitled "Thoughts on the Cause of the Present Discontents,"* 7.

20 There were numerous reviews of the book in June and later. See, for instance, "Burke's Thoughts Reviewed," in Almon, *Political Register*, 4:345–61.

21 (1726–92).

22 I.e., the London radicals, many of whom were involved with the Society of the Supporters of the Bill of Rights, which had recently been founded to promote radical objectives.

23 Burke, *Correspondence*, 2:150, Burke to Richard Shackleton [ante 15 August 1770].

24 (1735–84), MP 1770–80.

25 *Middlesex Journal*, 12 July 1770.

26 For which, see, for instance, H.T. Dickinson's chapter on "Defence of the Whig Establishment" in *Liberty and Property*, 162–92.

27 This argument is developed below, 175–86. See also Langford, "Old Whigs, Old Tories and the American Revolution," 106–30, especially 114, for an illustration of how the Rockinghams' Whig perspective affected their thinking in imperial and other matters.

28 It was agreed to at a Court of Common Council on 15 November 1770; see *Gentleman's Magazine* 40(1770):540, and *Annual Register* 13(1770):162. It was presented on 21 November; see *Annual Register* 13(1770):164.

29 Agreed to on 22 May; see *Gentleman's Magazine* 40(1770):234.

30 Presented on 13 June; ibid., 176.

31 Agreed to some time in late September as a result of efforts of John Calcraft and John Sawbridge; see PRO, Chatham Papers, 25:51, Calcraft to Lady Chatham, 12 August 1770; ibid., 25:76, Calcraft to Chatham [late September 1770].

32 Presented on 7 November; see *Annual Register* 13(1770):161.

33 Burke, *Correspondence*, 2:142, Richmond to Burke, 10 June 1770.

34 SCL, WWM, R1–1313, Armytage (3rd Baronet, 1734–83, MP 1761–68) to Rockingham, 16 September 1770.

35 SCL, WWM, R1–1307, Wedderburn to Rockingham, 11 August 1770.

36 Burke, *Correspondence*, 2:155, Burke to Rockingham, 7, 8 September [1770].

37 Nottingham University Library (NUL), Portland Papers (PWF) 5217, Hotham to Portland, 26 August 1770.

38 Ibid.; Burke, *Correspondence*, 2:151–2, Rockingham to Burke, 5 September 1770.

39 (1712–98).

40 Wyvill, *Political Papers*, 1:xxi.

41 SCL, WWM, R1–1314, Rockingham to Dowdeswell, 28 September 1770.

42 Wyvill, *Political Papers*, 1:31; *Gentleman's Magazine* 40(1770): 465–7; *Gazetteer*, 1 October 1770.

43 *Gentleman's Magazine* 40(1770):481.

44 The most authoritative account of this crisis is Goebel, *Struggle for the Falkland Islands*, 274–407.
45 The Manila Ransom was the sum of £2 million, which local authorities had promised the English commander at the taking of Manila in 1763 in order to avert the pillage of the city, and which the Spanish government had refused to authorize.
46 Except the southern secretary, Lord Weymouth (Thomas Thynne, 3rd Viscount Thynne, 1734–97).
47 *Gentleman's Magazine* 40(1770):439.
48 Ibid., 539; *Annual Register* 13(1770):161–2.
49 Ibid., 157.
50 Ibid., 161–2; *Gentleman's Magazine* 40(1770):539.
51 Chatham, *Correspondence*, 3:464n.
52 On 1 June 1770 (ibid., 459n).
53 Burke, *Correspondence*, 2:142, Richmond to Burke, 10 June 1770; PRO, Chatham Papers, 25:76, Calcraft to Chatham [September 1770].
54 PRO, Chatham Papers, 25:51, Calcraft to Lady Chatham, 12 August 1770; ibid., 25:76, Calcraft to Chatham [September 1770].
55 Chatham and Temple appear to have attempted to pressurize Rockingham through Richmond (ibid., 25:151, Temple to Chatham [May 1770]).
56 Chatham, *Correspondence*, 3:469, Chatham to Calcraft, 28 July 1770.
57 Albemarle, *Memoirs of Marquis of Rockingham*, 2:194.
58 SCL, WWM, R1–1358, Richmond to Rockingham, 12 February 1771.
59 Ibid.
60 BM, Hardwicke Papers, BL, Add. Ms. 35402:64, D. Wray to Hardwicke, 13 October 1770.
61 Walpole, *Memoirs*, 4:116–17.
62 PRO, Chatham Papers, 54:215, Rockingham to Chatham, 25 July 1770.
63 BM, Hardwicke Papers, BL, Add. Ms. 35375:73, John Yorke to Hardwicke, 1 August 1770.
64 Robert Henley, 1st Earl of Northington (c.1708–72). He was lord chancellor in both the Grenville and the Rockingham administrations and was lord president under Chatham. His primary attachment was to the king.
65 In 1770 Northington appeared as Tom Tilbury in the well known "Tête-à-Tête" portraits in *Town and Country Magazine* (2:345). In the "Histoire" annexed to the portrait and labelled "Tom Tilbury and Mrs. T..rr..t" rumours of a recent negotiation between Tilbury and the opposition parties for the formation of a new administration are mentioned.
66 PRO, Chatham Papers, 25:59. This message was enclosed in ibid., 25:57, Calcraft to Chatham, 18 September 1770. Over the next two months, the breakdown of the unity among the London radicals became public knowledge. In late October, Wilkes and Sawbridge had a bitter argument at a meeting of the Common Council which was recorded in all the news-

papers, and in November the first disputes between Wilkes and John Horne gained widespread attention.

67 BM, Hardwicke Papers, BL, Add. Ms. 35609:240, C.J. Reynolds to Hardwicke, 18 September 1770; PRO, Chatham Papers, 25:57, Calcraft to Chatham, 18 September 1770; NUL, PWF 5319, Hotham to Portland, 30 September 1770; ibid., 2212, Byng to Portland, 19 October 1770.

68 PRO, Chatham Papers, 25:55, Calcraft to Chatham, 8 September 1770.

69 BM, Hardwicke Papers, BL, Add. Ms. 35375:25, Yorke to Hardwicke, 1 August 1770.

70 PRO, Chatham Papers, 54:212, Rockingham to Chatham, 2 November 1770; Chatham, *Correspondence*, 3:491, Rockingham to Chatham, 20 November 1770.

71 The motion was made by Baron Craven (1738–91), an independent peer who normally supported opposition (Walpole, *Memoirs*, 4:93). The Rockinghams, however, had designed it (Chatham, *Correspondence*, 3:415, Rockingham to Chatham, 17 February 1770).

72 Walpole, *Memoirs*, 3:33.

73 *Annual Register* 13(1770):132.

74 Although the British navy may have been in rather poor shape at this stage, the sea forces of France and Spain were in a similar condition. Moreover, the Admiralty proved to be rather efficient at preparing the navy, and by Christmas Britain was in a much better position to wage war than either of her two potential enemies. See Tracy, "Falkland Islands Crisis of 1770," 40–76.

75 Burke, *Correspondence*, 2:164, Rockingham to Burke, 26 September 1770.

76 SCL, WWM, R1–1325, Lyttleton to Rockingham, 12 November 1770, and R1–1324, Temple to Rockingham, 12 November 1770.

77 See Rockingham's three letters to Chatham in November (Chatham, *Correspondence*, 3:489–91, 15, 20 November 1770; PRO, Chatham Papers, 54:212, Rockingham to Chatham, 2 November 1770).

78 In fact, Burke had warned the marquis in a letter of 7 and 8 September that the "Court is fully resolved to adhere to its present System, but that if, contrary to their expectation it should be found impossible to go on with the present instruments, they will send to Lord Chatham, not to your Lordship, or to the Grenvilles" (Burke, *Correspondence*, 2:157).

79 Chatham, *Correspondence*, 3:481, Chatham to Calcraft, 10 November 1770.

80 See below, 113.

81 Burke, *Correspondence*, 2:126–7, William Burke to William Dennis, [3,6] April [1770].

82 Cobbett, *Parl. Hist.*, 16:1034–81.

83 Ibid., 1040.

84 Ibid., 1046, 1052.

85 Chatham, *Correspondence*, 3:489–90, Rockingham to Chatham, 15 November 1770.

86 They asked for all the intelligence regarding the Falkland Islands received by the ministry during the twelve months preceding 12 September 1770 (Cobbett, *Parl. Hist.*, 16:1085–6).

87 Ibid., 1094; Almon, *Anecdotes of the Life of William Pitt*, 3:30.

88 See, for example, Lord North's speech on 13 November (Cobbett, *Parl. Hist.*, 16:1049–50).

89 Goebel, *Struggle for the Falkland Islands*, 309–11, 355–63.

90 *Journals of the House of Lords (Lords Journals)*, 33:49–51; *Journals of the House of Commons (Commons Journals)*, 33:138–9; BM, BL, Eg. Ms. 224:26–48.

91 Cobbett, *Parl. Hist.*, 16:1358–78.

92 Ibid., 1379–85.

93 Burke, *Correspondence*, 2:188, Rockingham to Burke [30 January 1771].

94 SCL, WWM, R1–1358, Richmond to Rockingham, 12 February 1771.

95 For a brief summary of the debate in Parliament from the government side, see Thomas, *Lord North*, 46–51.

96 *Lords Journals*, 33:54–5; Cobbett, *Parl. Hist.*, 16:1355.

97 Gilbert, "Political Correspondence of Charles Lennox, Third Duke of Richmond," 260, Richmond to Rockingham, 1 February 1771.

98 Ibid.

99 Cobbett, *Parl. Hist.*, 16:1359.

100 There is a list of the minority in *Bingley's Weekly Journal*, 23 February 1771.

101 For example, Dowdeswell's motion of 4 February calling on the government to inform the House whether or not France had interfered in the recent negotiations was defeated by a vote of 179–57.

102 Walpole, *Correspondence*, 23:239, Walpole to Mann, 4 October 1770.

103 Walpole, *Memoirs*, 4:179.

104 Ibid., 4:137.

105 Chatham, *Correspondence*, 4:23, Shelburne to Chatham, 26 November 1770.

106 Thomas, *Lord North*, 51.

107 Johnson, "Letters of William Samuel Johnson to the Governors of Connecticut," 9:473, Johnson to Trumball, 5 February 1771.

108 Chatham, *Correspondence*, 4:37, Temple to Chatham, 3 December 1770.

109 George III, *Correspondence*, 2:171, North to King, 16 November [1770].

110 Henry Bowes Howard, 11th Earl of Suffolk (1739–79).

111 On 22 January (*London Gazette*, 23 January 1771, 11111).

112 On 26 January (ibid., 27 January 1771, 11112).

113 Walpole, *Memoirs*, 4:174.

114 Thomas, 2nd Baron Lyttleton (1709–73); Thomas Villiers, 1st Baron Hyde (c. 1709–86), later (1776) 1st Earl of Clarendon.

115 Great Britain, HMC, *Abergavenny Mss.*, 3, "Minutes of Arrangements, Given to Mr. Rice," 21 January 1771.

116 SCL, WWM, R1–1350, Richmond to Rockingham, 21 January 1771.

117 Grenville had approximately five followers in the House of Lords at this time. Besides those mentioned above, they were John Hobart, 2nd Earl of Buckinghamshire (1723–93) and Robert Hamden, 4th Baron Trevor (1776–83).

118 Lawson, *George Grenville*, 292.

119 (1725–74), MP 1754–55, 1761–74.

120 (1729–1807), MP 1763–80.

121 (1733–1800), MP 1754–83; not to be confused with his father Thomas Townshend, (1701–80, MP 1722–74).

122 Lawson, *George Grenville*, 293.

123 See below, 152.

124 Hugh Percy, 1st Duke of Northumberland (c.1715–86).

125 Gilbert, "Political Correspondence of Charles Lennox, Third Duke of Richmond," 260.

126 *Lords Journals*, 33:65–7.

127 SCL, WWM, R1–1352, Richmond to Rockingham [22 January 1771].

128 Chatham, *Correspondence*, 4:29, Camden to Chatham, 28 November 1770.

129 SCL, WWM, R1–1352, Richmond to Rockingham [22 January 1771].

130 William Legge, 2nd Earl of Dartmouth (1731–1801).

131 SCL, WWM, R1–1352, Richmond to Rockingham [22 January 1771].

132 NUL, PWF 6727, Meredith to Portland, 20 July 1765.

133 Burke, *Correspondence*, 2:210, Burke to O'Hara, 2 April 1771.

134 Ibid.

CHAPTER SIX

1 Burke, *Correspondence*, 2:194, Rockingham to Burke, 14 February 1771.

2 Junius, *Letters of Junius*, 135–48, Junius to the *Public Advertiser*, 19 December 1769.

3 (1719–81), MP 1761–71.

4 Rea, *English Press in Politics*, 181.

5 (1722–79), MP 1768–79.

6 Rea, *English Press in Politics*, 82.

7 See, for example, Father of Condor, *A Letter Concerning Libels*; Junius, *Letters of Junius*, 177–85.

8 Ibid., 178.

9 See Namier and Brooke, *History of Parliament*, 3:189, 322–3.

10 Burke, *Correspondence*, 2:160, Burke to Rockingham, 23 September 1770.

11 Public Record Office (PRO), Chatham Papers, 25:179, Camden to Chatham, 11 November 1770.

12 Ibid., 179.
13 Chatham, *Correspondence*, 4:22–3, Shelburne to Chatham [26 November 1770].
14 Bodleian Library, North Papers, d, 13:143, [unknown] to Guilford, 24 November 1770.
15 Chatham, *Correspondence*, 4:22–3, Shelburne to Chatham [26 November 1770].
16 *Journals of the House of Lords (Lords Journals)*, 33:20; Walpole, *Memoirs*, 4:140.
17 (1735–89), MP 1768–89.
18 Chatham, *Correspondence*, 4:20, Shelburne to Chatham [26 November 1770].
19 (1744–92), MP 1768–74, 1776–90.
20 Chatham, *Correspondence*, 4:21.
21 Ibid., 30, Shelburne to Chatham [28 November 1770].
22 Cobbett, *Parl. Hist.*, 16:1211; British Museum (BM), British Library (BL), Eg. Ms. 223, 42–96.
23 Cobbett, *Parl. Hist.*, 16:1155.
24 Chatham, *Correspondence*, 4:32, Chatham to Calcraft [28 November 1770].
25 Ibid., 24, Chatham to Shelburne [26 November 1770].
26 BM, BL, Eg. Ms. 223:25; Sheffield City Library (SCL), Wentworth Woodhouse Muniments (WWM), R1–1335A, Chatham to Rockingham, 3 December 1770.
27 Chatham, *Correspondence*, 4:32, Chatham to Calcraft [28 November 1770].
28 Ibid., 4:32.
29 Ibid., 57, Calcraft to Chatham, 16 December.
30 Chatham, *Correspondence*, 4:32.
31 Ibid., 33, Calcraft to Chatham [28 November 1770].
32 Burke, *Correspondence*, 2:194–5, 14 February 1771.
33 Rockingham informed Portland of this in a letter of 11 December. See Nottingham University Library (NUL), Portland Papers (PWF) 9037.
34 PRO, Chatham Papers, 25:179, Camden to Chatham, 11 November 1770.
35 See, for instance, Holdsworth, *History of English Law*, 7:342–5.
36 Burke, *Correspondence*, 2:195, Rockingham to Burke, 14 February 1771.
37 SCL, WWM, R1–1357, Rockingham to Dowdeswell, 11 February 1771.
38 Burke, *Correspondence*, 2:170, Rockingham to Burke, 15 December 1770; ibid., 186, Burke to Rockingham [post 20 January, 1770].
39 SCL, WWM, R1–1356, Dowdeswell to Rockingham, 8 February 1771.
40 Ibid., Rockingham to Dowdeswell, 14 February 1771. In a letter to Rockingham two days later, Dowdeswell claimed that the changes he had proposed were meant to "rather strengthen our principle than shake it" (WCL, Dowdeswell Papers [16 February 1771]).
41 Ibid.

42 Burke, *Correspondence*, 2:210, Burke to O'Hara, 2 April 1771.
43 SCL, WWM, R1–1357, Rockingham to Dowdeswell, 11 February 1771.
44 Burke, *Correspondence*, 2:193, Rockingham to Burke, 14 February 1771.
45 SCL, WWM, R1–1356, Dowdeswell to Rockingham, 8 February 1771. There are three drafts of the preamble among Rockingham's papers at Sheffield: WWM, R1–1365A, B, and C. The third R1–1365C, is the one Dowdeswell eventually decided to use. It is slightly different from the other two drafts largely because it reflects Dowdeswell's last efforts to satisfy his allies.
46 Burke, *Correspondence*, 2:202, Burke to unknown journal [post 12 March 1771].
47 Ibid., 210, Burke to O'Hara, 2 April 1771.
48 (1731–92), MP 1760–84; not to be confused with his cousin of the same name.
49 Onslow first moved for the attendance of Richard Thomson of the *Gazetteer* on 8 February (Cobbett, *Parl. Hist.*, 17:58–62). On 12 March he moved for the attendance of seven more printers. They were John Wheble, William Woodfall, Henry Baldwin, Thomas Evans, Thomas Wright, Samuel Bladon, and John Miller (ibid., 75–7).
50 Ibid., 83–4. *Journals of the House of Commons (Commons Journals)*, 33:258–9.
51 (c.1731–1800).
52 BM, Wilkes Papers, BL, Add. Ms. 30871:69, Morris to Wilkes, 13 March 1771.
53 See Thomas, "John Wilkes and the Freedom of the Press."
54 (1735–84), MP 1770–80; (1725–93), MP 1768–74.
55 Oliver was committed on 25 March and Crosby on 27 March (*Commons Journals*, 33:286, 289).
56 See, for instance, *Public Advertiser*, 28, 29 March, 9 April 1771.
57 Burke, *Correspondence*, 2:178, Burke to O'Hara, 31 December 1770.
58 Cobbett, *Parl. Hist.*, 17:109.
59 Ibid.
60 The same ruling was made for Oliver.
61 Bristol University Library, Diary of Matthew Brickdale.
62 Ibid.
63 *Rockingham Memoirs*, 2:207, Rockingham to Dowdeswell, 28 March 1771.
64 *Public Advertiser*, 1 April 1771.
65 Burke, *Correspondence*, 2:241, Burke to William Baker, 26 September 1771.
66 *Public Advertiser*, 2 April 1771.
67 Chatham, *Correspondence*, 4:105, Shelburne to Chatham, 25 February 1771.
68 Ibid., 129, Chatham to Calcraft, 26 March 1771.
69 (1736–1812), later Horne Tooke.
70 On 9 April Horne, at a meeting of the Bill of Rights Society, moved after a violent altercation with Wilkes, "That the Society should be dissolved."

After being defeated by a vote of 26–24, he and his supporters formed a new society of their own known as the Constitutional Society (*Annual Register* 14[1771]:93–4).

71 Chatham, *Correspondence*, 4:146–7, Shelburne to Chatham [9 April 1771].
72 Ibid., 146–7; ibid., 155, Camden to Chatham [12 April 1771].
73 Ibid., 154, Temple to Chatham, 18 April 1771.
74 Ibid., 4:165, Chatham to Rockingham, 25 April 1771.
75 Walpole, *Memoirs*, 4:213.
76 Cobbett, *Parl. Hist.*, 16:220–7.
77 Burke, *Correspondence*, 2:205, Dowdeswell and Rockingham to Burke, [27] March 1771.
78 Ibid., 209, Burke to O'Hara, 2 April 1771.
79 Ibid., 209–10.
80 Chatham, *Correspondence*, 4:187, Chatham to Shelburne [10 January 1772].
81 Burke, *Correspondence*, 2:297, Rockingham to Burke, 22 December 1771.
82 Gilbert, "Political Correspondence of Richmond," 260, Richmond to Rockingham, 1 February 1771.
83 Cobbett, *Parl. Hist.*, 16:1355.
84 Ibid., 16:214.
85 SCL, WWM, R1–1373, Abingdon to Rockingham [May 1771].
86 Ibid., Rockingham to Dowdeswell, 11 February 1771.
87 Burke, *Writings and Speeches*, 2:318.
88 Gilbert, "Political Correspondence of Richmond," 329, Richmond to Rockingham, 15 March 1772.
89 SCL, WWM, R1–1413, Portland to Rockingham, 21 November 1772.

CHAPTER SEVEN

1 For instance, see the *Gentleman's Magazine* 41(1771):310–14.
2 An article signed "Roberto" appeared in the *Gazetteer* of 25 September attacking Trecothick, Baker, and Martin for their ineffectual subservience to Rockingham. It contributed to the further alienation of Rockingham's city friends from the radicals; see Burke, *Correspondence*, 2:241, Burke to William Baker, 26 September 1771; ibid., 245, Trecothick to Burke [8 October 1771].
3 Albemarle, *Memoirs of the Marquis of Rockingham*, 2:212, Rockingham to Dowdeswell, 19 December 1771; Nottingham University Library (NUL), Portland Papers (PWF) 9045, Rockingham to Portland, 26 July 1771.
4 Burke, *Correspondence*, 2:309, Burke to John Cruger, 30 June 1772.
5 Sheffield City Library (SCL), Wentworth Woodhouse Muniments (WWM), R1–1391.
6 Henry Frederick, Duke of Cumberland (1745–90).

7 1(1743–1808).

8 1st Baron Irnham (1713–87).

9 William Henry, Duke of Gloucester (1743–1805).

10 Printed in Brooke, *King George III*, 274.

11 Rumours about Gloucester's marriage to Maria Walpole, dowager Lady Waldegrave (1736–1807), widow of the king's former governor, had been rife for some time. They appear to have been kept from George III, however; see ibid., 277.

12 Clark, *English Society*, 42–118; Cannon, *Aristocratic Century*, especially 152, 161, 178–9. Many historians have argued the other side and demonstrated change in the eighteenth century. See, for instance, Corfield, *Impact of English Towns*; Gunn, *Beyond Liberty and Property*; and Langford, *Public Life and the Propertied Englishman*.

13 *Public Advertiser*, Thomas to printer, 20 November 1771. See also, ibid., Cumbrieniss to the D[uke] of C[umberland], 13 November 1771.

14 (1737–94)

15 Gibbon, *Letters*, 2:154.

16 *Public Advertiser*, 2 January 1772.

17 Ibid., 9 December 1771. In the *Public Advertiser* of 13 November 1771, it was reported that "the republican Party are very warm and zealous in the Defence of a late unpopular Marriage, but it is plain these Enemies to Kings rejoice at every Act that may lessen the Royal Family in the Eyes of the People."

18 By a vote of 300 to 64; see Cobbett, *Parl. Hist.*, 17:419, and *Journals of the House of Commons (Commons Journals)*, 33:584.

19 NUL, PWF 5359, Thomas Pitt to Portland, 12 March 1772.

20 There is a list of the Rockinghams who voted with government on this motion in the *Public Advertiser*, 17 March 1772.

21 Burke, *Correspondence*, 2:287, Burke to O'Hara, 18 November 1771.

22 See, for example, NUL, PWF 9062, Rockingham to Portland, 18 March 1772.

23 Ibid.

24 British Museum (BM), Hastings Papers, British Library (BL), Add. Ms. 29133:93, Sam Peckett to Hastings, 4 May 1772.

25 Ibid., 94.

26 Ibid.

27 (1716–89), MP 1756–82.

28 (1713–1802), MP 1768–96.

29 1st Baronet (c.1710–81), MP 1747–48, 1768–81.

30 (1719–95), MP 1741–84.

31 (d. 1778), MP 1772–78.

32 Hon. Richard Walpole (1728–98), MP 1768–84, and his brother Hon. Thomas Walpole (1727–1803), MP 1754–84.

33 NUL, PWF 5361, Pitt to Portland, 21 March 1772.

34 Ibid.
35 Fox, *Memorials and Correspondence*, 1:73, Fox to Ossory [February 1772]. The letter printed in this work is incomplete. For the manuscript itself, see BM, BL, Add. Ms. 47579:1.
36 Johnston, "Charles James Fox," 750–84.
37 Fox, *Memorials and Correspondence*, 1:73
38 Cobbett, *Parl. Hist.*, 17:420; NUL, PWF 5360, Pitt to Portland, 17 March 1772.
39 (?1707–77), MP 1756–77.
40 BM, BL, Eg. Ms. 239:6.
41 *Commons Journals*, 33:608; George III, *Correspondence*, 2:332, King to North, 23 March 1772; BM, Hardwicke Papers, BL, Add. Ms. 35610:180, Harris to Hardwicke, 23 March 1772.
42 Cobbett, *Parl. Hist.*, 17:388.
43 Burke, *Correspondence*, 2:309, Burke to Cruger, 30 June 1772.
44 See also Barré's speech (Cobbett, *Parl. Hist.*, 17:406).
45 *Public Advertiser*, 17 March 1772.
46 6th Baronet (1728–95), MP 1768–95.
47 7th Baronet (1719–94), MP 1753–60, 1768–90.
48 (1721–90), MP 1757–74, 1784–90.
49 2nd Baronet (1745–1813), MP 1768–1812.
50 BM, BL, Eg. Ms. 237:120.
51 (1727–1802), MP 1764–1802. These surveys (which are currently among the Abergavenny Mss at Eridge Castle) were used in Namier and Brooke, *History of Parliament*, to help evaluate the allegiances of the MPs in the House at this particular time. In dealing with the independent element I was able to borrow observations made in this work.
52 4th Baronet (1719–1804), MP 1768–1774.
53 (1738–77), MP 1761–76.
54 BM, BL, Eg. Ms. 237:120.
55 NUL, PWF 2665, Portland to Cavendish, 9 March 1772.
56 Ibid., Thomas Pitt to Portland, 21 March 1772.
57 Ibid., 9062, Rockingham to Portland, 18 March 1772.
58 For the Royal Marriage Act from the king's perspective, see Brooke, *King George III*, 267–77. Professor Brooke tells us that the act "was the personal measure of the King: apart from the Regency Act of 1765 the only legislative enactment which he proposed during the whole course of his reign" (275–6).
59 George III, *Correspondence*, 2:325, George III to North, 26 February 1772.
60 Cobbett, *Parl. Hist.*, 17:245.
61 Sykes, *Church and State*, 381–4.
62 There is a complete list of the minority in *Parliamentary Register*, 9:332–3.
63 Cobbett, *Parl. Hist.*, 17:290.

64 Ibid., 270–1.
65 Burke, *Correspondence*, 2:299, Burke to the Countess of Huntingdon [ante 6 February 1772].
66 Burke, *Writings and Speeches*, 2:359–64.
67 Ibid., 368.
68 BM, Egmont Papers, BL, Add. Ms. 47585:13, 2 April 1772.
69 George III, *Correspondence*, 2:335, North to the King [3 April 1772].
70 PRO, Chatham Papers, 53, pt. 2, 20, Price to Chatham, 3 April 1773.
71 Cobbett, *Parl. Hist.*, 17:440.
72 Burke, *Writings and Speeches*, 3:431–4.
73 See Sykes, *Church and State*, 386; Norman, *Church and Society*, 15; Hempton, "Religion in British Society," 201–13.
74 I agree with Clark's interpretation of Burke's essentially traditional position (*English Society*, 247–58).
75 See, Dickinson, *Liberty and Property*, 167–8.
76 See below, 176.
77 Ayling, *Edmund Burke*, 193–202.
78 See, Burke, *Writings and Speeches*, 3:376–9, 384–6.
79 Burke continued to support Catholic relief but only in Ireland (O'Brien, *Great Melody*, 468–84, 497–500, 511–21).
80 Ayling, *Edmund Burke*, 193–202.
81 See, Bradley, *Religion, Revolution and English Radicalism*, 91–120.
82 For a concise discussion of this process and source materials, see O'Gorman, "Pitt and the 'Tory' Reaction to the French Revolution," 21–38. See also Mitchell, *Charles James Fox*, 108–35.
83 SCL, WWM, R1–1876, to a representative of the Gentlemen of York, 30 December 1779.
84 Burke *Correspondence*, 2:309.

CHAPTER EIGHT

1 Sutherland, *East India Company*, 213–68; Bowen, *Revenue and Reform*, 119–89; Elofson, "Rockingham Whigs in Transition."
2 See, for example, Dow, *History of Hindostan*; Bolts, *Considerations on India Affairs*.
3 Walpole, *Correspondence*, 33:441, Walpole to Mann, 4 November 1772.
4 Nottingham University Library (NUL), Portland Papers (PWF) 9001, Rockingham to Portland, [early 1768].
5 See Donoughue, *British Politics and the American Revolution*, 24.
6 The stock ledgers are in the India Office Library, London.
7 Elofson, "Rockingham Whigs in Transition," 954–5.
8 Ibid., 955.
9 Ibid., 955–6.

10 Burke, *Correspondence*, 2:344, Rockingham to Burke, 24, 27, 28 October 1772.
11 William L. Clements Library (wcl), Dowdeswell Papers, Dowdeswell to Rockingham, 18 October 1772.
12 Sheffield City Library (scl), Wentworth Woodhouse Muniments (wwm), R1–1413, Portland to Rockingham, 21 November 1772.
13 Albemarle, *Memoirs of the Marquis of Rockingham*, 2:225.
14 Bowen, *Revenue and Reform*, 141.
15 Burke, *Correspondence*, 2:366, Burke to Dowdeswell, 6, 7 November 1772.
16 Ibid., 385, Burke to Rockingham, 23 November 1772.
17 For the latter bill, see O'Brien, *Great Melody*, 304–36.
18 Burke, *Correspondence*, 385, Burke to Rockingham, 23 November 1772. See also ibid., 384 and 351, Burke to Dowdeswell, 27 October 1772. I do not disagree with Dr Bowen that in the beginning the Rockingham leaders had some difficulty deciding what specific stand the party should take in Parliament. However, I have been able to find nothing to persuade me that the leaders were not unanimous that they should attempt to prevent the patronage and revenues of the company adding to the influence of the crown. This was the "principle they had committed themselves to in the past" and it was their "central policy" now (Elofson, "Rockingham Whigs in Transition," 958, 967, 978).
19 Ibid., 958–9.
20 See above, 4.
21 scl, wwm, R1–1409, Rockingham to Dowdeswell, 30 October 1772.
22 Burke, *Correspondence*, 2:370, Richmond to Burke, 15 November 1772. See also ibid., 368, Burke to Rockingham, 11 November 1772.
23 Ibid., 2:361–7.
24 scl, wwm, bk-1/399, A. Keppel to Burke, 6 November 1772.
25 scl, wwm, R1–1412, Rockingham to Dowdeswell, 17 November 1772.
26 scl, wwm, R1–1413, Portland to Rockingham, 21 November 1772.
27 wcl, Dowdeswell Papers, Dowdeswell to Rockingham, 8 November 1772. scl, wwm, R1–1412, Rockingham to Dowdeswell, 17 November 1772.
28 wcl, Dowdeswell Papers, Dowdeswell to Rockingham, 17 December 1772.
29 He appeared on 29 January 1773; see Burke, *Correspondence*, 2:423, Rockingham to Burke, 9 February 1773.
30 Burke, *Correspondence*, 2:390–1, Richmond to Burke, 2 December 1772.
31 scl, wwm, R1–1419, Dowdeswell to Rockingham, 20–22 December 1772.
32 Ibid.
33 Chatham, *Correspondence*, 4:252, Shelburne to Chatham, 27 February 1773.
34 Germain and Cornwall both joined the North cabinet during the American Revolution – Germain in 1775 as first lord of trade and secretary of state for America, and Cornwall in 1774 as a lord of the Treasury.
35 Thomas Townshend, Jr, had been joint paymaster general under Chatham, and he became secretary at war and then home secretary in

1782. His father had been under-secretary of state, 1724–30, and was closely connected with the Whig leadership under George II.

36 The twelve were Sir James Cockburn (1729–1804), MP 1772–84; Sir George Colebrooke (1729–1809), MP 1754–74; Henry Crabb Boulton (c.1709–73), MP 1754–73; Peregrine Cust (1723–85), MP 1761–75, 1776–85; George Dempster (1732–1818), MP 1761–68, 1769–90; Henry Fletcher (c.1727–1807), MP 1768–1806; Robert Gregory (?1729–1810), MP 1768–84; Robert Jones (d.1774), MP 1754–74; John Purling (?1722–1800), MP 1770, 1772–90; Thomas Rumbold (1736–91), MP 1770–75, 1780–84; John Stephenson (?1709–94), MP 1754–55, 1761–94; and Laurence Sulivan (c. 1713–86), MP 1762–74. These men were directors, 1772–73, or had been on the directorship for one or more years between 1768 and 1773. The two who offered resistance to the government were Sulivan and Gregory.

37 The nabobs were John Carnac (1720–1800), MP 1768–74; Eyre Coote (1726–83), MP 1768–80; Henry Crabb Boulton (also a director); William Frankland (1720–1805), MP 1768–74; Robert Palk (1717–98), MP 1767–87; Sir George Pigot (1719–77), MP 1765–77; Thomas Rumbold (also a director); Henry Strachey (1737–1810), MP 1768–1807; Francis Sykes (1732–1804), MP 1771–1804; and John Walsh (1726–95), MP 1761–80. Those whom we know supported the opposition in 1773 were Frankland (whom I would categorize as an independent Rockingham), Pigot, and Walsh.

38 Headed by John Burgoyne (1723–92), MP 1761–92.

39 For example, see BM, Hastings Papers, BL, Add. Ms. 29133:493–6, Caillaud to Hastings, 31 March 1773. For Burke's comments, see Burke, *Correspondence*, 2:350, Burke to Dowdeswell, 27 October 1772; ibid., 354–5, Burke to Rockingham, 29 October 1772. Clive occasionally tried to shift the blame onto the directors (Cobbett, *Parl. Hist.*, 17:851–2). Richmond made some charges against the directors which were reported in the *Public Advertiser* of 16 March.

40 SCL, WWM, R1–1419, Dowdeswell to Rockingham, 20–22 December 1772; *Annual Register* 16(1773):101–8. The City of London also petitioned the crown against government intervention; see *Gentleman's Magazine* 43(1773):346.

41 Sutherland, *East India Company in Eighteenth Century British Politics*, 187.

42 Cobbett, *Parl. Hist.*, 17:682.

43 Ibid., 568.

44 Ibid., 675.

45 Elofson, "Rockingham Whigs in Transition," 966.

46 *Journals of the House of Commons (Commons Journals)*, 34:365.

47 *Journals of the House of Lords (Lords Journals)*, 35:681.

48 Cobbett, *Parl. Hist.*, 17:855–82; Walpole, *Last Journals*, 1:198–9; Chatham, *Correspondence*, 4:263–4.

49 SCL, WWM, RI-1402, Rockingham to [Charles Turner, Autumn 1772].
50 (1732–1818).
51 O'Brien, *Great Melody,* 301–84.
52 Besides the evidence presented here, see ibid., 260–72.
53 Burke, *Correspondence,* 2:383, Burke to Rockingham, 23 November 1772.
54 See, ibid., 425, Burke to Charles O'Hara, 26 March 1773.
55 George Byng, 4th Viscount Torrington (1740–1812).
56 NUL, PWF 2343, Viscount Torrington to Portland, 25 October 1772.
57 SCL, WWM, R1–1443, Richmond to Rockingham, 10 September 1773.
58 For example, see Burke, *Correspondence,* 2:497, Rockingham to Burke [post 13 December 1773].
59 *Lords Journals,* 35:682.
60 Brooke, *Chatham Administration,* 50; Brewer, *Party Ideology and Popular Politics,* 257; O'Gorman, *Rise of Party,* 474.
61 SCL, WWM, R1–1413, Portland to Rockingham, 21 November 1772.
62 Sutherland, *East India Company in Eighteenth Century Politics,* 266–8.
63 WCL, Dowdeswell Papers, Dowdeswell to Rockingham, 18 July 1773.
64 Burke, *Writings and Speeches,* 2:264.
65 Langford, *First Rockingham Administration,* 282. The reader might also consult the *Thoughts on the Cause of the Present Discontents* for evidence of the Rockinghams' publicly declared admiration of George II (and implied criticism of George III); see Burke, *Writings and Speeches,* 2:266–7.
66 Burke, *Correspondence,* 3:381, 384, Burke to Fox, 8 October 1777.
67 SCL, WWM, R1–1810, Fox to Rockingham, 24 January [1779].
68 Elofson, "Rockingham Whigs and the Country Tradition."
69 Thomas, "Sir Roger Newdigate's Essays on Party," 399–400.
70 See Burke, *Writings and Speeches,* 2:215.
71 See below, 177–83.
72 *Commons Journals,* 33:608; George III, *Correspondence,* 2:334, King to North, 23 March 1772; BM, Hardwicke Papers, BL, Add. Ms. 35610:180, Harris to Hardwicke, 23 March 1772.
73 O'Gorman, *British Two-Party System,* 42.
74 *London Evening Post,* 17 April 1777.
75 NUL, PWF 9:140, Rockingham to Portland, 1 September 1780.
76 SCL, WWM, R1–1897, Rockingham to John Carr, 20 May 1780.
77 (1731–83), MP 1768–82.
78 O'Gorman, *Rise of Party,* 418.

CONCLUSION

1 William Ponsonby, 2nd Earl of Bessborough [I] (1704–93).
2 Sheffield City Library (SCL), Wentworth Woodhouse Muniments (WWM), R1–1442.

3   See *A List of the Absentees of Ireland*.

4   SCL, WWM, R1–1446, 20 September 1773.

5   SCL, WWM, R1–1449, 30 September 1773.

6   Burke, *Correspondence*, 2:471, Burke to John Bourke [12 October 1773].

7   John Fitzpatrick, 2nd Earl of Upper Ossory (1745–1818).

8   SCL, WWM, R1–1451, 16 October 1773; *Annual Register* 16(1773):217–18.

9   SCL, WWM, R3–9.

10   SCL, WWM, R1–1454, North to Devonshire, 21 October 1773.

11   SCL, WWM, R3–11, R3–44, R3–56, R3–156, R3–158.

12   SCL, WWM, R3–148, Ellis to Rockingham, 5 December 1773.

13   SCL, WWM, R3–15, Glynn to Rockingham [mid-November 1773]; ibid., R3–18, James Townsend to Rockingham, 4 November 1773; ibid., R3–24, Bull to Rockingham, 6 November 1773; Burke, *Correspondence*, 2:482, Burke to Rockingham, 7, 11 November 1773.

14   (c.1714–84), MP 1773–84, sheriff of London 1771–72, alderman 1772, lord mayor 1773–74.

15   Burke, *Correspondence*, 2:483.

16   Simon, 1st Earl Harcourt (1714–77).

17   *Harcourt Papers*, 9:92.

18   Ibid., 92, Harcourt to North, November 1773.

19   SCL, WWM, R3–41, Lord Bellamont to Rockingham, 7 November 1773.

20   7th Baronet (1735–99), later (1776) 1st Baron Bingham and (1795) 1st Earl of Lucan.

21   See, Thomas, *Tea Party to Independence*.

22   Burke, *Correspondence*, 2:475–6, Burke to Bingham, 30 October 1773.

23   See Burke, *Writings and Speeches*, 3:46, 288–9, 374–6.

24   SCL, WWM, BK-304, Bingham to Burke [26 November 1773].

25   See, for example, Mahoney, "Mr Burke's Imperial Mentality and the Proposed Irish Absentee Tax," 158–66.

26   SCL, WWM, R1–1466, Rockingham to Dowdeswell, 30 November 1773.

27   The copies at Sheffield are in his own hand.

28   See, Chatham, *Correspondence*, 4:303, Shelburne to Chatham, 30 October 1773.

29   Burke, *Correspondence*, 2:491, Burke to O'Hara, 19 November 1773.

30   Colley, *In Defiance of Oligarchy*, 152, 231, 264, 288, 292.

31   Ibid., 292.

32   SCL, WWM, R1–1412, Rockingham to Dowdeswell, 17 November 1772.

33   Burke, *Writings and Speeches*, 3:247, 251, 258, 288–9

34   William Pitt (1759–86), MP 1781–1806.

35   Mitchell, *Charles James Fox*, 136–57.

36   Burke, *Correspondence*, 3:384, Burke to Fox, 8 October 1777.

37   SCL, WWM, R1–1077, Savile to Rockingham, 31 July 1768.

38   See Namier, *England in the Age of the American Revolution*, 229–82;

Donoughue, *British Politics and the American Revolution,* 36–46.
39 De Berdt, "Letters," 347.
40 Ibid., 391, De Berdt to Thomas Cushing, 2 February 1770.
41 Burke, *Correspondence,* 2:528, 6 April 1774.
42 Ibid., 2:523, 2 February 1774.
43 Cobbett, *Parl. Hist.,* 17:1169–91. Lord John Cavendish spoke against the bill but only "in its present form" (1186).
44 It was retained in 1770 when the other duties were repealed.
45 BM, BL, Eg. Ms. 246:4.
46 India Office Library, East India Company court books, 81:384.
47 Ibid., 446.
48 (d.1791).
49 See above, 141.
50 SCL, WWM, R1–1423–5.
51 *Public Advertiser,* 21 February 1773.
52 See Thomas, *Townshend Duties Crisis,* especially 1–17.
53 Burke, *Correspondence,* 2:529, Burke to the Committee of Correspondence of the General Assembly of New York, 6 April 1774.
54 Ibid., 3:89–90, 5 January 1775.
55 Ibid., 2:70, Dowdeswell to Burke, 5 September 1769.
56 Ibid., 96, Burke to O'Hara, 24 October [1769].
57 Cobbett, *Parl. Hist.,* 17:176–8.
58 There is a partial and very inadequate list of the minority in the *Gazetteer,* 10 March 1772.
59 Cobbett, *Parl. Hist.,* 16:1165.
60 Ibid., 1049.
61 (1740–1822).
62 See Christie, *Myth and Reality,* 261–83; Black, *The Association,* 1–82; O'Gorman, *Rise of Party,* 408–15.
63 Bolingbroke, *Dissertation upon Parties,* 125.
64 *Cato's Letters,* 1:86–7, 21 January 1720.
65 See Dickinson, *Liberty and Property,* 167–8.
66 See above, 141, 143.
67 Rudé, *Wilkes and Liberty.*
68 *Parliamentary Register,* 3:432–41.
69 Cobbett, *Parl. Hist.,* 19:570. See also the speech of John Wilkes when introducing his reform bill in the House of Commons on 31 March 1776 (ibid., 18:1295).
70 See Browning, *Political and Constitutional Ideas of the Court Whigs;* Dickinson, *Liberty and Property,* 121–62.
71 *Parliamentary Register,* 3:29.
72 Burke, *Writings and Speeches,* 9:153.
73 SCL, WWM, R1–1420, Rockingham to Murray, 20 December 1772.

74 Burke, *Correspondence*, 2:188, Rockingham to Burke [30 January 1771].
75 Ibid., 2:181, Rockingham to Burke, 3 January 1771.
76 Ibid., 191, Rockingham to Burke, 3 February 1771.
77 Ibid., 193, Rockingham to Burke, 14 February 1771.
78 Burke, *Writings and Speeches*, 2:292.
79 SCL, WWM, R1–1219, Cavendish to Rockingham [July 1769].
80 Burke, *Writings and Speeches*, 3:68–9.
81 Ibid., 2:311.
82 Burke, *Correspondence*, 2:44, Burke to Rockingham 9 July 1769.
83 Ibid., 3:190, Burke to Rockingham, 22, 23 August 1775.
84 Ibid., 218, Burke to Richmond, 26 September 1775.
85 Brewer, "Rockingham, Burke and Whig Political Argument," 195.
86 SCL, WWM, R1–996, Rockingham to P. Wentworth, 3 March 1768.
87 Burke, *Writings and Speeches*, 3:466–7, 476–7.
88 Burke, *Correspondence*, 2:377, Burke to Richmond [post 15 November 1772].
89 Burke, *Writings and Speeches*, 2:264.
90 Cobbett, *Parl. Hist.*, 21:150.
91 Nottingham University Library (NUL) Portland Papers (PWF) 9123, Burke to Portland, 16 January 1780.
92 Mitchell, *Charles James Fox*.
93 See Elofson, "Rockingham Whigs and the Country Tradition," 111.
94 Burke, *Writings and Speeches*, 9:157.
95 Bolingbroke, *Dissertation upon Parties*.
96 Burke, *Writings and Speeches*, 2:315.
97 Ibid., 317–18.
98 The argument above, 94–5, is that Burke was defending one party, not the party system.
99 On 17 February 1771 (Bristol University Library, Diary of Matthew Brickdale).
100 Wyvill, *Political Papers*, 1:32.
101 (1709–87).
102 SCL, WWM, R1–1186.
103 BM, Grenville Papers, BL, Add. Ms. 42086:68, 17 July 1768.
104 Burke, *Writings and Speeches*, 2:443.
105 Ibid., 420.
106 Burke, *Correspondence*, 9:292, Burke to Laurence [ante 22 March 1797].
107 SCL, WWM, R1–1410, Savile to Rockingham [November 1773].
108 Albemarle, *Memoirs of the Marquis of Rockingham*, 2:231–4, 5 November 1773.
109 SCL, WWM, R1–156–29, Rockingham to Lady Rockingham, 21 November 1773.
110 See O'Brien, *Great Melody*, xxxii–lix.

111 SCL, WWM, R1–1389, Rockingham to Dowdeswell, 10 December 1771.
112 Burke, *Correspondence*, 3:388–9.
113 SCL, WWM, R1–1413, Portland to Rockingham, 21 November 1772.
114 Richmond, "The Duke of Richmond's Memorandum," 479.
115 SCL, WWM, R1–1420, Rockingham to Murray, 20 December 1772.
116 Thomas Wentworth, 1st Earl of Strafford (1593–1641).
117 SCL, WWM, R1–1402, Rockingham to Turner [autumn 1772].
118 See Mitchell, *Charles James Fox*, 56–66.
119 For the debate amongst historians, see Thomas, "Party Politics in Eighteenth-Century Britain."
120 Dickinson, *Liberty and Property*, 121–62.
121 See above, 12.
122 See above, 5.
123 See above, 6 and n.
124 See in particular Hill, *British Parliamentary Parties, 1742–1832*; O'Gorman, *British Two-Party System*.

APPENDIX

1 Meredith actually broke with the Rockinghams in this period (see above, 117–18). However, letters that he wrote to the marquis during the petitioning movement in the summer of 1769 (for example, SCL, WWM, R-1237) suggest that he still considered himself a member of the party at that time.
2 O'Gorman, *Rise of Party*, 224–8 and n.
3 Rogers, *Protests of the House of Lords*, vol. 2.
4 See, for instance, his letter to the marquis in October 1770 (SCL, WWM, R1-1351).

Bibliography

PRIMARY SOURCES

Manuscripts

BERKSHIRE RECORD OFFICE
Hartley Papers

BODLEIAN LIBRARY
Clarendon Papers
Colebrooke Letters, Ms. Evy. lett. d. 350, ff. 35–53
Dashwood Papers
North Papers
Sulivan Papers

BOSTON PUBLIC LIBRARY
Ms. 224

BRISTOL UNIVERSITY LIBRARY
Matthew Brickdale's Parliamentary Diaries

BRITISH MUSEUM
Adair Papers, BL, Add. Mss. 50829–30, 53800–15
Buckinghamshire Papers, BL, Add. Ms. 22359
Cartaret Webb Papers, BL, Add. Ms. 22132, 215–68
Cavendish's debates of the House of Commons for the years 1768–74, BL, Eg.
     Mss.
Dashwood Papers, BL, Eg. Ms. 2136
Egmont Papers, BL, Add. Ms. 47585
Francis Papers, BL, Add. Mss. 40761–2

Germain et al., BL, Add. Ms. 39779
Grenville Papers, BL, Add. Mss. 42084, 42086, 52087
Hardwicke Papers, BL, Add. Mss. 35039, 35362, 35368, 35375, 35402, 35404, 35425, 35428–30, 35451, 35501, 35502, 35568, 35608–11, 35613
Hastings Papers, BL, Add. Mss. 29132–3
Holland House Papers, BL, Add. Mss. 47568, 47579–85, 47589–91, 47594
Liverpool Papers, BL, Add. Mss. 38206, 38207, 38305, 38306, 38398, 38469, 38470
Martin Papers, BL, Add. Mss. 41354, 41361
Mitchell Papers, BL, Add. Mss. 6822, 6834
Moore Papers, BL, Add. Ms. 12440
Newcastle Papers, BL, Add. Mss. 32988–92, 33001, 33002, 33030, 33031, 33037, 33041, 33045, 33048, 33056, 33059–61, 33072, 33082, 33087–92, 33096, 33097
Pelham Papers, BL, Add. Mss. 33095, 33096, 33099, 33125, 33129
Stevens Transcripts, BL, Add. Mss. 42258, 42264, 42265
West Papers, BL, Add. Mss. 34728, 34735
Wilkes Papers, BL, Add. Mss. 30866, 30868, 30870, 30871, 30877,30881, 30892
Woodfall Papers, BL, Add. Mss. 2774, 2775, 2778–80

CHATSWORTH HOUSE
Devonshire Papers

HISTORY OF PARLIAMENT TRUST TRANSCRIPTS
Germain Papers (original in William L. Clements Library)
Sandwich Papers (original with V. Montagu Esq.)

HOUSE OF LORDS RECORDS OFFICE
Lords Minute Books
Lords Sessional Papers

INDIA OFFICE LIBRARY
Clive Papers
East India Company Court Books
East India Company Stock Ledgers

IPSWICH AND EAST SUFFOLK RECORD OFFICE
Albemarle Papers

NORTHAMPTONSHIRE RECORD OFFICE
Fitzwilliam Papers

NOTTINGHAM UNIVERSITY LIBRARY
Portland Papers

PUBLIC RECORD OFFICE
Chatham Papers PRO 30/8
Grenville Papers PRO 30/29
Inspector General's Accounts of Imports and Exports, Customs 16/1

SHEFFIELD CITY LIBRARY
Wentworth Woodhouse Muniments, Rockingham and Burke Papers

STAFFORDSHIRE RECORD OFFICE
Dartmouth Papers

WARWICKSHIRE RECORD OFFICE
Newdigate Papers

WILLIAM L. CLEMENTS LIBRARY, MICHIGAN
Dowdeswell Papers

Periodicals

Annual Register, or a View of the History Politicks, and Literature of the Year ...
Bingley's Weekly Journal
Daily Advertiser
Gazetteer and New Daily Advertiser
General Evening Post
Gentleman's Magazine and Historical Chronicle
Lloyd's Evening Post and British Chronicle
London Chronicle
London Evening Post
London Gazette
London Magazine
Middlesex Journal
Public Advertiser
St. James's Chronicle, or the British Evening Post
The Town and Country Magazine, or the Universal Repository of Knowledge, Instruction and Entertainment

Published Correspondence and Contemporary Material

An Address to Protestant Dissenters. London, 1773.
Albemarle, Earl of, ed. *Memoirs of the Marquis of Rockingham and His Contemporaries.* 2 vols. London, 1852.
Almon, J. *Anecdotes of the Life of the Right Honourable William Pitt.* 6th ed. London, 1792.

– *Biographical, Literary and Political Anecdotes of Several of the Most Eminent Persons of the Present Age*. London, 1797.
– *History of the Late Majority*. London, 1765.
– *Memoirs of a Late Eminent Bookseller*. London, 1790.
– ed. *The Political Register and Review of New Books*. 5 vols. London, 1767–72.
An Analysis of the Thoughts on the Cause of the Present Discontents and of the Observations on the Same. London, 1770.
Barrow, R., ed. *The Pillars of Priestcraft and Orthodoxy Shaken*. 4 vols. New ed. London 1768.
Bateson, M., ed. *A Narrative of the Changes in the Ministry 1765–1767*. London, 1898.
Beckford, William. *Memoirs of William Beckford of Fonthill*, ed. C. Redding. Vol. 1. London, 1859.
Bedford, Duke of. *The Correspondence of John, Fourth Duke of Bedford*, ed. Lord John Russell. Vol. 3. London, 1846.
Blackburne, F. *Reflections on the Fate of a Petition for Relief in the Matter of Subscription, Offer'd to the Honourable House of Commons, February 6th, 1772*. London, 1772.
Blunt, R., ed. *Mrs. Montagu, Her Letters and Friendships*. 2 vols. London, 1923.
Bolingbroke, Lord. *A Dissertation upon Parties. In Several Letters to Caleb D'Anvers, Esq*. 3rd ed. London, 1739.
– *Lord Bolingbroke: Historical Writings*, ed. I. Kramnick. Chicago, 1972.
Bolts, W. *Considerations on Indian Affairs*. London, 1777.
Boswell, J. *An Account of Corsica: The Journal of a Tour to That Island, and Memoirs of Pascal Paoli*. 3rd ed. London, 1769.
Brown, A.E. *John Hancock His Book*. Boston, 1898.
Burgh, J. *Political Disquisitions; or An Enquiry into Public Errors, Defects, and Abuses*. 3 vols. London, 1774.
Burke, Edmund. *The Correspondence of Edmund Burke*, ed. T.W. Copeland et al. 10 vols. Cambridge, 1958–78.
– *Edmund Burke: Letters, Speeches and Tracts on Irish Affairs*, ed. C.M. Arnold. London, 1881.
– *Edmond Burke on Government, Politics and Society*, ed. B.W. Hill. Sussex, 1975.
– *Selected Letters of Edmund Burke*, ed. H.C. Mansfield, Jr. Chicago, 1984.
– *The Works of the Right Honourable Edmund Burke*. 6 vols. 2nd ed. London, New York, Toronto, 1906.
– *The Writings and Speeches of Edmund Burke*, ed. P. Langford et al. 7 vols. to date. Oxford, 1981–.
Calendar of Home Office Papers of the Reign of George III. Vol. 2, ed. Q. Reddington. London, 1878–79. Vol. 3, ed. R.A. Roberts London, 1881.
A Candid Refutation of the Charges Brought against the Present Ministers in a Late Pamphlet, Entitled the "Principles of the Late Changes Impartially Examined." London, 1765.

Cartwright, F.D. *Life and Correspondence of Major John Cartwright.* London, 1826.

Cato's Letters: Essays on Liberty, Civil and Religious and Other Important Subjects. 2 vols. New York, 1971.

Cavendish, Sir Henry. *Sir Henry Cavendish's Debates of the House of Commons in the Thirteenth Parliament of Great Britain, 1768–74,* ed. J. Wright. 2 vols. London, 1841–43.

Channing, E., and A. Coolidge, eds. *The Barrington Bernard Correspondence and Illustrative Matter 1760–1770.* Cambridge, Mass., 1912.

Chatham, Earl of. *Correspondence of William Pitt, Earl of Chatham,* ed. W.S. Taylor and J.H. Pringle. Vols. 3, 4. London, 1839.

Chesterfield, Earl of. *The Letters of Philip Dormer Stanhope, Fourth Earl of Chesterfield,* ed. D. Dobree. Vol. 6. London, 1932.

Clementson, John. "The Parliamentary Diary of John Clementson, 1770–1772," ed. P.D.G. Thomas. *Camden Miscellany,* 4th ser., 13 (1974): 143–67.

Clive, R. *An East India Budget Containing Many Precious Stones, Diamonds, Rubies &c. of the First Water and Magnitude.* [London], 1773.

Cobbett, W., ed. *The Parliamentary History of England from the Earliest Period to the Year 1803.* Vols. 16, 17, 18. London, 1803.

Coke, Lady Mary. *The Letters and Journals of Lady Mary Coke.* 4 vols. London, 1889–96.

A Collection of Letters and Essays in Favour of Public Liberty, 1764–1770. London, 1774.

A Collection of Papers Designed to Explain and Vindicate the Present Mode of Subscription Required by the University of Oxford from All Young Persons at their Matriculation. Oxford, 1772.

A Collection of Tracts on the Subjects of Taxing the British Colonies in America, and Regulating Their Trade. London, 1773.

Commerce of Rhode Island: 1726–1800. Massachusetts Historical Society, 7th ser., 9, 10 (1914–15).

Considerations of the Propriety of Requiring a Subscription to Articles of Faith. 2nd ed. London, 1774.

The Controversial Letters of John Wilkes Esq., the Rev. John Horne and Their Principal Adherents, with a Supplement Containing Material Anonymous Pieces. London, 1771.

"Correspondence between William Strahan and David Hall, 1763–1777." *Pennsylvania Magazine of History and Biography* 10 (1886): 86–99 et seq.

Cust, Lady E.L. and Sir J., eds. *Records of the Cust Family.* Vol. 3. London, 1927.

De Berdt, Dennys. "Letters of Dennys De Berdt, 1757–1770." *Publications of the Colonial Society of Massachusetts* 131 (1910–11): 293–461.

A Defence of the Considerations on the Propriety of Requiring a Subscription to Articles of Faith in Reply to a Late Answer from the London Press. London, 1774.

Dempster, George. *Letters from George Dempster to Sir Adam Ferguson, 1756–1813*, ed. J. Ferguson. London, 1834.

Dow, A. *History of Hindostan.* London, 1772.

Dowdeswell, W. *The Sentiments of an English Freeholder on the Decision of the Middlesex Election.* London, 1769.

Elliot, G.F.S. *The Border Elliots and the Family of Minto.* London, 1897.

Father of Candor. *A Letter Concerning Libels.* London, 1771.

Fitzmaurice, Lord E. *The Life of William Earl of Shelburne.* Vol. 2. London, 1876.

Forester, M. *A Defence of the Proceedings of the House of Commons in the Middlesex Election.* London, 1770.

Fox, Charles James. *Memorials and Correspondence of Charles James Fox*, ed. Lord John Russell. 2 vols. London, 1853.

Francis, Sir Philip. *Memoirs of Sir Philip Francis, K.G.*, ed. Q. Parkes and H. Merivale. 2 vols. London, 1867.

Francis, Sir Philip, et al. *The Francis Letters, by Sir Philip Francis and Other Members of the Family*, ed. B. Francis and E. Keary. 2 vols. London, 1901.

Franklin, Benjamin. *The Papers of Benjamin Franklin*, ed. L.W. Laboree. Vols. 15, 16, 17. New Haven, 1971–73.

– *The Writings of Benjamin Franklin*, ed., A.H. Smyth. Vols. 5, 6. New York, 1907.

Franklin, Benjamin, and Richard Jackson. *Letters and Papers of Benjamin Franklin and Richard Jackson 1753–1785.* Philadelphia, 1947.

Fraser, W., ed. *Memorials of the Family of Wemyss.* Edinburgh, 1888.

Gage, Thomas. *The Correspondence of General Thomas Gage with the Secretaries of State and with the War Office and the Treasury, 1763–1775*, ed. C.E. Carter. New Haven, 1931, 1933.

Garrick, David. *Private Correspondence of David Garrick.* 2 vols. London, 1831–32.

"Garth Correspondence," ed. J.W. Barnwell. *South Carolina Historical and Genealogical Magazine* 30 (1929).

George III. *Letters from George III to Lord Bute, 1755–66*, ed. R. Sedgwick. London, 1937.

– *Correspondence of King George the Third from 1760 to December 1783*, ed. Sir J. Fortescue. 6 vols. London, 1927.

Gibbon, Edward. *The Letters of Edward Gibbon*, ed. J.E. Norton. Vol. 1. London, 1956.

Grafton, Duke of. *Autobiography and Political Correspondence of Augustus Henry, Third Duke of Grafton*, ed. W. R. Anson, 1898.

Gray, C., ed. "Charles Gray's Parliamentary Notebook." Historical Manuscripts Commission, 14th report, 9:316–50.

Great Britain. Historical Manuscripts Commission. *Abergavenny Manuscripts* (no. 15).

– *Buccleuch Manuscripts* (no. 45).

– *Charlemont Manuscripts* (no. 28).

– *Dartmouth Manuscripts* (no. 20).

– *Denbigh Manuscripts* (no. 68).
– *Donoughmore Manuscripts* (no. 27).
– *Foljambe Manuscripts* (no. 41).
– *Hastings Manuscripts* (no. 78).
– *Laing Manuscripts* (no. 72).
– *Lothian Manuscripts* (no. 62).
– *Polworth Manuscripts* (no. 67).
– *Round Manuscripts* (no. 38).
– *Rutland Manuscripts* (no. 24).
– *Stopford-Sackville Manuscripts* (no. 49).
– *Various Collections: Knox* (no. 55, vi).
– *Various Collections: Wood* (no. 55, viii).
– *Weston Underwood Manuscripts* (no. 10).
The Grenville Papers, ed. W.J. Smith. 4 vols. London, 1852.
Guttridge, G.H., ed. *The American Correspondence of a Bristol Merchant, 1766–76: Letters of Richard Champion.* University of California Publications in History, 22 (1934): 1–27.
The Harcourt Papers, ed. E.W. Harcourt. Vols. 7, 8, 9. Oxford, 1905.
Hardy, F. *Memoirs of the Political and Private Life of James Caulfield, Earl of Charlemont.* 2 vols. London, 1812.
Harris, G. *The Life of Lord Chancellor Hardwicke with Selections from His Correspondence, Diaries, Speeches and Judgements.* 3 vols. London, 1847.
Haywood, S., and Lefft, C. *The Right of Protestant Dissenters to a Complete Toleration.* 2nd ed. London, 1787.
Hickey, William. *Memoirs of William Hickey*, ed. A. Spencer. 4 vols. London, 1913–25.
Hoffman, R.J.S. *Edmund Burke New York Agent, with His Letters to the New York Assembly and Intimate Correspondence with Charles O'Hara 1761–1776.* Philadelphia, 1956.
Hollis, Thomas. *Memoirs of Thomas Hollis*, ed. F. Blackburne. London, 1780.
Hume, David. *The Letters of David Hume*, ed. J.Y.T. Greig. Vol. 2. Oxford, 1932.
Ibbetson, J. *A Plea for the Subscription of the Clergy to the Thirty-nine Articles of Religion.* London, 1778.
Ilchester, Countess of, and Lord Stavordole. *The Life and Letters of Lady Sarah Lennox, 1745–1826.* Vol. 1. London, 1901.
Ilchester, Earl of, ed. *Letters to Henry Fox, Lord Holland.* London, 1915.
Jebb, D.J. *Letters on the Subject of Subscription to the Liturgy and Thirty-nine Articles.* London, 1772.
Jesse, J.H. *George Selwyn and His Contemporaries.* London, 1843.
Johnson, Samuel. *False Alarm.* London, 1770.
– *The Letters of Samuel Johnson*, ed. R.W. Chapman. 3 vols. Oxford, 1952.
– *Memoirs of the Life and Writings of the Late Dr. Samuel Johnson.* London, 1785.

– *Thoughts on the Late Transaction Respecting Falkland's Islands.* London, 1771.

Johnson, William Samuel. "Letters of William Samuel Johnson to the Governors of Connecticut." *Collections of the Massachusetts Historical Society,* 5th ser., 9 (1914): 211–490.

Journals of the House of Commons. Vols. 32, 33, 34. London, 1803.

Journals of the House of Lords. Vols. 33, 34, 35. London, n.d.

Junius. *Letters of Junius,* ed. C.W. Everett. London, 1927.

Keppel, T. *The Life of Admiral Viscount Keppel.* Vol. 1 London, 1842.

Kimball, G.S., ed. *The Correspondence of the Colonial Governors of Rhode Island 1723–1775.* Vol. 2. Boston and New York, 1902–03.

Kippis, A. *A Vindication of the Protestant Dissenting Ministers with Regard to Their Late Application to Parliament.* 2nd ed. London, 1773.

Knox, W. *The Present State of the Nation: Particularly with Respect to Its Trade, Finances, etc. etc. Addressed to the King and Both Houses of Parliament.* London, 1768.

Leinster, Duchess of. *Correspondence of Emily, Duchess of Leinster,* ed. B. Fitzgerald. Dublin, 1949–57.

"A Letter from the Marquis of Rockingham to Sir William Mayne on the Proposed Absentee Tax of 1733," ed. J.E. Tyler. *Irish Historical Studies* 8 (1952–53): 367.

A Letter to the Earl of Bute. London, 1771.

A Letter to the Gentlemen, Clergy, and Freeholders of the County of Middlesex. London, 1768.

A Letter to Protestant Dissenting Ministers. London, 1772.

A List of the Absentees of Ireland, and an Estimate of the Yearly Value of Their Estates and Incomes Spent Abroad. 3rd ed. Dublin 1769.

Macaulay, C. *Observations on a Pamphlet Entitled "Thoughts on the Cause of the Present Discontents."* London, 1770.

Malmesbury, Earl of, ed. *A Series of Letters from the First Earl of Malmesbury, His Family and Friends from 1745 to 1820.* Vol. 1. London, 1870.

Mason, F.N., ed. *John Norton and Sons, Merchants of London and Virginia.* 2nd ed. Newton Abbot, 1968.

Meredith, Sir W. *The Question Stated, Whether the Freeholders of Middlesex Lost Their Right, by Voting for Mr. Wilkes at the Last Election? In a Letter from a Member of Paliament to On of His Constituents.* London, 1769.

Minchinton, W.E., ed. *Politics of the Port of Bristol in the Eighteenth Century.* Bristol Record Society Publications, no. 23, 1963.

Morison, S.E., ed. *Sources and Documents Illustrating the American Revolution 1764–1788 and the Formation of the Federal Constitution.* Oxford, 1923.

Olson, A.G. *The Radical Duke: The Career and Correspondence of Charles Lennox, Third Duke of Richmond.* Oxford, 1961.

Osborne, Sarah Byng. *Letters of Sarah Byng Osborne: 1721–1773,* ed. J. McClelland. Stanford University, 1930.

Paine, T. *Common Sense*. London, 1776.

The Parliamentary Register, or History of the Proceedings and Debates of the House of Commons (1774–80). Vol. 3. London, 1803.

Phillimore, R. *The Memoirs and Correspondence of George, Lord Lyttleton*. Vol. 2. London, 1845.

Plumer, William. *Letters of William Plumer to William Henry Cavendish Bentinck, Third Duke of Portland*, ed. R.W. Goulding. London, 1909.

The Political Monitor Exhibiting the Present State of Affairs in Ireland. Dublin, 1772.

Porter, K.W. *The Jacksons and the Lees*. Vol. 1. Cambridge, Mass., 1937.

Pownall, T. *The Administration of the Colonies*. 4th ed. London, 1768.

The Principles of the Late Changes Impartially Examined. 2nd ed. London, 1765.

Proceedings and Debates of the British Parliaments Respecting North America, 1754–1783, ed. R.C. Simmons and P.D.G. Thomas. 6 vols. New York, 1982–86.

Richmond, Duke of. "The Duke of Richmond's Memorandum, 1–7 July 1766," ed. A.G. Olson. *English Historical Review* 75 (1960): 475–82.

Robertson, C.G. ed. *Select Statutes, Cases and Documents*. 8th ed. London, 1947.

Rogers, J.E. Thorold, ed. *A Complete Collection of the Protests of the House of Lords*. Vol. 2. Oxford, 1875.

Ryder, Nathaniel. "Parliamentary Diaries of Nathaniel Ryder, 1764–67," ed. P.D.G. Thomas. *Camden Miscellany* 23, 4th ser., 7 (1969): 229–351.

The Sentiments of an English Freeholder on the Late Decision of the Middlesex Election. London, 1769.

The Sentiments of the Old Whigs upon a Place Bill. 2nd ed. London, 1740.

Shebbeare, J. *A First Letter to the People of England on the Present Situation and Conduct of National Affairs*. 4th ed. London, 1756.

A Sketch of the Secret History of Europe since the Peace of Paris. London, 1772.

The Statutes at Large. London, 1786.

Stevens, A. *Memoirs of John Horne Tooke*. Vol. 1. London, 1918.

Tucker, J. *An Apology for the Present Church of England as by Law Established, Occasioned by a Petition Laid before Parliament for Abolishing Subscriptions, in a Letter to One of the Petitioners*. 2nd ed. Gloucester, 1772.

Walpole, Horace. *Horace Walpole's Correspondence*, ed. W.S. Lewis. Vols. 1, 4, 5, 10, 14, 15, 16, 23, 28, 31, 32, 35, 36, 39. London, 1937.

– *Horace Walpole's Memoirs of the Reign of King George III*, ed. G.F.R. Barker. 4 vols. London, 1894.

– *The Last Journals of Horace Walpole during the Reign of George III, 1771 to 1783*, ed. A. Francis Steuart. Vol. 1. London, 1910.

– *Letters of Horace Walpole*, ed. P. Toynbee. Vols. 6, 7, suppt. 1, 2, 3. Oxford, 1904, 1918, 1925.

Whitworth, Sir C. *State of the Trade of Great Britain in Its Imports and Exports; Progressively from the Year 1679*. London, 1776.

Wilkes, John. *The Correspondence of the Late John Wilkes with His Friends, etc.*, ed. J. Almon. 5 vols. London, 1895.

Wyvill, C., ed. *Political Papers, Chiefly Respecting the Attempt of the County of York, and Other Considerable Districts ... to Effect a Reformation of the Parliament of Great Britain*. 6 vols. York, 1794.

Young, A. *Six Months Tour through the North of England. Containing an Account of the Present State of Agriculture, Manufactures and Population in Several Counties of This Kingdom*. 4 vols. 2nd ed. London, 1771.

SECONDARY SOURCES

This is a selected bibliography that does not include the standard works of reference.

Anderson, G.P. "Pascal Paoli: An Inspiration to the Sons of Liberty." *Publications of the Colonial Society of Massachusetts* 16 (1924–26): 180–8.

Andrews, C.M. "The Boston Merchants and the Non-Importation Movement." *Publications of the Colonial Society of Massachusetts* 19 (1916–17): 159–259.

Ashton, T.S. *An Economic History of England: The Eighteenth Century*. London, 1955.

– *Economic Fluctuations in England 1700–1800*. Oxford, 1959.

Ayling, S. *Edmund Burke: His Life and Opinions*. New York, 1988.

Baxter, W.T. *The House of Hancock in Boston, 1724–75*. Cambridge, Mass., 1945.

Black, E.C. *The Association: British Extra-Parliamentary Political Organization 1769–1773*. Cambridge, Mass., 1963.

Bleakley, H. *Life of John Wilkes*. London, 1917.

Bonsall, B. *Sir James Lowther and Cumberland and Westmorland Elections, 1754–75*. Manchester, 1960.

Bowen, H. *Revenue and Reform: The Indian Problem in British Politics 1757–1773*. Cambridge, 1991.

Bradley, J.E. *Religion, Revolution and English Radicalism: Nonconformity in Eighteenth-Century Politics and Society*. Cambridge, 1990.

Brewer, J. "English Radicalism in the Age of George III." In *Three British Revolutions: 1641, 1688, 1776*, ed. J.G.A. Pocock, 323–67. Princeton, 1980.

– "The Misfortunes of Lord Bute: A Case Study in Eighteenth-Century Political Argument and Public Opinion." *Historical Journal* 16 (1973): 3–43.

– "Party and the Double Cabinet: Two Facets of Burke's Thoughts." *Historical Journal* 14 (1971): 3–21.

– *Party Ideology and Popular Politics at the Accession of George III*. Cambridge, 1976.

– "Rockingham, Burke and Whig Political Argument." *Historical Journal* 18 (1975): 188–201.

- *The Sinews of Power: War, Money and the English State, 1688–1783.* New York, 1989.

Brooke, J. *The Chatham Administration, 1766–68.* London, 1956.

- *King George III.* London, 1972.

Brown, P. *The Chathamites.* London, 1967.

Browning, R. *The Duke of Newcastle.* New Haven, 1972.

- *Political and Constitutional Ideas of the Court Whigs.* London, 1982.

Bryant, D.C. "Burke's Present Discontents: The Rhetorical Genesis of a Party Testament." *Quarterly Journal of Speech* 42 (1956): 115–26.

Burns, A. *History of the British West Indies.* London, 1954.

Butterfield, H. *George III, Lord North and the People.* Cambridge, 1952.

Cannon, J. *Aristocratic Century: The Peerage of Eighteenth-Century England.* Cambridge, 1984.

- *Parliamentary Reform, 1640–1832.* Cambridge, 1973.

Carrington, D. "The Corsican Constitution of Pasquale Paoli 1755–69." *English Historical Review* 88 (1973): 481–503.

Chaffin, R.J. "The Townshend Duties of 1767." *William and Mary Quarterly,* 3rd ser., 27 (1970): 90–121.

Chapman, G.W. *Edmund Burke: The Practical Imagination.* Cambridge, Mass., 1967.

Christie, I.R. "The Anatomy of the Opposition in the Parliament of 1784." *Parliamentary History* 9 (1990): 50–77.

- "The Changing Nature of Parliamentary Politics, 1742–1789." In *British Politics and Society from Walpole to Pitt,* ed. J. Black, 101–22. London, 1990.

- *Crisis of Empire: Great Britain and the American Colonies 1754–1783,* London, 1976.

- *The End of North's Ministry 1780–1782.* London, 1958.

- "The Marquis of Rockingham and Lord North's Offer of a Coalition, June–July 1780." In his *Myth and Reality, in Late Eighteenth-Century British Politics and Other Papers,* 109–32. London, 1970.

- *Myth and Reality in Late Eighteenth-Century British Politics and Other Papers.* Berkeley and Los Angeles, 1970.

- "Party in Politics in the Age of Lord North's Administration." *Parliamentary History* 6 (1987): 47–68.

- "Was There a 'New Toryism' in the Earlier Part of George III's Reign?" *Journal of British Studies* 5 (1965–66): 60–71.

- *Wilkes, Wyvill and Reform.* London, 1962.

Christie, I.R., and B.W. Laboree. *Empire or Independence 1760–1776.* Oxford, 1976.

Clark, D.M. *British Opinion and the American Revolution.* London, 1930.

Clark, J.C.D. "The Decline of Party, 1740–1760." *English Historical Review* 93 (1978): 517–19.

- *English Society, 1688 – 1832*. Cambridge, 1985.
- *Revolution and Rebellion: State and Society in England in the Seventeenth and Eighteenth Centuries*. Cambridge, 1986.

Cobban, A. *Edmund Burke and the Revolt against the Eighteenth Century.* London, 1929.

Cochrane, J.A. *Dr. Johnson's Printer: The Life of William Strachan*. London, 1964.

Colley, L. "Eighteenth-Century English Radicalism before Wilkes." *Transactions of the Royal Historical Society,* 5th ser., 31 (1981): 4–21.

- *In Defiance of Oligarchy: The Tory Party, 1714–60*. Cambridge, 1982.

Collyer, C. "The Rockingham Connection and Country Opinion in the Early Years of George III." *Proceedings of the Leeds Philosophical and Literary Society* 71 (1952–55): 251–75.

- "The Rockinghams and Yorkshire Politics, 1742–1761." Publications of the Thoresby Society, *Thoresby Miscellany* 41 (1954): 352–82.

Cone, C.B. *Burke and the Nature of Politics: The Age of the American Revolution*. University of Kentucky, 1957.

Connell, B. *Portrait of a Whig Peer*. London, 1957.

Copeland, T.W. *Edmund Burke: Six Essays*. London, 1950.

Corfield, P.J. *The Impact of English Towns*. Oxford, 1982.

Currey, C.B. *The Road to Revolution: Benjamin Franklin in England, 1765–75*. New York, 1968.

Davies, A.M. *Clive of Plasie*. London, 1939.

Davis, R. *The Rise of the English Shipping Industry in the Seventeenth and Eighteenth Centuries*. London, 1962.

Dickerson, O.M. *The Navigation Acts and the American Revolution*. Philadelphia, 1951.

Dickinson, H.T. "The Eighteenth Century Debate on the Glorious Revolution." *History* 61 (1976): 28–45.

- *Liberty and Property: Political Ideology in Eighteenth-Century Britiain*. London, 1977.

Donoughue, B. *British Politics and the American Revolution, 1773–75*. London, 1964.

Elofson, W.M. "The Rockingham Whigs and the Country Tradition." *Parliamentary History* 8 (1989): 90–115.

- "The Rockingham Whigs in Transition: The East India Company Issue 1772–1773." *English Historical Review* 104 (1989): 947–74.

Feiling, K.G. *The Second Tory Party 1714–1832*. London, 1938.

Fitzgerald, P. *The Life and Times of John Wilkes, M.P.* London, 1888.

Foord, A. *His Majesty's Opposition: 1714–1830*. Oxford, 1964.

Forrest, Sir G.W. *The Life of Lord Clive*. 2 vols. London, 1918.

Gilbert, A. "The Political Correspondence of Charles Lennox, Third Duke of Richmond: 1765–84." D PHIL thesis, Oxford University, 1956.

Gipson, L.H. *The Coming of the Revolution: 1763–75*. New York, 1962.

Goebel, J. *The Struggle for the Falkland Islands: A Study in Legal and Diplomatic History.* New Haven, 1927.

Graham, J.A. *Memoirs of John Horne Tooke.* New York, 1828.

Gunn, J.A.W. *Beyond Liberty and Property: The Process of Self-Recognition in Eighteenth-Century Political Thought.* Kingston and Montreal, 1983.

– *Factions No More.* London, 1972.

Guttridge, G.H. "David Hartley, M.P., An Advocate of Conciliation 1774–1783." *University of California Publications in History* 14 (1926): 231–40.

– "The Early Career of Lord Rockingham 1730–1765." *University of California Publications in History* 44 (1952).

– *English Whiggism and the American Revolution.* Berkeley and Los Angeles, 1963.

Hamer, M.T. "From the Grafton Administration to the Ministry of North." PH D thesis, Cambridge University, 1971.

Harlow, V.T. *The Founding of the Second British Empire, 1763–93.* 2 vols. London, 1952–54.

Harrington, V.D. *The New York Merchants on the Eve of the American Revolution.* New York, 1935.

Hayton, D. "The 'Country' Interest and the Party System, 1689– c. 1720." In *Party Management in Parliament, 1660–1784,* ed. C. Jones, 42–65. New York, 1984.

Hempton, D. "Religion in British Society 1740–1790." In *British Politics and Society from Walpole to Pitt 1742–1789,* ed. J. Black. Hampshire and London, 1990.

Hill, B.W. *British Parliamentary Parties, 1742–1832.* London, 1985.

Hinkhouse, F.J. *The Preliminaries of the American Revolution as Seen in the English Press, 1763–1775.* New York, 1926.

Hoffman, R.J.S. *The Marquis: A Study of Lord Rockingham, 1730–1782.* New York, 1973.

Holdsworth, Sir W.S. *A History of English Law.* Vol. 10. London, 1938.

Holzman, J.M. *The Nabobs in England: A Study of the Returned Anglo-Indian.* New York, 1926.

Hoppit, J. *Risk and Failure in English Business, 1700–1800.* Cambridge, 1987.

Horn, D.B. *Great Britain and Europe in the Eighteenth Century.* Oxford, 1967.

Hughes, E. *North Country Life in the Eighteenth Century.* 2 vols. London, New York, Toronto, 1965.

Innes, J. "The King's Bench Prison in the Later Eighteenth Century: Law, Authority and Order in a London Debtor's Prison." In *An Ungovernable People: The English and Their Law in the Seventeenth and Eighteenth Centuries,* ed. J. Brewer and J. Styles, 250–98. London, 1980.

James, F.C. *Ireland in the Empire 1686–1770: A History of Ireland from the Williamite Wars to the Eve of the American Revolution.* Oxford, 1973.

Jensen, M. *The Founding of a Nation: A History of the American Revolution 1763–1776.* New York, 1968.

Jesse, J.H. *Memoirs of the Life and Reign of King George the Third*. London, 1867.

Johnston, D.T. "Charles James Fox; From Government to Opposition 1771–1774." *English Historical Review* 89 (1974): 750–84.

Johnston, E.M. *Great Britain and Ireland, 1760–1800*. Edinburgh, 1963.

Kammen, M.G. *A Rope of Sand*. New York, 1968.

Kemp, B. "Crewe's Act 1782." *English Historical Review* 68 (1952): 258–63.

– *Sir Francis Dashwood: An Eighteenth Century Independent*. London, 1967.

Kramnick, I. *Bolingbroke and his Circle: The Politics of Nostalgia in the Age of Walpole*. Cambridge, Mass. 1968.

Langford, P. *The First Rockingham Administration, 1765–66*. Oxford, 1972.

– "Old Whigs, Old Tories, and the American Revolution." *Journal of Imperial and Commonwealth History* 8 (1980): 106–30.

– *A Polite and Commercial People, England, 1727–1783*. Oxford, 1989.

– *Public Life and the Propertied Englishman 1689–1798*. Oxford, 1991.

– "The Rockingham Whigs and America, 1763–73." In *Statesmen Scholars and Merchants*, ed. P. Whiteman, J.S. Bromley, and P.G.M. Dickson. Oxford, 1973.

Lascelles, E. *The Life of Charles James Fox*. London, 1939.

Lawson, P. *George Grenville: A Political Life*. Oxford, 1984.

– "George Grenville and America: The Years of Opposition, 1765–1770." *William and Mary Quarterly*, 3rd ser., 37 (1980): 561–76.

Lord Bute: Essays in Re-enterpretation, ed. K.B. Schweizer. Leicester, 1988.

Lucas, R. *Lord North, Second Earl of Guildford, K.G., 1732–1792*. 2 vols. London, 1913.

Macaulay, Lord. *Essay on Lord Clive*, ed. B. Wilson. New York, 1930.

– *Essay on the Earl of Chatham*. London, 1887.

MacCabby, S. *English Radicalism 1762–1785*. London, 1955.

MacKay, R.F. *Admiral Hawke*. Oxford, 1965.

Maclean, J.N.N. *Reward Is Secondary: The Life of a Political Adventurer and an Inquiry into the Mystery of "Junius."* London, 1963.

Magnus, P. *Edmund Burke: A Life*. London, 1939.

Mahoney, T.H.D. "Mr. Burke's Imperial Mentality and the Proposed Irish Absentee Tax of 1773." *Canadian Historical Review* 35 (1956): 158–66.

Mair, P. *From Resistance to Revolution: Colonial Radicals and the Development of American Opposition to Britain, 1765–1776*. London, 1773.

– "John Wilkes and American Disillusionment with Britain." *William and Mary Quarterley*, 3rd ser., 20 (July 1963): 3–32.

Mansfield, H.C.S. *Statesmanship and Party Government: A Study of Burke and Bolingbroke*. Chicago, 1965.

Marshall, P.J. *The Impeachment of Warren Hastings*. London, 1965.

– *Problems of Empire: Britain and India 1757–1813*. London, 1968.

Miller, J.C. *Origins of the American Revolution*. 2nd ed. Stanford, 1959.

Minchinton, W.E. *The Growth of English Overseas Trade in the Seventeenth and Eighteenth Centuries*. London, 1969.
– *The Trade of Bristol in the Eighteenth Century.* Bristol Record Society, 1957.
Mitchell, L.G. *Charles James Fox*. Oxford, 1992.
– *Charles James Fox and the Disintegration of the Whig Party.* Oxford, 1971.
Money, J. *Experience and Identity: Birmingham and the West Midlands*. Manchester, 1977.
Morley, J. *Burke*. London, 1923.
Murray, R.H. *Edmund Burke: A Biography.* Oxford, 1931.
Namier, Sir L. *Crossroads of Power*. London, 1962.
– *England in the Age of the American Revolution*. 2nd ed. London, 1961.
– *The Structure of Politics at the Accession of George III*. 2nd ed. London, 1957.
Namier, Sir L., and J. Brooke. *Charles Townshend*. London, 1964.
– *History of Parliament: The House of Commons: 1754 to 1790*. 3 vols. London, 1964.
Newman, B. *Edmund Burke*. London, 1927.
Norman, E.R. *Church and Society in England 1770–1970*. Oxford, 1976.
Norris, J. *Shelburne and Reform*. London, 1963.
O'Brien, C.C. *The Great Melody: A Thematic Biography and Commented Anthology of Edmund Burke*. Chicago, 1992.
O'Gorman, F. *Edmund Burke: His Political Philosophy.* London, 1973.
– "Edmund Burke and the Idea of Party." *Studies in Burke and his Time* 11 (1969–70): 131–42.
– *The Emergence of the British Two-Party System, 1710–1832*. London, 1982.
– "Party and Burke: The Rockingham Whigs." *Government and Opposition*. 3 (1968): 92–110.
– "Pitt and the 'Tory' Reaction to the French Revolution 1789–1815." *Britain and the French Revolution, 1789–1815*, ed. H.T. Dickinson, 21–38. Hampshire and London, 1989.
– *The Rise of Party in England: The Rockingham Whigs 1760–1782*. London, 1975.
– *Voters, Patrons and Parties: The Unreformed Electoral System of Hanoverian England*. Oxford, 1989.
Olson, A.G. *Anglo-American Politics, 1660–1775: The Relations between Parties in England and Colonial America*. Oxford, 1973.
Owen, J.B. *The Rise of the Pelhams*. London, 1957.
Pares, R. *King George III and the Politicians*. 2nd ed. Oxford, 1967.
Parkinson, C.N. *The Rise of the Port of Liverpool*. Liverpool, 1952.
Parssinen, T.M. "Association, Convention, Anti-Parliament in British Radical Politics, 1771–1848." *English Historical Review* 88 (1973): 481–503.
Pemberton, W.B. *Lord North*. London, 1938.
Peters, M. "The 'Monitor' on the Constitution, 1755–1765: New Light on the Ideological Origins of English Radicalism." *English Historical Review* 86 (1971): 706–27.

Phillips, J. *Electoral Behavior in Unreformed England: Plumpers, Splitters and Straights*. Princeton, 1982.

Porritt, E. *The Unreformed House of Commons: Parliamentary Representation before 1832*. 2 vols. Cambridge, 1903.

Postgate, R. *That Devil Wilkes*. rev. ed. London, 1956.

Prior, J. *Life of the Right Honourable Edmund Burke*. 5th ed. London, 1854.

Ramsay, J.F. *Anglo-French Relations 1763–70*. University of California Publications in History, 17, no. 3 (1939): 143–246.

Rea, R. *The English Press in Politics 1760–1775*. Lincoln, Neb., 1962.

Reid, L. *Charles James Fox: A Man for the People*. London, 1969.

Reitan, E.A. "Edmund Burke and the Civil List 1769–82." *The Burke News Letter* 8 (1966): 604–18.

– "The Civil List in 18th Century British Politics: Parliamentary Supremacy versus the Independence of the Crown." *Historical Journal* 9 (1966): 318–37.

– "The Civil List, 1766–77: Problems of Finance and Administration." *Bulletin of the Institute of Historical Research* 47 (1974): 186–201.

Ritcheson, C.R. *British Politics and the American Revolution*. Norman, 1954.

Robbins, C. *The Eighteenth Century Commonwealthman*. Cambridge, Mass. 1959.

– "The Strenuous Whig: Thomas Hollis of Lincoln"s Inn."*William and Mary Quarterly*, 3rd ser., 7 (1950): 406–54.

Roberts, M. *Splendid Isolation, 1763–1780*. Reading, 1970.

Robertson, M. "Scottish Commerce, and the American War of Independence." *Economic History Review*, 2nd ser., 9 (1956–57): 123–31.

Rogers, N. *Whigs and Cities: Popular Politics in the Age of Walpole and Pitt*. Oxford, 1989.

Royle, E., and Walvin, J. *English Radicals and Reformers, 1760–1848*. Brighton, 1982.

Rubini, D. *Court and Country, 1688–1702*. London, 1967.

Rudé, G. *Wilkes and Liberty: A Social Study of 1763 to 1774*. Oxford, 1962.

Sainsbury, J. *Disaffected Patriots: London Supporters of Revolutionary America 1769–82*. Kingston and Montreal, 1987.

Savadge, W.R. "The West Country and American Mainland Colonies, 1703–83, with special reference to the Merchants of Bristol." B LITT thesis, Oxford University, 1957.

Schlesinger, A.M. *The Colonial Merchants and the American Revolution, 1763–83*. New York, 1917.

– *Prelude to Independence: The Newspaper War on Britain, 1764–1776*. 1st ed. New York, 1958.

Schumpeter, E.B. *English Overseas Trade Statistics, 1697–1808*. Oxford, 1960.

Shelton, W.J. *English Hunger and Industrial Disorders*. London, 1973.

Sherrard, O.A. *A Life of John Wilkes*. London, 1930.

– *Lord Chatham and America*. London, 1958.

Shy, J. "Thomas Pownall, Henry Ellis, and the Spectrum of Possibilities, 1763–1775." In *Anglo-American Political Relations 1675–1775*, ed. A.G. Olson and R.M. Brown, 155–86. New Brunswick, 1970.

Sosin, J.M. *Agents and Merchants*. Lincoln, Neb. 1965.

Stephen, L. "Chatham, Francis and Junius." *English Historical Review* 3 (1888): 233–49.

Sturgess, G. "The Rockingham Whigs 1768–1774." MA thesis, Manchester University, 1972.

Sutherland, L.S. "The City of London and the Opposition to Government 1668–1774. In *London in the Age of Reform*, ed. J. Stevenson, 1–29. Oxford, 1977.

– *East India Company in Eighteenth Century Politics*, Oxford, 1952.

– "Edmund Burke and the First Rockingham Ministry." *English Historical Review* 47 (1932): 46–72.

– "Edmund Burke and the Relations between Members of Parliament and their Constituents." *Studies in Burke and His Times* 10 (1968): 1005–21.

Sykes, N. *Church and State in England in the Eighteenth Century*. Hamden, Conn., 1962.

Thomas, P.D.G. "The Beginning of Parliamentary Reporting in Newspapers 1718–1774." *English Historical Review* 74 (1959): 623–30.

– *British Politics and the Stamp Act Crisis: The First Phase of the American Revolution, 1763–1767*. Oxford, 1975.

– "Charles Townshend and American Taxation in 1767." *English Historical Review* 83 (1968): 33–51.

– "Check List of M.P.s Speaking in the House of Commons, 1768 to 1774." *Bulletin of the Institute of Historical Research* 35 (1962): 220–6.

– "John Wilkes and the Freedom of the Press (1771)." *Bulletin of the Institute of Historical Research* 33 (1960): 86–98.

– *Lord North*. London, 1976.

– "Party Politics in Eighteenth-Century Britain: Some Myths and a Touch of Reality." *British Journal for Eighteenth-Century Studies* 10 (1987): 205–15.

– "Sir Roger Newdigate's Essay on Party, c.1762." *English Historical Review* 102 (1987): 399–400.

– *Tea Party to Independence: The Third Phase of the American Revolution, 1773–1776*, Oxford, 1991.

– *The Townshend Duties Crisis: The Second Phase of the American Revolution, 1767–1773*. Oxford, 1987.

Throsler, P.A. *Pasquale Paoli: An Enlightened Hero, 1725–1807*. London, 1970.

Tracy, N. "The Falkland Islands Crisis of 1770: Use of Naval Force." *English Historical Review* 90 (1974): 40–65.

Trelvar, W.D. *Wilkes and the City*. London, 1917.

Trevelyan, G.O. *The Early History of Charles James Fox*. London, 1881.

Tuberville, A.S. *A History of Welbeck Abbey and Its Owners, 1755–1879*. 2 vols. London, 1839.

Tucker, R.W., and D.C. Hendrickson. *The Fall of the First British Empire: Origins of the War of American Independence*. Baltimore, 1982.

Underdown, P.T. "Burke as M.P. for Bristol." PH D thesis, London University, 1963.

Valentine, A. *Lord George Germain*. Oxford, 1962.

– *Lord North*. Norman, 1967.

Veitch, G.S. *The Genesis of Parliamentary Reform*. London, 1913.

Von Ruville, A. *William Pitt Earl of Chatham*. London, 1907.

Watson, D. "Barlow Trecothick and Other Associates of Lord Rockingham during the Stamp Act Crisis." MA thesis, Sheffield University, 1958.

– "The Relations between the Duke of Newcastle and the Marquis of Rockingham and Mercantile Interests in London and the Provinces, 1761–1768." PH D thesis, Sheffield University, 1968.

– "The Rockingham Whigs and the Townshend Duties." *English Historical Review* 84 (1969): 561–5.

Wector, D. *Edmund Burke and His Kinsmen*. Boulder, 1939.

Williams, A.F.B. *The Life of William Pitt, Earl of Chatham*. 2 vols. London, 1913.

Wilson, R.G. *Gentlemen Merchants: The Merchant Community in Leeds 1700–1830*. Manchester and New York, 1971.

Winstanley, D.A. *Lord Chatham and the Whig Opposition*. Cambridge, 1912.

Index

Abdy, Sir Anthony, 24, 25, 47, 64, 67, 68, 70, 72, 103, 204n83

Abergavenny, Earl of, 23

Acourt, William, 204n83

Albemarle, Earl of, 14, 22, 39

American Revolution, 6, 13, 25, 95, 143, 156, 157, 161–2, 165–71, 173, 174, 186–7, 193. *See also* North America

Anne, Queen, 97

Archer, Lord, 23

Armytage, George, 68, 105

Aufrere, George René, 23

Augusta of Saxe Gotha, mother of George III, 29, 30, 83, 85

Bagot, Sir William, 5, 12, 13, 25, 97, 139, 142, 192

Baker, William, 102–3, 105–6, 128, 132, 190

Baldwin, Henry, 230n49

Barré, Col. Isaac, 46, 49, 50, 56, 113, 114, 127, 212n106

Barrow, Charles, 24

Beauclerk, Aubrey, 204n83

Beaufort, Duke of, 79

Beckford, William, 12, 13, 46, 49, 50, 56, 84, 85, 99, 103–4, 109–10, 151

Bedford, Duke of, 28, 29, 51

Bedford party, 12, 27, 28,

30, 31, 33, 38, 40, 89, 95, 154, 192

Bellas, George, 214n15

Bellas, Henry, 70

Bentinck, Lord Charles Edward, 204n78

Bessborough, Earl of, 14, 159–60, 163

Bingham, Charles, 161–2

Blackett, Sir Edward, 139, 202n22

Bladon, Samuel, 230n49

Bolingbroke, Viscount, 94, 183–4

Bollan, William, 52

Boroughbridge, 65

Boston, 50, 51, 53

Boston Port Bill (1774), 169

Boston Tea Party, 161, 165–6, 168–9

Boswell, James, 210n65

Bowen, Hugh, 148

Bradley, James, 11, 41

Brett, Sir Percy, 79

Brewer, John, 62

Bristol, 11, 63, 67, 180

Brooke, John, 9, 10, 39, 81

Brunswick, House of, 134

Bucarrelli, Governor, 106

Buckinghamshire, 67, 72, 73, 75

Buckinghamshire, Earl of, 228n117

Buenos Aires, 106

Bull, Frederick, 160–1

Burgoyne, John, 236n38

Burke, Edmund, ix, 3, 21, 22, 23, 26, 50, 64, 69, 78, 82, 85, 101–2, 111, 118, 124, 125, 129, 132, 135, 138, 181, 182, 191; and American conflict, 43–4, 50, 52–4, 87–8, 168–9; and Clive, 152–3; constitutional opinion, 101–2, 119, 180; and Corsican issue, 46; and Dowdeswell, 19; and East India Company, 148, 149, 153–4; and Falkland Islands issue, 113–14; and Irish absentee tax, 160–3, 188; and juries issue, 122; and London remonstrance (1770), 86; *Observations on a Late State of the Nation*, 18, 27, 58, 200n35; and petitioning campaign, 72, 73; and printers issue, 127; and religion, 141–3; and Rockingham party, 3, 18–20, 92, 177, 190, 192; and secret influence, 30; *Thoughts on the Cause of the Present Discontents*, 7–8, 10, 17, 18, 20, 27, 31, 32, 35, 61, 67, 88–95, 99, 101–2, 103–4, 108–9,

15, 17, 23, 24, 36, 37, 49, 57, 60, 65, 70, 78, 79, 81, 82, 84, 86, 121, 122, 129, 130, 135, 136, 137, 192; and America, 42–4, 50–4, 87–8, 167, 169, 170–1; character, 14, 17–18, 20, 165, 190, 191; constitutional opinion, 34, 66–7, 83, 92, 154; and East India Company issue, 148, 149; and Falkland Islands issue, 114–15, 227n101; and juries issue, 124, 185; *Observations on a Late State of the Nation*, 58; and petitioning campaign, 61, 66–8, 71, 154; and power, 26, 34; and printers issue, 127, 129; revenue officers bill (1770), 96, 97–8, 99, 104; and Rockingham party, 17–18, 19, 20, 49, 66, 92, 192; and Tea Act, 170–1; and union movement, 39, 34, 83, 84, 85, 88–9, 165, 187–8

Drake, William, 200n20, 202n24
Dring, Jerome, 68
Dundas, Sir Lawrence, 136
Dunning, John, 79, 158, 174
Durham County, 138

East India Company, 5, 20, 22, 24, 38, 116, 145–58, 171–2, 173, 185, 188, 191
East Indies, 111, 145
economic reform, 7, 8–9, 67, 96, 158, 174, 182, 193
Elizabeth I, 135
Ellis, Welbore, 160
Essex, 24
Evans, Thomas, 230n49

Falkland Islands conflict, 106–7, 110–18, 119, 120, 123, 127, 129, 145, 173, 176

Fenwick, Thomas, 204n78
Fitzwilliam, Earl of, 23, 169
Fletcher, Henry, 47–8, 204n78, 236n36
Fox, Charles James, 7, 137, 155, 157, 165, 182, 192
France: and Corsica, 45–6; and Falkland Islands conflict, 106–7, 111, 114. *See also* French Revolution
Frankland, Thomas, 23
Frankland, William, 23, 236n37
French Revolution, 143, 144, 176, 193
Fuller, Rose, 50, 137

Genoa: and Corsica, 45–6
George I, 24
George II, 7, 24, 134
George III, 5, 7, 11–12, 25, 28, 39, 74, 80, 81, 84, 86, 90, 105, 113, 115, 120, 133, 134, 140, 142, 159, 176, 193; and Grenville, 44
Germain, Lord George, 102, 116–17, 150, 190
Gibbon, Edward, 134
Gloucester, Duke of, 133
Glynn, Sgt John, 50, 120 122, 214n15
Glynne, Sir John, 202n25
Grafton, Duke of, 33, 37, 38, 80; resignation, 79
Grafton administration, 49; and Wilkes, 55–7
Grafton party, 12, 13
Granby, Marquis of, 79
Gregory, Robert, 24, 41, 150, 236n36
Grenville, George, 28, 38, 29, 61, 166; and America, 50–4, 87–8, 166, 186–7, 212n117; character, 39–40, 44–5, 190; Controverted Elections Bill, 96–7, 98, 99, 172; death, 113; and Dowdeswell, 57, 83, 84; and Middlesex election, 56–7; and Portland-Lowther conflict, 49; and

union movement, 75–7, 78–9, 83, 84, 87–8, 89, 187–8, 190. *See also* Grenville administration; Grenville party
Grenville, James, 79
Grenville administration, 118
Grenville party, 12, 13, 27, 28, 29, 31, 33, 39–40, 58, 63, 72, 85, 94, 95, 99, 102, 111, 154, 192, 193; and America, 42, 50–4; and Corsica, 45–6; and Falkland Islands conflict, 113; and Portland-Lowther conflict, 49; and union movement, 57–9, 75–7, 78–9, 82, 89, 111, 116–17, 166, 187–8
Grey, Earl, 7, 157

Hanbury, John, 23
Hanover, House of, 4, 24, 25, 32, 85, 134, 156
Harcourt, Earl, 161
Hardwicke, 1st Earl of, 80
Hardwicke, 2nd Earl of, 79–80
Harrison, Joseph, 53, 186
Harrowden, 149
Hastings, Warren, 152
Hedon, 65
Herbert, Henry, 96
Hewett, John, 14, 24
Hill, B.W., 11
Hill, Richard, 200n20
Hillsborough, Earl of, 51
Hoghton, Henry, 138, 142, 202n25
Horne, John, 128
Horton, Anne, 133
Hotham, Beaumont, 204n78
Hume, David, 81
Huntingdon, Earl of, 79, 117
Huske, John, 50
Hussey, Richard, 79
Hussey, William, 202n21
Hyde, Baron, 116